THE ENCYCLOPEDIA OF DREAMS

"My purpose in writing this book is to help others discover the treasure in their own dreams—treasure that can provide guidance throughout various trials and stresses of life. Our dreams often speak to us in symbols, and we must learn to decipher them. I do not believe that there are any hard and fast interpretations of the images that appear in dreams. Every dream is unique, colored by the dreamer's own experiences, attitudes, associations, hopes and fears. Nonetheless, there are many images that appear in dreams that have widespread or universal symbolic content. I believe that understanding these meanings can lead to a fuller understanding of the specific dream content. If this book can serve as a helpful guide, then its purpose will be fulfilled." —ROSEMARY ELLEN GUILEY

ROSEMARY ELLEN GUILEY is a journalist specializing in paranormal and mystical experience. She is a member of both the American and London Societies for Psychical Research and the Academy of Religion and Psychical Research. Her works include *Harper's Encyclopedia of Mystical and Paranormal Experience*, *The Miracle of Prayer*, and *Angels of Mercy*.

THE ENCYCLOPEDIA OF DREAMS

Symbols & Interpretations

ROSEMARY ELLEN GUILEY

BERKLEY BOOKS, NEW YORK

THE ENCYCLOPEDIA OF DREAMS:
SYMBOLS AND INTERPRETATIONS

A Berkley Book / published by arrangement with
Crossroad Publishing Company

PRINTING HISTORY
Crossroad Publishing Company edition published 1993
Berkley edition / July 1995

ISBN: 0-425-14788-6

BERKLEY®
Berkley Books are published by The Berkley Publishing Group,
200 Madison Avenue, New York, New York 10016.
BERKLEY and the "B" design
are trademarks belonging to Berkley Publishing Corporation.

PRINTED IN THE UNITED STATES OF AMERICA

10 9 8 7 6

For those who seek to understand
their dreams

Contents

Acknowledgments

This book came together with the indispensable help of several individuals. I would like to express my deep appreciation to James G. Matlock, parapsychologist and doctoral candidate in anthropology, for his assistance on the chapters concerning multicultural dream beliefs and the paranormal aspects of dreams; to Doreen M. Beauregard, for her assistance on the chapters concerning the history of dreams and dream research, and dream recall; and to Robert M. Place, an expert on alchemy, for his assistance on the material concerning dreams and alchemy. Finally, I would like to thank Werner Mark Linz, chairman and chief executive officer of The Continuum Publishing Company, for giving me the opportunity to write this book, and Mike Leach, publisher of Crossroad, for his editorial guidance. I also wish to thank Bruce S. Trachtenberg for his support.

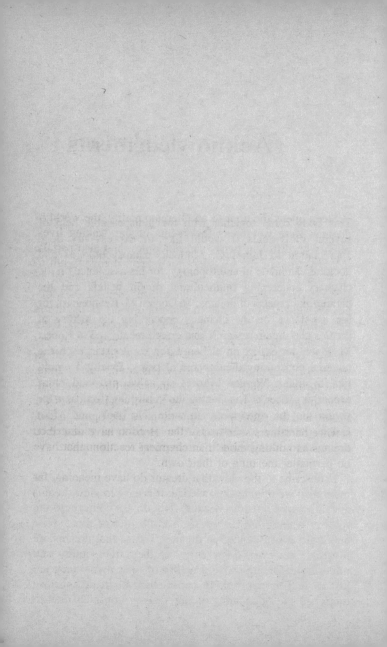

Preface

Sleep opens the door to an alternate reality, the world of dreams. Here we replay the events of our waking lives, often with different twists and outcomes, and also partake in adventures of the bizarre. Quite often, dreams seem to be loaded with meaning, but the meaning is difficult to separate from the surreality of the dreams themselves. Modern Western science tends to dismiss dreams as having at best a limited significance. Sigmund Freud considered them as messages from the unconscious that expressed "day residues," or rehashes of events in waking life, as well as repressions and unfullfilled wishes. His pupil, Carl G. Jung, went further, to outline a dream landscape filled with symbolic images of deep meaning, precognitive glimpses of the future, and telepathic communication. At the opposite end, science hardliners such as J. Allan Hobson have described dreams as nothing more than chemical reactions that have no particular meaning of their own.

I subscribe to the view that dreams do have meaning, far more than we might acknowledge. It is easy to view dreams as fantasies or illusions because they do not conform to the rules of waking-life reality. In fact, all rules of time, space and logic are suspended in dreams. To say that dreams are illusions, however, deprives us of their true vitality and importance. Dreams have a reality of their own—they are just as real as our waking consciousness. In dreams, we transcend the boundaries of our waking consciousness to experience consciousness on more subtle levels. These levels are more subjective, as opposed to the objective reality we experience with our five physical senses. The subjectivity does not render dreams any less "real." By delving into our dreams, and attuning ourselves to their subjective reality, we stand to learn much about ourselves and our relationships to others and to the cosmos.

This fundamental wisdom about the reality of dreams has been understood and accepted universally since ancient times. The early Greeks and Romans, for example, believed that when the body was asleep, the soul became free to travel, especially to nonworldly, dreamlike realms wherein dwelled the lesser spirits who mediated between humans and the gods. Plato called this realm the *metaxu,* or "the between." Here the human soul had experiences and encounters that had the same validity as experiences had during waking life. What made the dream experiences special, however, were their supernatural characteristics. In dreams, it was possible to meet the gods, to see the future and to be healed of illness and disease. Similarly, shamanic cultures have accessed this same alternate, dreamlike reality for the same purposes. And Tibetans have looked to dreams for information about past lives.

These same opportunities for extraordinary information and healing powers continue in the dream-lives of modern people, though we seldom think of dreams as supernatural, or of having their own reality. Today we seldom think about meeting the gods in our dreams, but we are creatively inspired by dreams. Many arrived at answers to questions and solutions to problems that had eluded them in waking consciousness. Physicist Neils Bohr saw the model for the atom in a dream, and the nineteenth-century Russian chemist Mendeleev had a dream vision of the periodic table of elements. Artist William Blake was shown a process for copper engraving in a dream; the inexpensive production technique then enabled him to make a living from his mystical illustrations. Author Robert Louis Stevenson received the idea for *The Strange Case of Dr. Jekyll and Mr. Hyde* in a dream, and poet William Coleridge wrote his fragment, *Kubla Khan*, word for word as he remembered it from a dream. He might have completed his work had he not been interrupted while committing it to paper. When he returned to his task, he discovered, unhappily, that it had evaporated from memory. Dreams are fleeting—they must be recorded immediately upon awakening if we are to retain and benefit from their content.

The examples of the creative results of inspired dreams can go on. The ancients would have called these ideas and revelations gifts from the gods, delivered in the only medium possible where divine and earthly can meet: the dream.

We in the modern West no longer consult dream diviners for information about the future, but we do continue to see the future ourselves in dreams. Precognitive warnings of catastrophes and disasters are not uncommon, occuring even in dreams of persons who are not affected by the forthcoming events themselves. Perhaps one of the most dramatic cases concerned a landslide of coal in Aberfan, Wales, on October 21, 1966. The coal tumbled down on a school, killing twenty-eight adults and 116 children. For weeks beforehand, numerous persons experienced advance warning of the disaster, many in dreams. In the early twentieth century, a British aeronautics engineer, J. W. Dunne, attempted to develop a scientific hypothesis to explain his own precognitive dreams, which concerned both trivial matters of daily life, and major events Dunne subsequently read about in the newspaper. His "Theory of Serial Time" posited an Absolute Time created by God, which was divided into layers in different dimensions. These layers could be viewed from different perspectives at different times. The scientific community rejected Dunne's ideas, but they are comparable to the ancients' idea of the *metaxu,* a nonphysical between-state where our definitions of space and linear time are suspended.

Finally, we in modern times are returning to the idea that dreams have profound healing power, not just of the psyche, but of the body as well. The ancient Greeks established healing temples devoted to the god Asclepius, where the ill came for ritual dream incubations. Since dreams were regarded as real events and not imaginary, the conditions were created at these temples to induce dreams that would cure the individual's complaint. If a dream included certain symbols associated with Asclepius, such as an olive tree, a serpent, a bearded man or a handsome youth (especially associated with miraculous cures, or rejuvenation), then the dreamer would be cured. If the person did not have a healing dream, then he or she sought to receive the cure through a vision.

Our Western dualistic philosophy that separates mind and body, matter and spirit, has led us away from using our thoughts and dreams to influence our health. Various Western spiritual traditions, such as Christian Science, have kept a focus on the use of prayer, thought and faith to effect healing through God. It was not until the early twentieth century, however, that attention returned to dreams as harbingers of health. Perhaps the best examples are the observations of Jung, who realized that certain dreams of his patients portended catastrophic illness. Specifically, these images were of horses—a metaphor for the body—who suffered injury or destroyed themselves.

More recently, researchers such as Patricia Garfield, a clinical psychologist and dream expert, have recognized that dreams have the power to help heal the body as well as warn of impending illness. In her book, *The Healing Power of Dreams* (Simon & Schuster, 1991), Garfield relates her own experiences with injury and healing dreams. After she suffered a broken wrist, Garfield in her dreams underwent a radical transformation. Every phase in her slow and painful recovery was dramatized by specific dream content. Garfield's experiences were supplemented by her work with patients who recounted their own healing dreams during the recovery from illness and injury. She also interviewed health care professionals and analysts. She discovered how dreams contain crucial bits of information about the condition of the body, which are not generally recognized. She also realized how much the ancients knew about the healing power of dreams—knowledge we'd lost through dualistic philosophy.

My purpose in writing this book is to help others discover the treasure in their own dreams—treasure that can provide guidance throughout the various trials and stresses of life. Our dreams often speak to us in symbols, and we must learn to decipher them. I do not believe that there is any hard and fast interpretation of the images that appear in dreams. Every dream is unique, colored by the dreamer's own experiences, attitudes, associations, hopes and fears. Nonetheless, there are many images that appear in dreams that have widespread or universal symbolic content. I believe that understanding these meanings can lead to a fuller understanding of the specific dream content.

The definitions of symbols provided in this book are drawn from myth, alchemy and modern dreamwork. I have kept the focus on Western traditions, since meanings of symbols can vary by culture. In modern dreamwork, some attention is paid to plays on words and slang in dreams. While I do believe that these interpretations can have merit, I have not incorporated them into this work, in order to focus on the most universal meanings of the symbols.

Ideally, the reader should take the definitions given herein and see if they resonate with the dream. Some may hit right on target, others may hit obliquely. Personal shadings and associations should always be applied. Ultimately, it is only the dreamer who can correctly interpret a dream, and not an outside source, be it a book, friend or analyst. If this book can serve as a helpful guide, then its purpose will be fulfilled.

PART I

The Science of Dreams

What Is a Dream?

Dreaming is a unique display, usually visual, that occurs during the night in order, I feel, to assess the impact of recent events on our lives. A dream is a remembered residue—in the form of creatively assembled visual metaphors.
—Montague Ullman and Nan Zimmerman[1]

In *The Interpretation of Dreams* (1900), Sigmund Freud proposed that dreams are disguised wishes arising from the unconscious mind; having been suppressed by the conscious mind, the wishes sneak into the sleeping brain in the form of dreams. Freud's theory has largely gone the way of the dinosaurs, particularly since an electroencephalograph (EEG) machine recorded rapid eye movement (REM) during sleep, and research into the physical nature of dreaming began.

What is a dream? There is no definitive answer to this question. The neuroscientific versus psychoanalytical debate about precisely what causes dreams and what is their function rages on. In this chapter we will examine the possible answers that have been offered by neurological and cognitive science researchers.

The Physical Act of Dreaming

The process of dreaming originates in the brain stem and is controlled by two neurotransmitters that turn dreams on and off. The "on switch" uses acetylcholine to begin the dream and the "off switch" uses norepinephrine and serotonin to end it. When the latter two chemicals are suppressed, the acetylcholine allows electrical signals to be sent to the cortex. (Norepinephrine and serotonin are also necessary to imprint messages in long-term memory, which may explain why we forget the majority of our dreams. Since the two chemicals are suppressed during the dreaming process, dreams cannot be stored in long-term memory.) The brain stem neurons also start a sinusoidal (resembling a sine curve) wave known as a theta rhythm in the hippocampus—a seahorse-shaped brain structure believed responsible for memory storage. Meanwhile, the nerves that usually carry information from the outside world shut down.

If the dream occurs during the REM phase of sleep, the sleeper experiences increased heart and respiration rates and a state of temporary paralysis. The brain stem freezes muscular activity to prevent the sleeper from acting out his or her dream. Experiments have been performed on cats in which the neural fibers that inhibit movement during REM were cut; the cats then moved freely and acted out their REM dreams. (Another interesting result of the surgery was the cats' loss during the waking state of their "curiosity reflex," which causes them to remain cautiously still in unfamiliar environments. Instead, presented with strange surroundings, these cats were unusually mobile.[2]) A few rare people *do* act out their REM dreams. Clonazepam, a drug used to treat epilepsy, has been used for this disorder.[3]

The Activation-Synthesis Hypothesis

One of the greatest opponents of the psychoanalytical approach to dream research is J. Allan Hobson, author of *The Dreaming Brain* (1988). His theories are based on the belief that the mind *is* the brain.

Hobson, with former collaborator Robert W. McCarley, developed the activation-synthesis hypothesis to explain dreams. It proposes that the higher-level neurons, upon receiving messages from the brain stem, rather than from the five senses, behave as if those messages *are* coming from the usual sources; consequently the neurons search memory to generate an interpretation of the messages. For example, if neurons fire in the part of the brain that controls balance, the cerebral cortex generates a dream about falling. And if we dream that we are being chased or threatened but cannot move to protect ourselves, it is because the brain is confused by the REM "paralysis" and interprets it as a genuine threat, which then surfaces in the dream.

This hypothesis may explain why dreams are primarily visual: the cells in the visual center are being activated. Hobson believes that the brain stem also activates the limbic brain, or emotional center, which may explain the emotional nature of our dreams.

While Hobson does agree that dreams have a psychological significance, he stresses that their meaning is right on the surface. To explain, Hobson says, "I walk out this door and I see the coatrack standing there. It's got *my* coat on it, *my* hat, but when I look at it, I see a person. It's happened fifty times. I fill in, I project . . . That's clear evidence that in the waking state I'm taking bits of form and filling in the holes. And that's what happens in dreams."[4]

Psychiatrist Ernest Hartmann is another researcher who interprets the elements of dreams according to what is happening physically in the brain. He believes that the high levels of dopamine present during REM are the cause of instinctual behavior in dreams, since dopamine in the waking state is associated with neural energizing. Likewise, the low serotonin levels bring about dream "hallucinations."[5]

Hartmann also believes that a basic organizational pattern of the brain, perhaps genetically determined, is responsible for what he terms "boundary thickness." He describes people who are prone to recurrent nightmares as having thin boundaries—they are more open and sensitive, become quickly involved in relationships, are perhaps too trusting, and usually do not identify strongly with groups of any kind. Artists and creative people also fall into this category.[6]

Different Types of Dreams

Dreams differ substantially according to when in the sleep pattern they occur—during the REM stage, at sleep onset (these are known as hypnagogic dreams), and at other non-REM (NREM) phases.

There are four stages of sleep. As the sleeper descends through Stages One through Four, brain waves decrease in frequency. After reaching Stage Four, the sleeper reverses the process and ends up back in Stage One, which is then called Emergent Stage One. This is when most REM dreaming happens.

REM Sleep

The physical science of dreams began in earnest in 1953, when researchers at the University of Chicago discovered that rapid eye movement and particular brain wave patterns are physical signals that a dream is in progress. Most dream research since then has focused on the REM stage.

All mammals (except the spiny anteater), as well as a

few birds and reptiles, experience REM sleep. In humans, the aging process parallels a gradual decrease in the percentage of time spent in this phase. Fetuses as young as twenty-three weeks spend nearly all their time in REM, and newborns spend about eight hours per day in REM. Up to fifty percent of the sleep of infants and small children is spent in REM. Adult sleep is twenty percent REM, and for the elderly only fifteen percent. Most scientists believe this is because REM sleep plays a part in the learning process.

While studying REM, sleep researcher William Dement discovered that there is a connection between the way the eyes move and what is happening in the concurrent dream. When his subjects displayed uninterrupted vertical or horizontal eye movements, he awakened them to ask about the content of their dreams. Vertical eye movements corresponded to dreams about standing at the foot of a cliff and looking up, climbing a ladder and looking up and down, looking at the top of stairs, and watching leaflets falling from a blimp. The subject with steady horizontal eye movements dreamt of two people throwing tomatoes at each other.[7]

Researchers also discovered that people who tend to forget their dreams show a greater amount of rapid eye movement, which is associated with greater amounts of activity in the dream. However, when these people did remember the content of their dreams, it was rather bland and inactive. Further investigation showed that it takes greater eye movement to look away from an object than to look at it. Thus the "nonrecallers" were most likely "looking away from" or avoiding their dreams.[8]

Four or five REM stages occur nightly, at ninety-minute intervals; the length of each session increases as the night goes on, until the average adult has spent about two hours in REM by morning. However, people suffering from certain mental or neurological disorders often experience abnormal REM stages.

In persons suffering from depression, the first REM stage occurs too early (about twenty to sixty-five minutes into sleep instead of ninety minutes) and lasts too long (twenty to thirty minutes instead of five to ten). Their REM periods are more variable in length and have more rapid eye movement than is normal.[9] Narcoleptics are even more REM-prone; they go directly into the REM phase upon falling asleep. (Another interesting characteristic of narcoleptics is their ability to be wide awake—or behave as if wide awake—and yet show the brain wave patterns of deep sleep.)

Somnambulism, or sleepwalking, is a form of behavior one might logically connect to the REM dream stage; however, this does not appear to be so. Studies have found it actually occurs during deeper, non-REM sleep, and that the walker's brain sends out an alpha wave, which is typical of a relaxed waking state.[10]

People awakened during REM sleep are highly likely to remember their dreams, which differ from NREM dreams in their vividness, complexity and generally bizarre nature. A faint external stimulus occurring during REM may be recognized in the sleeper's dream; for example, "a draft of air on the exposed skin of a dreamer may be depicted in the dream as a raging tornado."[11]

NREM/Sleep Onset Dreaming

Despite all the attention that REM has received in dream research, it must be remembered that we also dream outside the REM stage. NREM dreams are generally more logical and echo current or recent events in the dreamer's life.

Hypnagogic dreams are those occurring at the onset of sleep, often in the gray "twilight" between consciousness and unconsciousness. Primarily verbal and less complex than REM dreams, they are often described more as thinking or worrying than dreaming—like echoes of the thoughts on your mind just before falling asleep. For example, a person thinking just before sleep about buying a birthday present for a friend might hear that friend talking about their birthday in the dream. "At sleep onset, the human organism seems to shy away from disturbing thoughts and feelings, with this tendency strongest among those persons least able to tolerate such content."[12] Dreams that occur during daytime napping are usually also of this type.

Lest hypnagogic dreams seem dull in comparison to REM dreams, it must also be noted that they are very similar to experiences in sensory deprivation, meditation, and psychedelic drug use; features include soft whispering, one's name being called, a feeling of strangeness, starts or jerks, and a sensation of floating or falling. Most so-called out-of-body experiences happen during this stage. And although these dreams are primarily verbal, the visual element that does exist is often intense. As frequently happens in LSD experiences, there are lights and colors that develop into simple, geometric patterns or sometimes complex designs. Bloated or distorted faces are often seen.

The following hypnagogic dream was experienced by one sleep subject:

> While waiting for sleep he became aware of an indescribable something, which rose from the feet and hands, and taking eight or ten seconds to reach the head, there ending in a sound like the crash of glass houses breaking in a hail-storm with a vivid flash of yellow light.[13]

Some dreamers have reported that their hypnagogic visions, particularly the frightening ones, remained even after they opened their eyes. One man told of having a vision of a spider and seeing it briefly on his pillow when he opened his eyes. A woman dreamed of a friend and saw him standing beside her bed after she opened her eyes; he then vanished. Another man reported seeing an angel in the same fashion.[14]

The Effects of Drugs on Dreaming

Tranquilizers decrease dream time and often cause distortions, while barbiturates make dreams more thought-like. LSD increases dream time as does nicotine withdrawal; the dreams of those who have just given up smoking also tend to be more intense.[15]

Why We Dream

Most scientists agree that dreaming—at least, REM dreaming—plays a part in the learning process.

Researcher Jonathan Winson, author of *Brain and Psyche*, looks to the spiny anteater, or echidna, for answers about dreams and learning. The echidna is an egg-laying mammal (monotreme) and is the only mammal that does not experience REM sleep. Its brain is very similar to the human brain in that its prefrontal cortex is huge in relation to the rest of its brain. The mammals that have evolved from the monotreme, such as the opossum, have a much smaller prefrontal cortex than their predecessors, but they do experience REM sleep.

Winson suggests that REM dreaming in these mammals took over the functions that the large prefrontal cortex performs for the echidna. If it is the prefrontal cortex that formulates memories into strategies for future conduct, the echidna uses its large prefrontal cortex to do this in the waking state—as the "memories" are being experienced. For mammals of higher intelligence, such as humans, to learn in the same manner would require an extremely over-sized prefrontal cortex, larger than the skull could accommodate. So, says Winson, nature came up with an alternative: REM sleep. REM allows us to incorporate new information received during the day while the brain is "off-line."

Backing up Winson's theory is the fact that theta waves are active in the hippocampus during REM, and the hippocampus is involved in memory processing. In humans, the hippocampus doesn't become functional until the age of two, and Winson believes it is at this point that REM sleep takes on its interpretive function.[16]

Dream Deprivation

It is understood that dreaming is a necessary physiological function, since people prevented from REM dreaming become anxious or even panicky, fatigued, irritable, and have difficulty concentrating and remembering. If deprived of sleep long enough, they eventually dream while awake, i.e., they hallucinate. When finally allowed their REM, their brains compensate for lost time by greatly increasing the percentage of sleep spent in the REM stage. Much of the evidence of this, as well as theories of dreams as part of the learning process, comes from experiments in dream and sleep deprivation.

In one experiment, a group of college students was taught two mental tasks on the same day—one a simple word association game, the other the complex Wff'n'Proof logic game. That night the students were divided into four groups: some slept undisturbed, some were kept awake all night, some were awakened only during NREM sleep, and some were awakened each time they entered REM. The next day, all the students performed equally well on the easy word association game. But on the difficult logic game, those who were allowed to sleep all night or deprived only of NREM sleep seemed to have greater mastery over the game than those who lost REM sleep or didn't sleep at all.[17]

Researcher Rosalind Dymond Cartwright has conducted dream deprivation studies that demonstrate dreaming's role in coping with problems. In one study, volunteers were presented with a hypothetical problem and asked to come up with realistic solutions to it several hours later. In the meantime, some of the volunteers were kept awake and the others allowed to sleep; of those who slept, some were awakened before they went into REM sleep. The next day, the volunteers who had REM sleep came up with realistic solutions to the problem, whereas those deprived of REM created simplistic, unrealistic solutions. Another of Cartwright's experiments involved a university counseling program. The program had a problem with students in need of psychotherapy dropping out after only a few sessions. Cartwright found that students who were awakened during REM sleep and asked to recall their dreams were more likely to stay in therapy than those who did not recall dreams.[18]

Psychiatrists Chester Pearlman and Ramon Greenberg conducted an experiment that also demonstrates REM's coping strategies. Sleep volunteers were shown a shocking movie clip twice. Before the second showing, some students were allowed to sleep and dream while others were deprived of REM sleep. At the second showing, those who were allowed REM sleep were not as upset as they had been at the first showing. But those deprived of REM were just as upset as they had been the first time.[19]

Dreaming to Forget

Nobel laureate Francis Crick and theoretical biologist Graeme Mitchison proposed that dreams function not to help us remember but to help us forget. They refer to false information, obsessive connections, and the generally incorrect storage of memory that can occur when the neocortex is overloaded. During REM, pontine-geniculate-occipital cortex (PGO) waves from the brain stem hit the neocortex and false information is erased. This is how the brain rids itself of bad connections, they said; it unlearns them. In Crick and Mitchison's view, trying to remember our dreams actually may be an unhealthy thing to do.[20]

Other Possible Biological Functions of Dreaming

Replenishing. During REM sleep, there are higher levels of hormones in the body than at other times. Some scientists believe that REM helps to maintain the proper balance of hormones. It has also been suggested that, since some neurons are dormant during REM, this period may function to restore and replenish them.

During NREM sleep great amounts of growth hormone, which is responsible for body tissue renewal, enter the bloodstream. Ian Oswald proposes that REM sleep performs the same job in brain tissue repair. For example, senile people get very little REM sleep, and it has been shown that their brains actually shrivel from lack of cell renewal.[21]

Diagnostic. It is possible that traumatic dreams act as warning signals of serious physical illness. Robert C. Smith of Michigan State University questioned patients receiving cardiac catheterization for possible—but not yet diagnosed—heart disease to find out if dreams can act as early indicators of illness. He found that many of the patients who did have heart disease had dreams involving death (men) or separation/disruption of personal relationships (women), even though they were unaware of their illness. The severity of the patient's condition also paralleled the number of death/separation dreams they had.[22]

The following death dream was reported by a man admitted to the hospital and found to have cancer of the pancreas; he had the dream one week prior to being admitted:

> My brother and I visited our old house . . . , and mother was there in her casket. It was all black except for a weird glowing red stripe end-around. She tried to get out, but then fell back and seemed to disappear; she was a goner for sure now. We took her to the cemetery and almost got killed ourselves in a flood on the way.[23]

Life-sustaining. Robert Vertes, a professor of neuroscience, suggests that dreams prevent the sleeping brain from falling into permanent unconsciousness or even death. During sleep, he says, the brain is in a coma-like state, and dreaming keeps it activated.[24]

What We Dream About

While some ponder why we dream, other researchers keep track of the content of our dreams and how it relates to age, sex, and physical handicaps, among other things.

Sex Differences

The differences in the dreams of men and women tend to reflect their sex roles in the waking state. The dreams of men feature outdoor and unfamiliar settings and physical activity. Men don't usually notice details of clothing and color in their dreams, and they dream of other men more than women.[25]

In their dreams women often notice facial features and clothing details, aggressive behavior tends to be verbal rather than physical, conversation rather than physical action dominates, and the settings are typically familiar, indoor environments. Women dream of men and women in equal numbers.

However, as females' roles in society have changed and continue to change, so have their dreams. For example, women are increasingly seeing themselves as aggressors in their dreams.[26]

Calvin Hall and Bill Domhoff feel that men dream primarily of men because their unresolved conflicts are with men rather than women. Likewise, women dream proportionately because their conflicts with the two sexes are equal.[27]

Dreams During Pregnancy

Pregnant women's dreams contain a great number of references to animals, water, buildings and their mothers. For example:

I am swimming in the ocean, trying to get to the shore. There's a strong undertow that keeps me from going very far but I'm not worried. The water feels pleasantly warm and I'm only a few yards from a house which is built right out into the water. . . . Then I notice my mother . . . looking out one of the windows. She's smiling and waving to me. Next I notice the water around me is full of turtles of all kinds! Most are huge and they're swimming right along beside me.[28]

The stage of pregnancy seems to correspond to the content of the dream, particularly when animals—which probably represent the fetus—are involved. For example, women in their second trimester are likely to dream of amphibians (as in the example above), while women in the later stages of pregnancy are likely to dream of kittens, puppies, baby rabbits, etc.

Children's Dreams

The sex difference is evident in children's dreams also. Girls tend to show more fear as well as positive emotions, while boys tend to show more anger.[29] The "fear dream" is very common in children generally. Fear of animals in dreams is more common among boys than girls, and girls tend to dream of mammals while boys dream of non-mammals.[30] At seven years of age, burglars are popular stars in children's dreams.[31]

David Foulkes believes that dreaming in children develops at a rate parallel to conscious intelligence and visuo-spatial skills. He states that before the age of seven, children's dreams are passive; they do not "star" in their own dreams. (Adults, on the other hand, star in their own dreams 95 percent of the time, and only 6 percent of that time is as a passive observer). Before age five, says Foulkes, dreams are static images with little emotional content, featuring primarily animals and fatigue/sleep themes. By age five or six, story lines and movement develop, but there is still no self-representation.[32]

There are those who disagree somewhat with Foulkes' theory:

We must still address the many anecdotal and clinical reports of narratively complex and bizarre dreams in children two and three years old, parents' reports of telltale confusion in awakening children that may indicate dreaming in the first and second years, and the powerful nightmares and anxiety dreams of very young children.[33]

There is evidence that even very young infants are experiencing dreams of some type during their sleep. Certain social behaviors such as smiling as well as expressions of disdain, perplexity, and amusement appear in infants during REM sleep before they appear in the waking state.[34]

Dreams of the Elderly

The dreams of the elderly often concern "lost resources for coping with problems" and a vague sense of apprehension and confusion. For example: "I lost my way traveling. I had to ask many strangers where to go. I'm not sure I got where I was going;" "I'm in my friend's house, but with bigger rooms, and I lost my coat. I keep finding my coat and losing it." Often if there is a solution to the dream problem, it involves receiving food, soothing and physical comfort.[35]

Animal Dreaming

Of course, it is very difficult to determine what, if anything, animals dream about during REM. However, in one experiment, monkeys were trained to press a lever when a particular scene appeared on a screen. Later while sleeping, the monkeys were observed to press the lever, as if dreaming of the same scene.[36]

Color vs. Black-and-White

Edwin Kahn et al. found that color was present in 70 percent of the dreams of their subjects; however, it took some prompting to discover this. They believe that color is present in most dreams but that it is usually ignored in dream *reporting,* just as it often is in descriptions of waking events.[37]

Dreams of the Blind and Deaf

Color is most definitely present in the dreams of the congenitally deaf—vivid, brilliant color. Although color is also featured in the dreams of deaf people who lost their hearing after birth, it is not as prominent.

There is no evidence that those blind from birth see in their dreams, although REM movement is present. Those who lost their vision after birth claim to have sight in their dreams, and the more recent the loss the more likely they are to see in their dreams. The dreams of the blind also feature sound and touch more prominently than the dreams of seeing persons.

Dreams of Depressed People

It has already been mentioned that the REM patterns of depressed people are abnormal. Content analysis of their dreams has shown that depressed persons have lower dream recall, and that there is less detail in those that are recalled. There are fewer strangers and fewer people overall in their dreams, and the story lines tend to be stuck in the past.[38]

Dream Lucidity

A lucid dream is one in which the dreamer is aware that he or she is dreaming. For example:

I dreamed that I was walking by the water on the . . . shore. It was morning; the sky a light blue; the foam-

flecked waves were greenish in the sunshine. I forget just
how it happened, but something told me I was dreaming.
. . . I decided to prolong the dream and continued my
walk, the scenery now appearing extraordinarily vivid
and clear. Very soon my body began to draw me back.
I experienced dual consciousness: I could feel myself lying in bed and walking by the sea at one and the same
time. Moreover, I could dimly see the objects of my bedroom, as well as the dream scenery. I willed to continue
dreaming. . . . My will triumphed. . . . My bedroom faded
altogether from my vision, and I was out on the shore
feeling indescribably free and elated.[39]

The "double awareness" of lucid dreaming noted in the
description above is a characteristic also common to flying/
floating dreams and out-of-body experiences. The latter two
are believed by some to be caused by a double awareness
of dreamt and actual body position.[40] Interestingly, perhaps
paradoxically, the paralysis associated with REM is generally deeper during lucid dreaming—the same person who
may be free floating or flying is physically more paralyzed
than the non-lucid dreamer.[41]

Most of us experience dream lucidity rarely; however
some people have a propensity for it. Lucid dreaming is
closely associated physiologically with meditation, according to EEG measurements of alpha waves occurring in both
states. Indeed, meditators have more lucid dreams than non-
meditators, particularly if they have been practicing for a
long time. Whereas most lucid dreams are relatively realistic, the lucid dreams of long-time meditators tend to include images of white light, experiences of flying or
floating, and encounters with spiritual beings.[42]

Many lucid dreamers also experience what is known as
"false awakening," in which they dream that they have
woken up; this often occurs after a lucid dream.

Some dream researchers and therapists have found that the ability to dream lucidly and control the content of dreams can be taught (a talent particularly valuable to nightmare victims). For example, in a Stanford University experiment, volunteers fell asleep wearing special masks that detect REM sleep and turn on a flashing red light. The flashing red lights could be seen by the sleepers and they were thus alerted that they were dreaming.[43]

The following method for learning lucid dreaming (without any special equipment) was suggested by researcher Stephen LaBerge to one of his subjects. He instructed her to silently repeat the phrase ''I'm dreaming'' while counting (''One, I'm dreaming, two, I'm dreaming,'' etc.) during sleep onset. She did this and found that eventually she *was* dreaming. After doing this for a week, she was able to dream lucidly without the ''I'm dreaming'' mantra.[44]

(For more on lucid dreamwork techniques, see chapter 6.)

[I]f all the eye movements of REM sleep are randomly generated by a madman in the brain stem, how are lucid dreamers able to voluntarily execute eye-movement signals in accordance with pre-sleep agreements? Of course, the answer . . . is that the Hobson-McCarley hypothesis *cannot* be the whole story. I believe Hobson and McCarley are right about much of what they say about *physiological* determinants of the form of dreams; it is evident that dreams also have *psychological* determinants, and therefore any satisfactory theory of dream content ought to include both.[45]

Although neuroscientists have made some headway in dissecting the physical aspects of dreaming, perhaps the many unanswered questions indicate that it does not all come down to chemistry. The long-standing rift between physical and psychoanalytical dream interpreters may be bridged by the interdisciplinary approach that is gradually developing.

> When we make the interdisciplinary bargain we give up any right to stop the dialogue we have begun. . . . The bargain is precisely this: we enter a dialogue with others, and we pledge to remain faithful to the dialogue wherever it may go, wherever it may take us. . . . For my part, I believe the risks of not making this bargain are far worse—the risks of falling into a safe, secure narrowness of vision which protects our autonomy but prevents us from deepening our knowledge and widening our understanding.[46]

NOTES

1. Montague Ullman and Nan Zimmerman, *Working with Dreams*, p. 70. Los Angeles: Jeremy P. Tarcher, Inc., 1979.

2. Harry T. Hunt, *The Multiplicity Of Dreams*, p. 29. New Haven, CT: Yale University Press, 1989.

3. Sharon Begley, "The Stuff That Dreams Are Made Of," *Newsweek* (August 14, 1989): 43.

4. Edward Dolnick, "What Dreams Are (Really) Made Of," *The Atlantic Monthly* (July 1990): 42.

5. Hunt, *op.cit.,* p.24

6. "Dreamchasers," *Psychology Today* (April 1989): 60.

7. Calvin Trillin, "The Discovery of Rapid Eye Movements." In *The New World of Dreams*, edited by Ralph L. Woods and Herbert B. Greenhouse, p. 277. New York: Macmillan Publishing Co., 1974.

8. Ann Faraday, *Dream Power*, p. 52. New York: Berkley Books, 1972.

9. Lynne Lamberg, "Night Pilot," *Psychology Today* (July/ Aug. 1988): 35–42.

10. Gay Gaer Luce, "Sleepwalking Not Related to Dreams." In *The New World of Dreams*, edited by Ralph L. Woods and

Herbert B. Greenhouse, p. 334. New York: Macmillan Publishing Co., 1974.

11. Ullman and Zimmerman, *op. cit.*, p. 69.

12. David Foulkes, "How Do Hypnagogic Dreams Differ from REM Dreams?" In *The New World of Dreams*, edited by Ralph L. Woods and Herbert B. Greenhouse, p. 324. New York: Macmillan Publishing Co., 1974.

13. Hunt, *op. cit.*, p. 182.

14. Ian Oswald, "Drowsy Dreams Are Micro-Dreams." In *The New World of Dreams*, edited by Ralph L. Woods and Herbert B. Greenhouse, p. 318. New York: Macmillan Publishing Co., 1974.

15. Herbert Greenhouse, "The Effect of Drugs on Dreaming." In *The New World of Dreams*, edited by Ralph L. Woods and Herbert B. Greenhouse, pp. 390–391. New York: Macmillan Publishing Co., 1974.

16. Jonathan Winson, "The Meaning of Dreams," *Scientific American* (November 1990): 95–96.

17. "Dreamchasers," *Psychology Today* (April 1989): 60.

18. Lamberg, *art. cit.*, pp. 35–42.

19. Dianne Hales, "The Late Show: What's Behind the Drama in Our Dreams," *Mademoiselle* (May 1985): 234.

20. Winson, *art. cit.*, p. 87.

21. As discussed in Faraday, *op.cit.*, pp. 32–33.

22. Robert C. Smith, "Traumatic Dreams as an Early Warning of Health Problems." In *Dreamtime and Dreamwork*, edited by Stanley Krippner, p. 227. Los Angeles: Jeremy P. Tarcher, 1990.

23. *Ibid.*, p. 226.

24. Rae Corelli, "An Awakening Debate," *Maclean's* (April 23, 1990): 43.

25. Sarah Boxer, "Inside Our Sleeping Minds," *Modern Maturity* (Oct.–Nov. 1989): 48.

26. Begley, *art. cit.*, p. 43.

27. Calvin Hall and Bill Domhoff, "The Difference Between Men and Woman Dreamers." In *The New World of Dreams*, edited by Ralph L. Woods and Herbert B. Greenhouse, p. 16. New York: Macmillan Publishing Co., 1974.

28. Patricia Maybruck, "Pregnancy and Dreams." In *Dreamtime and Dreamwork*, edited by Stanley Krippner, pp 146–147. Los Angeles: Jeremy P. Tarcher, 1990.

29. Ursula Niederer, "Children's Home Dreams: Content and Relation to Anxiety," *ASD Newsletter* (Jan./Feb. 1990): 3.

30. Robert L. Van de Castle, "Animal Figures in Dreams: Age, Sex, and Culture Difference," *ASD Newsletter* (March/April 1990): 1.

31. Charles W. Kimmins, "The Dreams of Children." In *The New World of Dreams*, edited by Ralph L. Woods and Herbert B. Greenhouse, p. 29. New York: Macmillan Publishing Co., 1974.

32. David Foulkes, Michael Hollifield, Laura Bradley, et al., "Waking Self-Understanding, REM-Dream Self Representation, and Cognitive Ability Variables at Ages 5–8," *Dreaming* (March 1991): 41–51.

33. Hunt, *op. cit.*, p. 43.

34. H. Roffwarg, J. Muzio and W. Dement, "Ontogenetic Development of the Human Sleep-Dream Cycle," *Science* 152: 604–619.

35. Kenneth Z. Altshuler, Martin Barad and Alvin I. Goldfarb, "Dreams of the Aged." In *The New World of Dreams*, edited by Ralph L. Woods and Herbert B. Greenhouse, pp. 36–37. New York: Macmillan Publishing Co., 1974.

36. Allison Truett and Henry Van Twyver, "The Sleep and Dreams of Animals (II)." In *The New World of Dreams*, edited by Ralph L. Woods and Herbert B. Greenhouse, p. 355. New York: Macmillan Publishing Co., 1974.

37. Edwin Kahn, William Dement, Charles Fisher and Joseph E. Barmack, "Most People Dream in Color." In *The New World of Dreams*, edited by Ralph L. Woods and Herbert B. Greenhouse, pp. 363–364. New York: Macmillan Publishing Co., 1974.

38. Deidre Barrett and Michael Loeffler, "The Effect of Depression on Dream Content," *ASD Newsletter* (March/April 1990): 4.

39. C. Green, *Lucid Dreams*. London: Hamish Hamilton, 1968.

40. Harry T. Hunt. *The Multiplicity of Dreams*, p. 197. New Haven, CT: Yale University Press, 1989.

41. Jayne I. Gackenbach, "Women and Meditators as Gifted Lucid Dreamers." In *Dreamtime and Dreamwork*, edited by Stanley Krippner, p. 245. Los Angeles: Jeremy P. Tarcher, 1990.

42. *Ibid.*

43. Begley, *art. cit.*, p. 43.

44. Stephen LaBerge, *Lucid Dreaming*, p. 135. Los Angeles: Jeremy P. Tarcher, 1985.

45. *Ibid.*, p. 187.

46. Kelly Bulkley, "Interdisciplinary Dreaming: Hobson's Successes and Failures," *Dreaming* (Sept. 1991): 233–234.

2

Cross-Cultural Beliefs About Dreams

If an Ashanti man from West Africa dreams that he has made love to a married woman, he must hurry out first thing in the morning to the garbage heap (which doubles as the women's latrine) and solemnly whisper, "O midden heap, I have dreamed an evil dream, grant that it may never happen like that." One must carry any bad dream away to the midden, which is where everything bad is deposited.[1]

If an Ashanti man dreams of making love to a woman he has not slept with, it means he will never have her, because his soul has already possessed hers.[2] In the Melanesian Trobriand Islands, this sort of dream has a different meaning—it signifies that the woman has been performing love magic, that she desires the man, and he will rush off in the morning to find her.[3]

These illustrations reflect some basic attitudes toward dreams typical of such peoples as the Ashanti and the Trobrianders. The first Ashanti dream was prophetic, but the prophesied event could be avoided through the proper conduct of a prescribed ritual. The meaning of the second Ashanti dream reveals something basic about the understanding of dreams in tribal societies—dreams are assumed to represent the memories of the soul's adventures during the night. In both Ashanti dreams, the dreamer's soul is believed actually to have made love to the soul of the

woman he dreamed about. The same is true of the Trobriand dream, but here the spiritual lovemaking is presumed
to have been brought about through magical actions on the
part of the woman.

The idea that dreams represent the nocturnal adventures
of the soul may have been humankind's earliest understanding of these imaginary creations of the sleeping brain. For
that reason, anthropological accounts are a good place to
start unraveling the meaning of dreams. There are other
reasons to begin with these accounts, as well.

Although historically most recorded traditions of dream
interpretation view the dream as related more directly to
the mind and body of the dreamer than is true of tribal
societies, the same general classification of dreams holds
good in both cases. Not only this, but in one important
respect—the idea that dreams foretell the future in some
way, that they carry omens, auguries, or prophecies—
dream interpretation in tribal cultures resembles that of
many other traditions. As we will see later, the forward-
looking aspect of dreams was lost in the twentieth century
with Freud and his followers, but has been regained with
Jung.

The Animistic Outlook

While tribal cultures differ from each other in many
ways, they share a common outlook on the world, called
"animistic" by British anthropologist Edward Tylor in his
book, *Primitive Culture* (1871).[4] As Tylor portrayed it, animism is a system of beliefs about souls and spirits and
their place in the natural world. Not only human beings,
but lower animals and plants, and even things we would
consider inanimate, such as stones, are endowed with souls.
In addition, the animistic world is populated by nature spirits, evil spirits, and supernatural beings of various kinds.

Animism is dualistic—it asserts a distinction between the body on the one hand, and the spirit or soul on the other. The physical body is thought of as a container, the soul as its content. At death, the soul leaves the body permanently, but it may also leave during life, during what we call out-of-body and near-death experiences. Illness is due to the soul's getting into trouble during its wanderings, its absence from the body for a prolonged period of time, or the invasion of the sleeper's body by some foreign entity; for these reasons, dreams may be used to help diagnose and treat illness.

Modern religions have accustomed us to the idea of a single, indivisible soul, but in the animistic view the soul may be multifaceted, if not multiple. A single human body may be home to more than one soul. These souls may each have different functions during the life of the individual: one may be in charge of the breath, one of the intellect, another of the bones, etc., and they may have different fates after death. One may cease to exist, another may travel to the Land of the Dead, while a third may return to the living in the body of a newborn child. Where there is but a single soul, different facets may be in charge of different aspects of the body during life, and the soul may split apart after death.

Reincarnation beliefs are common in animistic societies, but the belief in multiple or multifaceted souls means the soul may simultaneously reincarnate *and* exist in the Land of the Dead. The soul residing in the Land of the Dead may return to visit living persons in their dreams, and may appear to them in the waking state as an apparition.

Many animistic societies have what is called a "mythic charter"—a system of stories that tells about the creation of the world and the beings who founded the society whose myths these are. The mythic charter acts as a model or guide to the conduct of life. Things are done in a certain way because that is the way they were done by the founders during the mythic age. For the Australian Aborigines, the mythic age is still alive and continuing parallel to the real world, and at night a person's soul leaves this world and enters that realm (appropriately enough, called the "Dream-time").

For the Aborigines there is thus a continuing interaction between the two realms, which provides a means for "updating" the mythic charter as real-life events require. In other societies, the mythic age is situated in the past, but the mythic charter may be updated through the dictates of supernatural beings who appear in dreams. In this way, dreams provide both a link with the mythic past and a way of keeping it relevant to present concerns.

Animistic Dream Types

Dream researcher Harry T. Hunt identifies four types of dreams common to animistic societies.[5] The classifications below follow his, although the examples given are different:

1. Incidental personal dreams, the most common and least important type of dream. Incidental dreams are understood to be based on personal desires and experiences—what Freud called "day residues" (see chapters 4 and 6). The dreams described at the beginning of this chapter are incidental dreams.

2. Diagnostic or prognostic dreams, which indicate illness and help to prescribe remedies. Dreams of this sort may at the same time be "pathogenic," that is, they themselves may bring or cause sickness to the dreamer. In pathogenic dreams, the soul undergoes some illness-causing adventure, such as a visit to the Land of the Dead, or the dreamer is invaded by a malignant entity, such as an evil spirit or witch.

3. Omen dreams, which contain predictions or prophecies of future events. Many omen dreams may in fact be precognitive, that is, they may be based on some extrasensory awareness of things yet to come (see chapter 4). The predicted event may be avoided by sharing the dream or by acting it out, practices which some researchers have compared to modern psychotherapy. Auspicious omen dreams may also be sought through dream incubation, for instance, by inviting a dream the night before going off on a hunt or taking to the warpath.

4. Message dreams, often called "culture pattern dreams," in which the dreamer receives a message or a gift, most often from a supernatural being. Shamans induce message dreams as part of their training exercises, and they are commonly associated with seclusions that are a part of "initiations" into adult society at puberty. By introducing new elements into a culture, message dreams provide a way of "updating" the mythic charter by which people conduct their lives. They have sometimes inspired native revitalization movements, such as the Ghost Dance religion that swept across the United States in the latter part of the nineteenth century. A special type of message dream is the "announcing dream," in which a deceased person appears and announces the intention to be reborn to a particular woman.

These four types of dreams are not mutually exclusive. That is, although most dreams in animistic societies may be assigned to one of these categories, many dreams would fit into more than one category.

Diagnostic and Prognostic Dreams

Kolawa was a very attractive woman in her late twenties, the youngest and also the favorite wife of Akwando. Years earlier, Akwando had vied for Kolawa's hand against Ifanim. Upon losing, Ifanim married Kolawa's older and less attractive sister.

The first two children born to Akwando and Kolawa died in infancy. When their third child became seriously ill as well, Akwando was convinced that his misfortune was due to sorcery. He consulted diviners, but they were unable to come up with any likely candidates. Then Kolawa confessed that she had been having erotic dreams about Ifanim.

Kolawa's confession told Akwando everything he needed to know. He called a public meeting, and laid out his case against Ifanim. Kolawa was an honest woman, he told the crowd, and there was no reason to doubt her when she said that she had been having these dreams. Ifanim must be using magic so that his spirit could enjoy access to Kolawa's spirit, which meant that he, Akwando, had been cuckolded. Moreover, the same adulterous magic must be what was killing his children one after another. Ifanim proclaimed his innocence, but the evidence against him was ironclad, and in the end he promised to desist.

Ifanim's implied admission of guilt brought about a change in Akwando's attitude toward him. By the end of the day, the two men were again fast friends. They agreed that women were nothing but troublemakers—and in a dramatic gesture of solidarity, they divorced their wives! Within a few days, Kolawa was back with Akwando, but Ifanim was still separated from his wife when anthropologist Donald Tuzin left the area several months later.

Tuzin learned from a friend of Kolawa's that she had not come forth about her dreams earlier because, until it occurred to her that there might be a connection between these dreams and the illnesses and deaths of her children, she had not seen any harm in them. They were a secret between her and Ifanim.

After Kolawa's confession and the confrontation between Akwando and Ifanim, Kolawa ceased to dream of having sex with Ifanim, and her baby recovered completely.[6]

Kolawa, Akwando and Ifanim are Arapesh, from northeastern New Guinea. Tuzin relates the story of another Arapesh man, old Wolof, who one day suddenly went blind. Although Wolof's family tried various medicinal and magical cures, none helped, and Wolof himself was convinced that they could not help. He had dreamed that his deceased father had thrown what seemed to be ashes in his face and eyes, and this indicated that his blindness had a supernatural cause and would not respond to earthly remedies. For Wolof there was no special meaning in his father's having done this to him—his father was simply a representative of the ancestors, who were known to be capable of such things.[7]

Wolof's dream occurred the night of the day in which he had gone blind, and gave him the explanation for his blindness. Had the dream occurred on the previous night, that is, had it preceded rather than followed the onset of the blindness, it would have been considered "pathogenic," or illness-causing. Wolof's deceased father's action would have been interpreted as being the cause of the blindness, rather than simply as offering an explanation of it.

Psychoanalytically trained anthropologist George Devereux described a pathogenic dream reported to him by a Mohave Indian woman. The woman had become upset, anorectic, and severely depressed after having dreamt that a deceased relative cooked and served her a fish whose head, she realized after she had begun to eat the fish, was that of her dead mother. For the Mohave, who live in the southwestern United States, dreams about ghosts, especially about the ghosts of relatives, are believed to cause illness as a matter of course. Particularly dangerous are dreams that involve being fed by the dead, so the woman interpreted her malady as having been caused by the events of the dream.[8]

Figuring out what in a pathogenic dream is illness-causing is not always easy. An evil witch or sorcerer may disguise his identity by borrowing the shadow soul of another sorcerer, or he may assume an entirely different shape, so that he appears in the victim's dream in an impenetrable disguise.[9]

The connection between sickness and dreams is so strong that in every case of illness the shaman or medicine man promptly investigates the patient's dreams, in order to make the proper diagnosis and prognosis. The fact that any dream—whatever its ultimate relationship to the illness may turn out to be—is used for these purposes implies that all dreams, including incidental dreams and omen dreams, are viewed as symptoms of illness and as indications of its seriousness.[10]

Illness categories, however, are established in a society's mythic charter. Devereux describes how this works for the Mohave. "All illnesses were foreordained, established, and created at the time of creation. The event of creation included (in principle) at least one such concrete case of illness (e.g. gastroenteritis) and at least one actual cure of this illness. The illness "gastroenteritis" exists because there was a case of such an illness during creation, which was both a precedent and a "prophecy" that such illnesses would occur subsequently. Each case of this illness—a hundred years ago, today, and a hundred years hence—is thus a duplication of the mythical precedent and an implementation of the "prophecy" that that prototypical illness represented."[11]

Omen Dreams

The interpretation of omens in dreams—even what constitutes an omen—varies from one culture to another, so that in order to interpret a dream appropriately, one must know something about the culture of the dreamer. What is a good omen in one place may be a bad omen in another, and vice versa.

Soon after he began his fieldwork among the Quiche Maya of Guatemala, Dennis Tedlock dreamed that he was given an ear of corn from an unknown person at a party; opening the husk, he found the cob already roasted, with butter, salt, lime juice, and chili powder on it. He knew what this would have meant to the Zuñi, among whom he had previously worked: the unknown person would have been interpreted as either a deceased person or a witch out to poison him, and he would have been told that he should not have accepted the corn, much less opened it. It was lucky that he had not eaten the corn, or he would be destined to die soon.

The Zuñi medicine man to whom he would have reported the dream would have draped himself with a blanket and inhaled the fumes of a burning piñon stick. Then he would have put the stick in a glass of water, fished it out and marked Tedlock's chest with it, and instructed him to drink the water. He would have told him that it was a good thing that he had reported this bad dream, so that its portended ill effects could be averted. If the dream had been one in a series of bad dreams, the medicine man would have arranged for Tedlock to be whipped publicly and initiated into one of the Zuñi's secret societies.

Instead, the Quiche diviner to whom he reported his dream said that it was an extremely good dream, but since Tedlock had not eaten the unknown ancestor's gift, it was not yet completed. The next time he was offered food in a dream, Tedlock was told, he should accept it and eat it on the spot. Twenty days later Tedlock dreamt that another unknown person offered him a green banana which, upon opening, he discovered to be ripe. He promptly ate the banana, finding it very sweet. When he reported this dream, the diviner smiled and told him it was a good augury—he and his wife, Barbara, were being accepted by the ancestors.[12]

This difference in interpretation does not mean the Quiche do not have bad dreams or recognize bad omens— it is just that they do not regard all relatives in dreams in the same negative light the Zuñi do. The difference is connected to the different ways these two people think about the dreaming process. The Zuñi think of the dream as something which happens to them, whereas the Quiche believe they have active control over all dream actions. The Zuñi share bad dreams in the morning, but good dreams only after they have come true. Sharing bad dreams and then performing certain actions keeps them from being ''completed'' in waking life, whereas the events of a good dream are wanted, and therefore are kept to oneself until they can be completed. The Quiche share all dreams, good and bad, immediately on waking.[13]

The idea that dreamlife actions prefigure daytime events and that steps must be taken to prevent unwanted actions from coming to pass is found in many animistic peoples. The Zuñi block the fulfillment through ritual, but in other societies the same thing is accomplished by acting out bad dreams. Seventeenth-century Iroquois went so far as to act out all dreams, good or bad, on the theory that dreams were the soul's way of communicating with the body. Whatever the soul desired, it represented in a dream, and these desires had to be carried out in waking life or the soul would become angry and turn on the dreamer, causing him or her to become sick.[14]

The dreamed-of events might be quite elaborate. Once a Huron warrior returned to his village and said he had dreamed of one of the Huron's culture heros, He-who-holds-up-the-sky, in the guise of a little dwarf. He-who-holds-up-the-sky had demanded that he receive a sacrifice of ten dogs, ten porcelain beads from each cabin, a wampum belt ten rows wide, four measures of sunflower seeds, and an equal amount of beans. As for the warrior, he was to have two married women at his disposal for five days and five nights. If these demands were not met, item by item, He-who-holds-up-the-sky said, he would destroy the village. Needless to say, his demands were promptly met, including the provo for the dreamer.

Dreams with explicit sexual content were not unusual, and these too were carried out to the letter, to the disgust of the Jesuits who recorded them.

Dreams were acted out even when they were harmful to the dreamer. In 1642, a Huron man dreamed that a non-Huron had taken him captive and burned him to death. In order to keep this dream from coming true, fires were set in the building in which the Huron tortured their own captives, and the dreamer danced naked through them while his fellows burned him with torches. After subjecting himself to this abuse for some time, he dashed out of the circle, grabbed a dog that was being held for him, and paraded through the village cabins with it, praying that it be accepted in his place. The dog was finally killed with a club, roasted, and eaten at a public feast; the ritual was performed to keep something similar from happening to the man.[15]

Anthony Wallace, in writing about the Iroquois, made the point that since many dreams expressed something of self-interest to the dreamer, acting them out actually had a therapeutic function. A similar point is made about the

Senoi of the Malay Peninsula by Kilton Stewart, who visited them in 1935. Stewart likens breakfast in a Senoi household to a ''dream clinic,'' in which the father and older brothers listen to and analyze the dreams of all the children. After breakfast, the male members of the community gather together and discuss the dreams of the previous night.

Like the Mexican Quiche, the Senoi believe that they can outface and master all the forces and beings of the dream universe, and therefore are not scared of their dreams. From childhood, they are encouraged to control their dream activities. If a child reports being scared by a dream of falling, he or she is told this is a very good dream, because falling is the quickest way to get in touch with the powers of the spirit world. In the course of time, according to Stewart, fearful dreams of falling change into joyous dreams of flying.

Pleasurable dreams should be continued until they arrive at a resolution which, on waking, leaves one with something of beauty or of use to the group. One should always reach one's destination in flying dreams, meet the beings there, hear their music, see their designs, observe their dances, and learn their useful knowledge. The control over dreamlife described for the Senoi is not unlike that exercised by lucid dreamers (chapter 4).[16]

So strong is the idea that bad events are foretold by dreams, that if something bad happens, it may be assumed that there was a dream about it which was either not remembered or was not acted out. For the Zuñi, the idea that death is caused by the dead sharing food with the living is so strong that when a person dies, relatives often wonder aloud if he or she did not perhaps have such an ominous dream which they failed to report, thus allowing the dream events to be brought to completion.[17]

Because the soul's adventures at night are thought to

pave the way for actions during the day, dreams may be sought before setting off on an important undertaking. Michael F. Brown describes how dreams and visions induced by hallucinogenic plants are used by the South American Jivaro to ensure successful hunting. In one case, a hallucinogenic dream was believed to account for a cure, and was thus the opposite of pathogenic. A Jivaro man, afflicted by a native ailment whose major symptom was the inability to find game animals, ingested a hallucinogenic plant. Under its influence he dreamed he saw many animals, of all the desirable species, and shortly after having this dream, he became a successful hunter again.[18]

Message Dreams

Message and gift dreams are most common during seclusions and fasts that accompany initiations into adulthood or into secret societies, or which are a part of training to become a shaman or medicine man. The messages often are brought by a person's guardian spirit, who may be acquired at this time.

Puberty fasts (often called "vision quests") were once especially common among native North Americans. It was customary for the Ojibwa, for instance, to send boys aged ten to fifteen out to fast for six or seven nights, or until they had a dream or vision experience. Supernatural "grandfathers" were believed to take pity on the boys and "bless" them by offering to share their knowledge and power.

In one dream collected by A. Irving Hallowell, the supernatural first appeared disguised as a human being. Later he told the boy, "Grandchild, I think you are strong enough to go on without me." With this, he began dancing, and as he danced, he turned into a golden eagle. Looking down at himself, the boy found that he too was covered with feathers, and when the eagle took off toward the south, the boy followed. From this dream, the boy became aware that the golden eagle was his guardian spirit.

Similar dreams involving supernaturals may occur at other times, and to individuals who have not undergone the puberty fast, which is uncommon today. Hallowell describes a dream in which a man entered a house to find a small boy with a bow and two arrows. "I'm going to find out how strong you are," the boy told the dreamer, whereupon the dreamer took up a position in the middle of the room. When the boy shot his arrows, he managed to dodge them, then he and the boy exchanged places. The dreamer hit the boy with the second arrow he shot, although he did not kill him. Hitting the boy was not difficult, because, although he seemed to be moving constantly, he nevertheless stayed in the same place. The boy acknowledged that he had been beaten, then revealed that he was actually a type of insect, something like a fly. He told the dreamer that if he were ever in a fight, he should think of him; his body would quiver like his, and he would be invincible.[19]

Song is widely associated with spiritual power, and songs may be received from supernaturals in dreams. The most remarkable example of this is the Tibetan "Gesar," over a million lines long, containing sixteen distinct episodes and a cast of thousands—no doubt the longest ballad in the world. Balladeers, most of them illiterate, claim not to have learned the song in waking life, but to have inherited it in a dream from which they awake with a compulsion to sing—which they do with their eyes half shut and an air of intense concentration, for days on end.[20]

Kilton Stewart describes a type of gift-message dream of the Senoi which he presents as working-out of problems confronted by the dreamer in waking life. A falling tree that had wounded a man appeared in his dreams, explained that it wished to be his friend, then gave him a new and unknown rhythm to play on his drums. Another man shared some wild gourd seeds with his group, but they gave everyone diarrhea. That night he had a dream in which the spirit of the gourd seeds appeared to him, made him vomit up the seeds, and explained that they were only good as a purgative, for use when people were sick. The gourd seed spirit then gave the dreamer a song and taught him a dance which he could show his group on waking, thereby gaining recognition and winning back some of his self-esteem.[21]

J. S. Lincoln gave the name ''culture pattern dream'' to dreams involving supernatural beings or ancestral spirits which act in stereotypical ways, occur on set occasions (such as puberty fasts), or are required before one can attain certain levels of status (such as adulthood). Lincoln drew attention to the origin of songs, dances, and other cultural items in dreams of this sort, and concluded that ''a large part of primitive culture is a result of the dream, or more accurately a result of the psychological and cultural processes behind the dream. These processes are given form in the dream and influence the culture directly from the latter.''[22]

There is an obvious relationship between dreams and a society's mythic charter. As Hallowell pointed out in discussing the Ojibwa, the *dramatis personae* of dreams and myths are often the same. In fact, myths provide the main knowledge about the beings encountered in dreams. Since the myths are taken as true stories, and dreams as memories of actual experiences, dreams bring persons face-to-face with mythic beings.[23]

Waud Kracke makes a similar point in reference to the Parintinin Indians of Brazil. Dreams provide an avenue of communication with superhuman beings otherwise known primarily in myth. In dreams, some older members of the community, especially those with shamanistic aspirations, commune with these superhuman beings.[24] Because these same beings were involved in the creation of the society, it follows that through their interaction with people in dreams, the beings can introduce and sanction changes in a society which could be legitimated in no other way.

Stewart describes Senoi dreams that incorporate new elements and help to bring about social change. One Senoi man had a dream which helped to break down social barriers between his group and encroaching Chinese and Islamic colonies. A supernatural being showed the dreamer how to perform a new dance. Dancers only were required to change their dietary habits and to wear new clothing, in line with the cultural habits of their new neighbors, but the dance was so good that nearly all Senoi along the border chose to do so.[25]

Occasionally message dreams have had wider repercussions. Dreams and visions of a return to an age before the coming of the white man provided the inspiration for the Ghost Dance, a revivalist religion which began on the Great Plains and quickly spread all the way to the Pacific in the latter part of the nineteenth century, before it was put down by the U.S. Army.[26]

A special type of message dream is the "announcing dream," in which a deceased figure—usually a relative of the dreamer—appears and announces its intention to be reborn to the dreamer. This type of dream has been best studied by Ian Stevenson, a psychiatrist and psychical researcher. Stevenson has reported several such dreams from the Tlingit Indians of Alaska. In one example, a pregnant woman dreamed of two deceased relatives, Fred and Harry. The family believed that Fred had already been reborn, and in the dream Fred said: "Harry wants to come down here too." This led the dreamer's mother to predict that the pregnant woman would have a boy, which she did.

In another case, the grandmother of a pregnant woman had two dreams, in the course of which one of her dear deceased friends appeared to her. In the first dream, the deceased friend, a Mrs. Bigelow, was sitting at the edge of the pier next to the dreamer's house in a fishing village. Mrs. Bigelow was alone and silent. In the second dream, Mrs. Bigelow was going through the dreamer's house looking at the beds, all of which seemed to be in use or already assigned. Then she said: "I think Alice has room." Alice was the dreamer's pregnant granddaughter. The child later born to Alice was a girl, and she gave what Stevenson calls "quite impressive evidence of knowledge of the life and friends of Mrs. Bigelow."[27]

Animistic Dream Symbols

The contrast in the Zuñi and Quiche interpretations of Dennis Tedlock's dream, described above, should prepare us for the way many symbols take their meanings from their cultural context. In our Western culture, Freud would have downplayed the significance of the dreamed figure and instead emphasized the ear of corn and the banana, both of which he would have interpreted as unambiguous phallic symbols, indicating a latent dream content of a sexual nature.

The Freudian distinction between manifest (surface) and latent (unconscious) content of dreams is observed by many animistic peoples, but the concerns that influence the latent content are very different. The Jivaro, for instance, are very concerned with hunting, and take an erect penis in a dream to represent a snake, rather than the other way around.[28] Similarly, for the Parintintin of Brazil, a sexual dream predicts the killing of a tapir because the tapir, in a well-known myth, was the adulterous lover of a mythic figure.[29]

Mythic associations are one way that dream events may be interpreted. Other events are interpreted in line with some general symbol system current in the culture, whereas the meaning of other dreams is derived from a more direct process of association. In yet other dreams, particularly if they are of the incidental personal type, events are simply interpreted naturalistically, as the literal adventures of the soul.

Barbara Tedlock describes a dream in which her Quiche informant was uncertain of the most appropriate interpretation. The man dreamed he was about to enter onto a road when he saw a group of girls approaching on bicycles. There were some ten or twelve girls, and then he was riding ahead of them. The dreamer was unsure whether to interpret the dream by a process of direct association, as signaling a coming leadership role for him, or symbolically, as portending his death, because certain types of vehicles—buses and trucks—generally indicated that the dreamer was being taken away to the Land of the Dead.[30]

The most appropriate interpretation may depend on context, including the status of the dreamer in his or her society. Another of Barbara Tedlock's dream accounts, told to her by the Quiche dream interpreter to whom she and her husband were apprenticed, concerned this man's younger brother. The brother had once reported a dream in which he was embraced by their dead grandmother, after which she walked with him, laughing and talking, down a steep mountain path. The diviner interpreted this as a bad dream, and predicted the brother's death, because the walk had been down rather than up the hill (and indeed, the brother died within a year). Had his brother been a diviner himself, or had he even been in training to become one, however, he would have interpreted the same dream as a good dream. It occurred in the mountains, where the gods lived, and an ancestor appeared and talked and laughed with the dreamer.[31]

Jung was influenced by the animistic interpretation of

dreams in developing his own dream theory. He modeled his distinction between personal and archetypal dream symbols on the distinction between incidental and culture pattern dreams that he encountered on a visit to Hopi and Taos pueblos. In contrast to Freud, he placed the most stress on the dream figure, which he understood to represent an archetype, arising from the unconscious.

NOTES

1. R. S. Rattray, "Sex Dreams of the African Ashantis." In *The New World of Dreams*, edited by Ralph L. Woods and Herbert B. Greenhouse, pp. 117–118. New York: Macmillan, 1974.

2. *Ibid.*, p. 117.

3. Bronislaw Malinowski, "The Dream Is the Cause of the Wish." In *The New World of Dreams*, edited by Ralph L. Woods and Herbert B. Greenhouse, pp 118–119. New York: Macmillan, 1974.

4. Edward Burnett Tylor, *Religion in Primitive Culture*, vol. 2. New York: Harper Torchbooks, 1958.

5. Harry T. Hunt, *The Multiplicity of Dreams: Memory, Imagination and Consciousness*, p. 82. New Haven: Yale University Press, 1989.

6. Donald Tuzin, "The Breath of a Ghost: Dreams and the Fear of the Dead." *Ethos.* 1975, vol. 3: 555–578.

7. *Ibid.*, p. 571.

8. George Devereux, "Pathogenic Dreams in Non-Western Societies." In *The Dream and Human Societies*, edited by G.E. von Grunebaum and Roger Callois, pp. 213–226. Berkeley and Los Angeles: University of California Press, 1966. Pp. 224–226.

9. *Ibid.*, p. 225.

10. *Ibid.*, p. 223.

11. *Ibid.*, p. 219.

12. Barbara Tedlock, "Zuñi and Quiche Dream Sharing and Interpreting." In *Dreaming: Anthropological and Psychological Interpretations*, edited by Barbara Tedlock, pp. 105–131. Cam-

bridge: Cambridge University Press, 1987. Pp. 105–106.

13. *Ibid.,* p. 119.

14. Anthony F. C. Wallace, "Dreams and the Wishes of the Soul: A Type of Psychoanalytic Theory among the Seventeenth Century Iroquois." *American Anthropologist* (1958), vol. 60:234–248. P. 238.

15. Ibid., p. 239.

16. Kilton Stewart, "Dream Theory in Malaya." In *Altered States of Consciousness: A Book of Readings,* edited by Charles T. Tart, pp. 159–168. New York: Wiley, 1969.

17. Tedlock, *op. cit.,* p. 123.

18. F. Michael Brown, "Ropes of Sand: Order and Imagery in Aguaruna Dreams." In *Dreaming: Anthropological and Psychological Interpretations,* edited by Barbara Tedlock, pp. 31–54. Cambridge: Cambridge University Press. Pp. 162–163.

19. A. Irving Hallowell, "The Role of Dreams in Ojibwa Culture." In *The Dream and Human Societies,* edited by G. E. von Grunebaum and Roger Caillois, pp. 267–292. Berkeley and Los Angeles: University of California Press, 1966. Pp. 284–285.

20. Robert K. Denton, "Ethnographic Considerations in the Cross-Cultural Study of Dreaming." In *Dreams: A Sourcebook,* edited by Jayne Gackenbach, pp. 317–358. New York: Garland Press, 1989. P. 327.

21. Stewart, *op. cit.,* pp. 166–167.

22. Jackson S. Lincoln, *The Dream in Primitive Culture,* p. 93. Baltimore: Williams and Wilkins, 1935.

23. Hallowell, *op. cit.,* pp. 278–279.

24. Waud Kracke, "Myths in Dreams, Thought in Images: An Amazonian Contribution to the Psychoanalytic Theory of Primary Process." In *Dreaming: Anthropological and Psychological Interpretations,* edited by Barbara Tedlock, pp. 31–54. Cambridge: Cambridge University Press, 1987. P. 31.

25. Stewart, *op. cit.,* p. 167.

26. Weston La Barre, "The Dream, Charisma, and the Culture Hero." In *The Dream and Human Societies,* edited by G. E. von Grunebaum and Roger Caillois, pp. 229–235. Berkeley and Los Angeles: University of California Press, 1966.

27. Ian Stevenson, "Cultural Patterns in Cases Suggestive of Reincarnation among the Tlingit Indians of Southeastern Alaska."

Journal of the American Society for Psychical Research (1966), vol. 60:229–243. Pp. 237–238.

  28. Hunt, *op. cit.*, p. 85.

  29. Kracke, *op. cit.*, p. 33.

  30. Tedlock, *op. cit.*, pp. 121–122.

  31. *Ibid.*, pp. 125–126.

3

Nightmares

The nightmare is the dark side of the dream experience. Instead of images and scenes that give us pleasure or that we want to remember, the most striking features of any nightmare are feelings of dread, helplessness, and sometimes paralysis in the face of danger. While we are often sorry when our dreams end, some nightmares can be so terrifying that we actually wake up screaming.

Yet, like dreams, nightmares can offer some deeper insight into our inner selves, revealing a hidden anxiety or past trauma that is not evident during our waking hours.

Nightmares are not limited to any group of individuals and they are more prevalent than once believed. While some researchers have identified individuals whose mental and emotional states are common to chronic nightmare sufferers, terrifying dreams are also reported by large numbers of seemingly well-adjusted people.

The nightmare experience itself can differ from individual to individual, in both interpretation and intensity. In some, a nightmare can simply be dismissed as a bad dream. In others, a nightmare can be a living hell, filled with very vivid and violent episodes—so terrifying that one would opt to stay awake rather than risk the return of the dream during sleep.

Nightmares do not favor men over women or children over adults. Psychiatrist Ernest Hartmann has suggested that women are more likely to admit nightmares than men. He notes that in our society nightmares are not thought to be "especially manly" and are often associated with fear, which Hartmann says is an "image that is hard for adult men to accept for themselves."[1]

Nightmares are found in all cultures. In some, like ours, they are considered to be bad dreams, while in others they are regarded as harbingers of things to come.

Early societies believed that nightmares were visits from a variety of evil spirits. Later views held that the nightmare was the result of physiological factors, notably indigestion. It was theorized that sleeping on a full stomach would restrict the circulation of blood through the heart and lungs, and would bring on a nightmare. Or, undigested food would cause an irritation that would trigger a response in the nervous system, and would result in a bad dream.[2]

Another widely believed theory proposed that sleeping on your back interfered with the circulation of blood—a situation remedied by a nightmare, which forced the sleeper to wake up and shift position in bed.[3]

While most research today focuses on the psychological roots of the nightmare, there *is* ample evidence linking the experience to a variety of physical factors and influences, such as medication. For example, medicines used in treating high blood pressure, heart problems and Parkinson's disease are known to cause nightmares. Similarly, nightmares are frequently reported by people suffering high fevers, or who have undergone surgery. They can even be triggered by protein-rich foods, such as eggs, meat and cheese, which contain tryptophan, an amino acid.

In the early twentieth century, researchers began advancing psychological explanations for the nightmare. Sigmund Freud regarded a nightmare as a perversion of his wish-fulfillment theories of dreams. Instead of a dream which allows us to imagine some experience that we wish for,

Freud said, the nightmare represents a conflict so great in our minds that "no compromise can be arrived at" and that "sleep is broken and the subject wakes to his danger."[4]

Ernest Jones, a colleague of Freud's, formulated three conditions, which he described as "cardinal features" of a nightmare:

—agonizing dread

—a sense of oppression or heavy weight on the chest that interferes with breathing

—a feeling of helpless paralysis.[5]

Jones said that all nightmares are the result of deeply repressed sexual desires, and the worst are caused by feelings of incest.

The studies of nightmares by Jones and his immediate followers were done before the advent of the modern understanding of the stages of sleep. Since then, researchers have identified a variety of psychological and physiological influences relating to the nightmare experience.

Researchers believe that most nightmares occur during the REM stage of sleep. By comparison, dreams in NREM sleep are said to be more concerned with ordinary affairs of daily living, not the horrifying fantasies the mind can create when in the grip of a nightmare.

Also, many people report nightmares in which they feel paralyzed. This might be explained by the fact that during REM sleep, all motor activity is turned off.

Nightmares and Children

Some researchers hold that nightmares don't afflict children until age five,[6] while others say they can appear in one-year-olds.[7]

Nightmares of children usually involve strange people, monsters or animals. It is generally believed these nightmares are early anxiety dreams that result from children's internalized fears of a waking world still largely unknown to them. A child manifests these fears in the form of dreams in which he or she is being beaten, devoured or chased.[8]

What makes nightmares so troubling for young children, especially those under age five, is their inability to articulate to their parents what has happened; they are simply too young to know what a nightmare is and that it is nothing to be feared. As one researcher has noted, "In very young children, especially under the age of 4 or 5, the inability to establish, even after waking, that the nightmare's oppressors are not real, adds terror to the overwhelming quality of the nightmare experience."[9]

As children grow older and become more able to explain what has happened to them, they receive comfort from their parents in return. By the time children turn seven, they usually recognize nightmares as bad dreams.[10]

Nightmares and Adults

Anxiety causes nightmares for adults as well as for children. While adult anxieties are different, there are definite parallels between nightmares for both age groups. Children feel powerless and helpless in a world they're just getting to know. Adults have their moments of powerlessness and helplessness from stresses in a world they know well.

According to psychiatrist John E. Mack:

Nightmares occur in response to the characteristic danger situations that human beings confront in the course of development, beginning with the fear of strangers and the dread of abandonment in infancy and the fear of bodily injury in early childhood, and ending with the fears of failure, death and loss of function in adulthood and old age . . . Nightmares may become the prototypic expression of the activities that characterize each stage of development.[11]

It's no surprise, then, that nightmares are common among people preparing for a major exam in school, changing jobs, moving or grieving over the loss of a loved one. These are times when our anxiety levels are high or we feel helpless, sometimes out of control. Our nightmares reflect these feelings, taking the form of scenarios in which we're victims of circumstances beyond our control, unable to positively influence the outcome of a terrifying situation in which we find ourselves.

When the stress is removed, when we're made to feel safe again, the attacks subside. In tests done in sleep laboratories, even chronic nightmare sufferers report fewer bad dream experiences, perhaps due to a sense of protection afforded by the laboratory surroundings.

Chronic Nightmare Sufferers

Ernest Hartmann, author of *The Nightmare* (1984), conducted major studies involving chronic nightmare sufferers. He found that such individuals most frequently dreamed of being chased or attacked, and sometimes of being beaten, shot, stabbed or mutilated by their pursuers.

He described frequent nightmare sufferers as individuals who are more sensitive and more easily upset than most. They are open and trusting, and tend not to adopt a defensive posture, and so are more vulnerable. "The most accurate way to sum up the characteristics of these persons is to say that they have thin boundaries or permeable boundaries,"[12] Hartmann said. He also found that frequent nightmare sufferers show tendencies toward mental illness.[13]

I believe that frequent nightmare sufferers—vulnerable, open and sensitive persons with thin boundaries—constitute a group specifically vulnerable to schizophrenic illness.[14]

Interpretations of Nightmares

A number of scenarios are common to most nightmares. When they occur, they may be telling us about difficulties during our waking life that we're not properly dealing with. Common themes include:

Falling. When you fall in a dream, it could symbolize a feeling of failure, a fear of failure, or anxiety that you are in a situation over which you have no control.

Nudity. A dream in which you find yourself without any clothes on—a terribly embarrassing situation—could be a signal that you are experiencing an internal conflict resulting from feelings you are holding in check. Perhaps you want to release these feelings but are afraid of embarrassment.

Climbing. When you find yourself climbing but getting nowhere it could represent similar feelings you have about your progress in life.

Loosening or loss of teeth. The idea that teeth, which we believe are firmly rooted to our jaws, could suddenly fall out or become loose symbolizes a sense of insecurity.

Missing buses, trains or ships. A dream in which you fail to get to the bus or train station on time, or you find that you've been left behind, might suggest you don't feel you are getting where you want to go with your life.

Nightmares and ESP

All cultures have beliefs that sometimes foretell the future. Thus, nightmares that contain visions of death, injury and disaster may provide warnings of impending doom. In one study, half of the nightmare sufferers interviewed told researchers of various paranormal incidents they had experienced, including clairvoyance and precognition, as well as telepathy and out-of-body experiences.

Predictive nightmares, which are experienced by twice as many women as men,[15] are different from a typical nightmare. In these scenarios, the dreamer is not the victim but the observer.

A number of historical events have been predicted in dreams, including the assassination of the Archduke of Hungary that triggered World War I, and the sinking of the *Titanic*. Mark Twain dreamed of his brother's death in an explosion on a riverboat.

While it is difficult to know how much credence to give a nightmare said to predict the future, the *Journal of the Society for Psychical Research* has suggested using the following criteria to establish a link between a dream and event:

—The dreamer must have shared his or her prediction ahead of time.

—The time between when the event is supposed to occur and the nightmare must be brief.

—The suggested event must seem unlikely to occur.

—The dream must be a literal—not symbolic—representation of what is expected.

—There must be a definite link between what the dreamer experienced and what actually happens.[16]

(For more information on the paranormal nature of dreams in general, see chapter 4.)

NOTES

1. Ernest Hartmann, *The Nightmare*, pp. 33–34. New York: Basic Books, 1984.

2. Ernest M. Jones, *On the Nightmare*, pp. 31–33. New York: Liveright Publishing Corp., 1951.

3. *Ibid.*, pp. 27–28.

4. *Ibid.*, p. 43.

5. *Ibid.*, pp. 20–22.

6. Sandra Schulman, *Nightmare*, p. 76. New York: Macmillan Publishing Co., 1979.

7. Hartmann, *op. cit.*, p. 31.

8. John E. Mack, M.D., "New Facts About Nightmares." In *The New World of Dreams*, edited by Ralph L. Woods and Herbert B. Greenhouse, p. 330. New York: Macmillan Publishing Co., 1974.

9. *Ibid.*, p. 331.

10. Schulman, *op. cit.*, p. 78.

11. Mack, *op. cit.*, p. 331.

12. Hartmann, *op. cit.*, p. 104.

13. *Ibid.*, p. 107.

14. *Ibid.*, p. 107.

15. Schulman, *op. cit.*, p. 166.

16. *Ibid.*, p. 184.

4

Dreams and the Paranormal

All dreams can provide messages from the unconscious to the conscious. Sometimes one experiences an unusual dream which seems to contain elements of the paranormal, such as telepathy, precognition or clairvoyance. Other unusual dreams are characterized by a state of lucidity and a feeling of being out-of-body. Research has demonstrated that such dreams are not merely flights of fancy. Perhaps they are interfaces with alternate realities.

Lucid Dreams

A "lucid dream" is a dream in which one is aware that one is dreaming, and can control the events of the dream as they unfold. The name was given to such dreams in 1913 by a Dutchman, Frederik van Eeden (pronounced "Aiden"), himself a prolific lucid dreamer. He recorded about 500 of his own dreams; no fewer than 352 were lucid. Here is an example:

On the night of September 9, 1904, van Eeden dreamed he stood at a table before a window. On the table were various objects. He was perfectly aware that he was dreaming, and he considered what experiments he could make with the objects. He began with trying to break a glass by beating it with a stone, but it would not break. He tried hitting it with his fist, with all his might, realizing how dangerous this would be in waking life. At first the glass still did not break, but when he looked away and then looked back, it had broken. He threw the broken glass out the window, heard the tinkling as the fragments struck the ground, and observed how realistic the sound was. He saw two dogs run away from it quite naturally. He then noticed a decanter of claret on the table and decided to see if he could taste the wine if he drank some of it. With perfect clarity of mind, he reflected that it tasted just like wine.[1]

Van Eeden noted that flying or floating experiences in dreams were a sign that lucidity was in the offing. The lucid part of the dream was often initiated and accompanied by the sensation of flying. Sometimes he felt himself floating swiftly through wide spaces; once he flew backwards; another time, dreaming he was inside a cathedral, he flew up through the immense building at terrific speed.[2]

Lucidity typically arises out of a normal dream state. Some unusual circumstance makes the dreamer aware that he or she is dreaming. Frequent lucid dreamer (and out-of-body experiencer) Oliver Fox tells of the varying stages of lucidity in which he might become aware that he was dreaming of a woman who had four eyes. In the first stage, he would take it entirely naturally in the dream, and only realize the oddity upon waking. In the second stage, he would remark on the oddity, but not appreciate its significance. In the third stage, the four eyes would seem more anomalous, but still he would not become fully cognizant of their implication in the dream. This would happen only if he reached the fourth stage—realizing it was impossible for a woman to have four eyes, and that, if he was seeing one, he must be dreaming.[3]

Parapsychologist Celia Green gives the name "pre-lucid dreams" to those in which the dreamer "adopts a critical attitude toward what he is experiencing, even to the point of asking himself the question 'Am I dreaming?' but without realizing that he is in fact doing so.'' People who habitually ask themselves this question, and even argue with themselves during the dream about whether they are dreaming or not, do not necessarily go on to have fully lucid dreams. Green points out that this means pre-lucid dreams have at least some of the verisimilitude that characterize lucid dreams proper. This is particularly true of ''false awakenings,'' a not uncommon ending to lucid dreams, in which the dreamer seems to awaken and to get up, only to awaken for real a short while later and realize he or she has been dreaming all the while.[4]

Green identifies three ways, besides the dawning of the critical faculty, that lucidity may arise. It may be initiated by the stress of a nightmare, by a reminder of some habitual technique of introspective observation, or by a spontaneous recognition that the quality of the experience is in some indefinable way different from that of waking life.[5] One or more of these four ways are mentioned by many lucid dreamers as well as by dream researcher Stephen LaBerge,[6] and they do seem to cover the ways dream lucidity emerges. The dawning awareness of some incongruity with real life is perhaps the most common way, however.

Green's book *Lucid Dreams* (1968) was the first general study of the phenomenon, but lucid dreams are by no means new. Aristotle alluded to them when he wrote, ''For often, when one is asleep, there is something in consciousness which declares what then represents itself is but a dream.'' The earliest lucid dream in Western history was reported as early as A.D. fifth century, in a letter written by St. Augustine. The monk tells of the Roman physician Gennadius whose doubts about life after death were dispelled when he was brought to realize that if he had eyes with which to see the events of the dream while his body was asleep, those same eyes would be able to see after death.[7]

Lucid dreaming is also mentioned in certain ancient Tibetan Buddhist texts. Teachings on lucid dreams were one of six topics attributed to the Indian teacher Naropa, who lived in the tenth or eleventh century A.D. Among his students was the Tibetan lama Marpa, and it was with him that knowledge of lucid dream work entered Tibet. The teachings were intended for advanced monks, not for novices or for the hoi polloi. The lessons contain instructions on how to induce lucid dreams and how to change dreamed events. The ability to change events is said to help the dreamer understand the illusory nature of reality, and this understanding is supposed to carry over into waking life and thus to help further the monk on his spiritual path of renunciation and achievement of Nirvana.[8]

Until the last few years, scientific knowledge of lucid dreams was based on anecdotal accounts of experiencers, which allowed skeptical psychologists to class them with the paranormal and dismiss them as occult superstition. In the late 1970s, however, with the work of psychologist Stephen LaBerge, research moved into the laboratory. LaBerge's work is now well known through his best-selling book, *Lucid Dreaming* (1985).

LaBerge's experiments became possible with the discovery that dreams were associated with REM sleep and the development of EEG techniques for monitoring sleep states. The eyes are exempt from the paralysis that affects the rest of the body during REM sleep, and it occurred to LaBerge that a lucid dreamer might signal the presence of lucidity by moving his or her eyes in a certain signaling pattern. The success of lucid dreamers at this task made other studies feasible; as a result we now know that a dream takes about as long as the dreamed events would in real life. When a dream appears to tell a story stretched out over a considerable period of time or space, LaBerge hypothesizes, the dreaming brain has simply spliced together a series of scenes in the same way that a movie does—we spend two hours in the theater, and yet we may be told a story that spans a lifetime.[9]

There are indications that lucid dreams may differ in some ways from normal dreams (they may be more realistic, for instance), so it is clear how far the data collected on lucid dreams can be generalized to all dreams. Nevertheless, the ability of lucid dreamers to be active participants in experiments through eye signals has allowed researchers to study, in a much more precise way than was possible before, the correlations between dreams and what is going on in the body and in the external environment. LaBerge and his colleagues at the prestigious Stanford University Sleep Laboratory have studied lucid dreams in relation to a variety of physiological measures, with some astonishing results.

Lucid dreamers' respiration patterns have been found to match the respiration patterns of their dreamed selves—when the subject dreams of running, his or her respiration speeds up, and upon coming to a stop, the respiration gradually slows down. Researchers also found that counting and singing, which draw on opposite hemispheres of the brain, during a lucid dream were associated with appropriate brainwave activity.[10] Their most incredible findings, however, were made with dreamed sexual activity.

One of LaBerge's subjects, a woman whom he calls "Miranda," spent a night in the Stanford Sleep Laboratory while LaBerge and a fellow experimenter recorded sixteen channels of physiological data, including measures from a vaginal probe. The probe, designed to be worn while sleeping, measured muscle activity from two electrodes on its surface. Pulse amplitude, a measure of the blood flow to the vaginal walls, was obtained by means of an infrared light and a photocell detector in the probe. Light emitted from the probe was reflected back to the photocell to an extent that varied with changes in the amount of blood flowing to the vaginal walls. Experiments in the waking state had clearly demonstrated that when women become sexually aroused, their vaginal pulse amplitude shows a significant increase.

About five minutes into her fifth REM period of the night, Miranda had a three-minute lucid dream in which she was lying in bed and felt someone's hands rubbing her neck. The improbability of this made her realize that she was dreaming. In order to test her state, she decided to try to rise in the air, which she did, then flew out the window and over the Stanford campus. Flying through an archway, she came upon a group of people, and swooped down upon the first man she reached. She tapped him on the shoulder, and he came toward her, apparently understanding what was required of him. Already aroused by the flying, she reached orgasm quickly, and woke up shortly thereafter. The graph of vaginal blood flow measured in the laboratory agreed with every stage of the dream. During the dreamed sexual activity, her respiration rate, vaginal muscle activity, and vaginal blood flow all reached their highest levels of the night—exactly as they would have, had she experienced a real orgasm in waking life.

LaBerge next experimented with a male he calls "Randy." Randy went to sleep equipped with a penile strain-gauge, a device commonly used to measure sexual response in males. The gauge consists of a loop of flexible tubing, about an inch in diameter, filled with mercury. As it expands during an erection, the gauge's electrical resistance increases, allowing the polygraph to measure the extent of the enlargement of the penis. REM periods are normally accompanied by erections of varying degrees, but LaBerge hoped to observe a greater erection during dreamed sexual activity.

A bizarre detail made Randy realize that he was dreaming. He flew up through the roof like Superman, and, having landed in a house yard, wished for a girl. A cute teenager then walked out a patio door, accompanied by her mother. The mother seemed to know Randy, and with a wink sent her daughter out to play. They went into the backyard, where the girl took off her blouse, knelt on the ground, and kissed Randy sensually. Soon he felt himself about to climax, and signalled the onset of orgasm.

When Randy opened his eyes, he seemed to have awakened from a wet dream. But it proved to be a false awakening, and when he awoke for real a few minutes later he found that he had not ejaculated after all. LaBerge writes that this is a common happening in his own experience— after dreamed sexual activity, he may experience a false awakening in which he seems to have had a wet dream, when in reality he has not. As in Miranda's case, Randy's polygraph record showed a precise correspondence with his dream report. His penile strain gauge indicated that his erection, having begun shortly before the onset of the REM period, reached its maximal level at the point he was dreaming of reaching orgasm. Remarkably, a slow detumescence began almost immediately after the dream orgasm.[11]

Lucid Dreams and Out-of-Body-Experiences

A lucid dream is not the same thing as an out-of-body experience (OBE), but there are close connections between them. Lucid dreams frequently lead on to OBEs, although those who have had both say they are distinctly different states. Oliver Fox calls lucid dreams "Dreams of Knowledge" (because one has the knowledge that one is dreaming), and in the early days of his OBEs, believed that lucid dreams were their necessary precursors. He got into the habit of prolonging his Dreams of Knowledge so that he could experiment with them, and he noticed that the longer he went, the more he would feel a pain in the head—not the physical head, but the head of his "astral body." He knew instinctively that this was a call for him to give up the dream. His first OBE occurred on an occasion when he decided to see what would happen if he ignored the warning pain and pressed on. All at once he felt a "click" in his brain, and his body pulled no longer. He was free of his physical body.[12]

Celia Green thinks it is not possible to fully comprehend lucid dreams without considering their relationship to OBEs. She points out that the two types of experience are "philosophically indistinguishable" because in both "the percipient is observing a complete and self-consistent field of perception, and recognizes at the same time that he is in a state which differs from that of normal waking life." However, she notes differences. An OBE usually starts when a person is awake rather than asleep. OBErs tend to perceive the world even more realistically than do lucid dreamers. Precise and vivid representations of the world of normal experience are often associated with OBEs, whereas lucid dreams more often contain symbolic or fantastic elements. Experiencers usually report greater control of events during OBEs. Finally, during an OBE, the experiencer may feel himself or herself to have no body at all, something which is very rare with lucid dreams.[13]

After a careful comparison of lucid dreams and OBEs, psychologist Harvey Irwin concluded that the two states were distinct, neurologically as well as phenomenologically.[14] For many experiencers, there is no mystery here. They believe that during lucid dreams consciousness stays with the body and the dreamed events are simply imagined, and that with OBEs consciousness actually detaches itself from the body and the experiences are real. However, this interpretation is not fashionable among more "scientific" researchers. LaBerge, for instance, considers the OBE simply to be a variety of lucid dream.[15] Parapsychologist Susan Blackmore, who has described an OBE she had while high on hashish,[16] also prefers to interpret OBEs as psychological phenomena, akin to lucid dreams.[17]

Shared Dreams

According to researcher Herbert Greenhouse, there are many hundreds, perhaps even thousands, of cases of shared dreams on record. Shared dreams are dreams experienced the same night (perhaps at the same time) by two or more people. Greenhouse describes the case of a man who dreamed that he was killed by a burly man with a hatchet on the streets of New York. His assailant was holding him down and strangling him with one hand, while with the other hand he wielded the hatchet. He heard the cries of friends who were running to his rescue, but before they could reach him, the hatchet split his forehead and blood spurted over his face. The next day, a classmate told him that he had dreamed of hearing his anguished cries and of seeing him held down by a man with a hatchet. He ran to his rescue, along with some other friends, but before they could reach him, Henry was killed. The next week, Henry heard from another friend who had substantially the same dream. Fortunately for Henry, the events depicted in the dream did not come to pass.[18]

David Ryback, a psychologist who has studied psychic dreaming, thinks shared dreams are more common than we realize. He points out that unless a person happens to talk about a dream with another person upon waking, he or she is unlikely to learn that someone else dreamed the same thing. Some but not all the shared dreams in Ryback's collection are psychic; i.e., the dreamer dreams of an event that either happens simultaneously with the dreamed event (telepathic or clairvoyant) or else foreshadows a future event (precognitive). The dream described by Greenhouse is a shared dream that might have been precognitive, had the young man actually been killed as depicted. Ryback relates a shared dream that did come true. A woman and her husband, a pilot, both dreamed the same night that his plane was having trouble gaining sufficient altitude on take-off to get over some power lines. The next week this occurred and the plane crashed.

In most shared dreams, the dreamers live close to each other. Not uncommonly, they are husband and wife, or lovers sharing the same bed. But physical proximity is evidently less important than a psychological or emotional connection between the dreamers. Ryback describes a case in which one dreamer was in Atlanta and the other in Australia. A colleague of Ryback's awoke during the night to hear his wife pleading with him to get her childhood friend to stay. The friend had made the plane trip from Australia only to decide to leave after two days in Atlanta. Ryback's colleague told his wife her friend wasn't there; she must be having a dream. A few days later a letter arrived from the friend, saying she had had the strangest dream—that she had traveled to see them in Atlanta, only to decide after two days to come home. "Isn't that ridiculous to go all that way for just two days?" she asked. "I don't know why I dreamed that."[19]

The preceding shared dreams all occurred to the dreamers spontaneously, but some people are able to plan and induce a shared dream. Oliver Fox, the habitual OBEr and lucid dreamer, was once spending the evening with two friends, Slade and Elkington, when their conversation turned to the subject of dreams. Before parting they agreed to try to meet on the Southampton Common in their dreams that night. Fox dreamed he met Elkington on the Common as planned, but that Slade was not present. Fox realized that he was dreaming, and Elkington seemed to know he was dreaming as well. In the dream, the two men commented on Slade's absence, then the dream ended, and Fox awoke. The next day when he saw Elkington, Fox at first said nothing of his experience, but asked his friend if he had dreamed. "Yes," Elkington replied, "I met you on the Common all right, but old Slade didn't turn up. We had just time to greet each other and comment on his absence when the dream ended."[20]

Shared dreams have not yet been studied in relation to either lucid dreams or OBEs, but there is clearly a connection between them; perhaps it is only that two persons close to each other are likely to dream of the same thing at the same time. Yet, those dreams in which the different dreamers each seem to perceive a situation from different angles do suggest that some part of the dreamer is there in person—that the dreamed situation itself is in some way shared.

Telepathic Dreams

Shared dreams are by no means the only dreams that may be telepathic or precognitive. Perhaps because the mind is more relaxed during sleep, it seems to be particularly receptive to psychic connections between people at that time. Extrasensory (ESP) dreams form an important segment of all ESP experiences. It has been estimated that of about 7,000 cases of ESP studied by parapsychologists in the United States, over two-thirds involved dreams. Similar proportions have been reported from Germany. In a British study of 300 cases, forty percent were dreams. A survey of school children in India showed that about half of their ESP experiences were dreams.[21]

Louisa Rhine—whose husband, J.B. Rhine, was head of

the famous Parapsychology Laboratory once associated with Duke University—made a lifetime study of spontaneous ESP experiences. Rhine analyzed the cases described in letters sent to the Parapsychology Laboratory. She discovered that about forty percent of "contemporaneous" ESP (telepathy or clairvoyance) occurred in dreams, and she identified four basic forms these dreams took. Some of the dreams were realistic, almost photographic representations of reality. Other dreams represented dramatizations of real experiences, which might contain some fantasy content, although the message conveyed by the dream was true. A third type of dream was more unrealistic or imaginative, while a fourth was symbolic.[22]

Based on her study of ESP dreams as well as other psychic experiences, Rhine proposed a two-stage process for the presentation of ESP in consciousness. In the first stage, the ESP information was received, complete and undistorted, below the threshold of conscious awareness. In the second stage, the ESP information was presented to consciousness, and it was in this process that it might become distorted.[23]

Rhine further believed that the percipient was responsible for all ESP impressions, and that the apparent agent (sender) had no role to play. In other words, she believed that the percipient reached out with his or her ESP to get the information, and that no initiative from the agent was involved, even when the agent seemed to be the more interested party. This interpretation has always been controversial. Critics have pointed out that Rhine may have reached the conclusion she did because of certain biases in her material—in order not to prematurely rule out of consideration the full range of experiences, she accepted at face value all cases sent to the Parapsychology Laboratory that seemed to her to have credence. But her lack of follow-up investigations meant she had to work mainly with the accounts of the experiencers.[24]

In fact, even some of Rhine's own cases, such as the following, seem to contradict her model.

Earlier in the twentieth century, long-distance telephone connections were not as common as they are today, and a woman who had gone to visit her sister in St. Louis could not call her husband in Indianapolis to tell him when to expect her. She intended to send him a telegram, but she was already on the train when she realized that she had forgotten to do so—the train would get in at 2:00 A.M. and there would be no one at the station to meet her. Seeing no other recourse, she decided to try telepathy, and kept saying over and over to herself, "Meet the 2:00 A.M. train, meet the 2:00 A.M. train from St. Louis." When she got off the train, her husband was waiting for her on the platform. He had been sound asleep but something kept telling him to meet the 2:00 A.M. train from St. Louis. Finally he had gotten up and called the station, found that such a train was expected, and went to meet it.[25]

Psychiatrist Ian Stevenson, one of Rhine's critics, made a study of telepathic "impression" cases. In these cases, the psi signal came in the form of an impression or hunch rather than an image or concrete idea. Stevenson found that the majority of telepathic impression cases occurred when someone emotionally tied to the percipient was in some kind of distress, which suggested that a relationship—not just an individual—was vital for such cases to occur. In some cases, there was no intentional focusing by the agent, yet the percipient somehow gained knowledge of the agent's experience. In other cases the agent was thinking about the percipient and perhaps even trying to send a message, as in the dream described above. Some cases fit Rhine's model, whereas others did not. Stevenson pointed out that it was only through careful study of cases with interviews that one could tell which was which.[26]

If Rhine's idea that the percipient is invariably the active party in an ESP case has not stood up to scrutiny, her proposal of two stages to the ESP processes has faired better. It has even received support from an unexpected source—Sigmund Freud.

Freud belonged to both the Society for Psychical Research and the American Society for Psychical Research and, although he was originally skeptical of the validity of telepathy, he became more and more fascinated with it. Having perceived the psychoanalytic importance of telepathy, he was ready to give the weight of psychoanalysis to parapsychological investigation, but was dissuaded by his friend and colleague Ernest Jones. At that time—the 1920s—psychoanalytic ideas had not yet become as widely accepted as they are today, and Jones was afraid that an association between psychoanalysis and ESP would jeopardize the chances of psychoanalysis being taken seriously.[27]

Freud describes one case in which a man dreamed that his wife had had twins the night before his daughter gave birth to twins. The daughter lived in a distant town, and had handed in a telegram at about the same time that he had dreamed of the event. Freud interpreted the error in the dream—the transformation of the daughter into the wife—as representing the dreamer's repressed wish that his wife be like the daughter of his first marriage. He hypothesized that during the night the man had received a telepathic communication that his daughter had twins. "The dream work seizes on this information, allows his unconscious wish that his daughter should replace his second wife to act upon it, and thus emerges the singular manifest dream in which the wish itself is veiled and the message distorted." The dream functioned in the way all dreams functioned, according to Freud, but it worked with information received telepathically rather than with day residues.[28]

Freud went so far as to say that in showing the psychological meaningfulness of the error in the dream, his psychoanalytical interpretation had revealed the paranormal nature of a dream that otherwise would have been dismissed as of little consequence. In Rhine's terms, the psychological process that accounted for the transformation Freud identified occurred in the second stage of the ESP process.

Precognitive Dreams

However they occur, telepathic and clairvoyant dreams do not pose the philosophical challenge that precognitive dreams do. It is one thing to become aware of something going on somewhere else at the same time—it is quite another to become aware of an event before it actually happens.

Precognition, like telepathy, may occur in the waking state as well as in dreams but is more likely to occur in dreams. Of the precognitive experiences described in the letters Louisa Rhine studied, seventy-five percent occurred in dreams and only twenty-five percent while the percipient was awake.[29] Roughly the same proportions have been found by other researchers. About sixty percent of precognitive experiences involve dreams, another ten percent borderline states of sleep, either when falling asleep or waking up (the hypnagogic and hypnopompic states, respectively).[30]

Precognitive dreams may relate to seemingly trivial events in the life of the dreamer, but many of them refer to some traumatic episode, and some foreshadow disaster. Ian Stevenson collected precognitive experiences associated with the sinking of the *Titanic* in 1912. Of the nineteen cases he discovered, ten were precognitive; of the precognitive experiences, no fewer than eight involved dreams.[31]

Knowing that precognitions of disaster were common, psychiatrist J. C. Barker decided to see if he could find precognitive experiences connected with a disaster in the town of Aberfan, Wales, in 1966. A coal-tip on a mountainside above the town had fallen suddenly, burying a school and killing 144 people, 128 of them children. The accident shook Britain badly, and thus seemed to have the emotional quality necessary to stir up precognitive experiences.

The day after the disaster, Barker arranged for a request for premonitions to be published in the *Evening Standard*, an English newspaper. Within two weeks he received seventy-six replies. Sixty experiences related directly to Aberfan; of these, twenty-five were dreams. Almost all these experiences were reported by persons living nowhere near Aberfan and who had no personal connection with it, but one was that of a little girl, one of the victims. Two weeks before the disaster she told her mother she was not afraid to die, and that morning she told her she had dreamed of going to school, but the school wasn't there—"something black had come down all over it."[32]

How are experiences like these to be explained? Frank Podmore, an early member of the Society for Psychical Research, thought all apparent precognition could be explained as telepathy. Other researchers skeptical of the possibility of seeing the future have sought to explain precognition as psychokinesis: they believe the dreamer brings about the dreamed events unconsciously, in order to make them conform to the dream.[33]

Not all researchers have trouble conceiving of precognition, however. The English writer J.W. Dunne, who had many precognitive dreams, suggested that it might be as easy to see the future as the past. Analogous with Freud's "day residue," he proposed calling precognized events which turned up in dreams "future day residues."[34]

New York parapsychologist Nancy Sondow recorded 943 of her own dreams over a period of fifty months. Ninety-six of these dreams she judged precognitive on the basis of Dunne's criteria that two or more unusual or unexpected events occur together in both the dream and the future. More than half the precognized events occurred within a day of the dream, with a steep regular decline in the number of precognitive dreams the further the time from the event. She found indications in other dream accounts and in laboratory precognition experiments that accurate precognition falls off with the passage of time, and offered a model of branching "futures" to explain her results. She reasoned that if there were a variety of possible futures, and a dream picked up only one of these, the further in time the event was from the dream, the less likely it would have been dreamed accurately.[35]

The branching-futures model not only makes sense of Sondow's data and that from many other case studies; it helps us to understand why the dreamer may sometimes avert the precognized event by taking appropriate action—either changing plans to avoid a situation, or by recognizing a situation that was dreamed and so taking appropriate action.

Through a response to a dream, the nineteenth-century suffragette Susan B. Anthony once saved herself from a fire by leaving the hotel where she was staying.[36] In a more recent case, a woman dreamed that her twenty-month-old daughter had climbed up onto a window ledge and was gaily babbling when she started to lose her balance and fall. The mother awoke in a panic and ran to check on her daughter, only to find her sound asleep in her bed. But three weeks later, when she had gone to bring in clothes off the line, she realized her daughter had not followed her as usual. She ran back into the house and up to her daughter's room, only to find her on the windowsill as she had dreamed. She caught the toddler just in time and lifted her to safety.[37]

Sometimes intervention is impossible, either because incomplete or erroneous information is dreamt, or because the event was of such a nature that it probably would have been impossible to change, anyway. In such case, the psychic function of the dream may be to prepare the dreamer for the event.[38]

Experiments with Dream ESP

Collecting accounts of dreams, classifying and analyzing them, provides a good beginning to the understanding of psychic dreams. But in most fields of science, systematic description is not enough—scientists want to take their studies into the laboratory, where they have control over the situation, and can better rule out chance and other normal factors that may enter into a dream. In many psychic experiences, the similarity between the psychic impression and the event with which it is apparently associated is so striking that chance would seem to be a very strained explanation for it. Just how far a circumstance is from chance cannot be precisely quantified the way it can be in the lab.

One of Louisa Rhine's justifications for not investigating the cases described in the letters sent to the Parapsychology Laboratory was that she was only hoping to identify problems to be followed up in the experimental setting. In fact, her studies were never used in this way.[39] But the famous experiments in dream ESP conducted between 1962 and 1974 at the Maimonides Medical Center in Brooklyn had their most direct inspiration in a similar source. Psychiatrist Montague Ullman, like Freud and other therapists before him, noticed indications of what seemed to be telepathic content in his patients' dreams, and he wanted to find out whether there was anything to it.

The experiments began at the Parapsychology Foundation, where its director, medium Eileen Garrett, acted as percipient. After this pilot series proved successful, the work moved to Maimonides, where Ullman was director of the Community Mental Health Center. Psychologist Gardner Murphy arranged for Maimonides to receive a grant to support the establishment of a dream laboratory—the first in the world to deal entirely with psychic dreaming.

A "target" picture was drawn according to a number chosen from a random number table. When EEG recordings showed that the percipient was in REM sleep, and therefore likely to be dreaming, the agent opened the designated envelope and began to concentrate on it. When the REM period was over, the subject would be wakened by a voice over the intercom and asked to report any dream he or she had. The sender would usually try to send one picture per night, but the sleeper would be awakened after each dream session. In the morning, the sleeper would be shown the "pool" of eight pictures from which the target was chosen, and asked to rank them. Often, the dreamer's dream reports would be ranked against the pictures by an independent series of judges. Very often, there was considerable similarity between the picture and what was dreamed.

Even more creative means were employed in precognition experiments. These often would not require the subject to pick up on a picture, but would expose the subject to a "full sensory" bombardment. This treatment would take place in the morning, after the dream reports were all in. Its purpose was to determine whether the dreams were reflected in the morning treatment accorded the subject.[40]

Not all series conducted at Maimonides were successful, but enough were that the overall record was highly significant statistically. The results were impressive enough that some experimenters tried to replicate them elsewhere. These "replications" differed from the original experiments in various ways, and they unfortunately were largely unsuccessful. In one replication study, the percipient was Robert Van de Castle, considered the "Prince of Percipients" at Maimonides because he scored a hit each of the eight nights in his dream series. The replication series was conducted at the University of Wyoming, under the direction of dream investigator Fewkes, and in a review of experimental ESP experiments published in the *Handbook of Parapsychology*, Van de Castle speculates how the different experimental situations may have affected the different results.

Although the experimental design was very similar to the one at Maimonides, some psychological differences in the way the experiments were conducted may have played a role in the outcomes. One difference was the interpersonal climate in each of the two laboratories. At Maimonides, everyone was extremely friendly and outgoing, whereas interactions with the staff at Wyoming were much more formal and detached. Another major difference was that at Wyoming the dream sessions were conducted over a two-week period, whereas at Maimonides a similar study had been spaced over forty-four weeks.[41]

There have been a few other experimental studies of dreams. One reported by Van de Castle did not have a laboratory setting. The percipients were about seventy members of a youth camp, aged sixteen and up. The agent was a female staff member who tried to send a colored magazine picture to all the campers. The following morning, the campers each ranked a series of five pictures for correspondence to their dreams. "Hits" were those ranked 1 or 2, "misses" the pictures ranked 4 or 5. There were more hits than misses on each of four nights, and the overall proportion of hits to misses was statistically significant.[42]

Van de Castle concludes his review of psychic dreams by noting motivation as a consistent factor in dreams occurring spontaneously—in daily life, in a therapeutic situation, and in the laboratory. He suggests that paranormal dreaming be considered the end product of a complex motivational configuration blending some need on the part of the "percipient" with behavioral or emotional activity on the part of the "agent." Like Ian Stevenson, but unlike Louisa Rhine, he holds that percipient and agent are each responsible in different ways for psychic dreams.[43]

Past-Life Memories in Dreams

In *Memories, Dreams, Reflections* (1961), Jung wrote about a series of dreams he had which seemed to describe the reincarnation of a friend of his. Because he is unaware of other such dreams, he says, he prefers not to describe this one. "I must confess, however, that after this experience I view the problem of reincarnation with somewhat different eyes, though without being in a position to state a definite opinion."[44]

It is too bad that Jung didn't tell us more about his reincarnation dream. It sounds as if it may have been an "announcing dream" of the sort described in chapter 2. In this type of dream, a woman, her husband, or other relative or close friend has a dream in which a figure appears, and "announces" its intention to be reborn to the woman.

People may have memories of previous lives themselves. Ian Stevenson has described numerous cases, mostly of children, who claim to have past-life memories that check out in detail—to the point that the persons they talk about can be identified. Children most often recall past lives while in the waking state, but adults may sometimes have apparent memories in their dreams.[45]

Meditation instructor Frederick Lenz collected 127 accounts of reincarnation memories from adults, nineteen of them while the persons were dreaming. He concluded that the "dream remembrances" differ from ordinary dreams in four ways:

1. Dream remembrances are accompanied by sensations completely unlike those they experienced from any other dream.

2. The dreamers are aware they are seeing one or more of their past lives.

3. Unlike most dreams, which normally fade after several hours or months, dream remembrances are so vivid that the dreamer can describe even the slightest details of the dream years later.

4. After someone has had a remembrance dream, his or her attitude toward death and dying changes.[46]

Author D. Scott Rogo tested Lenz's conclusions by advertising in psychic periodicals for people to write to him about their experiences. Seven of the twenty cases responding were dream cases, a much larger proportion than Lenz's. But the dreams in Rogo's collection were also vivid or repetitive, and they were just as emotionally powerful for the dreamer.

It is in the nature of such experiences that, although they are emotionally powerful for the dreamer, there is little about them that will prove their reality to other persons. Most such dreams lack the sort of "veridical" (truthful) content parapsychologists seek when trying to authenticate paranormal experiences. This is true of the cases published by Lenz—but Rogo does describe some veridical reincarnation dreams.

In one case, a woman had repetitive dreams about trying

to cross a river on a narrow suspension bridge swaying high over an expanse of water. She approached the bridge in various ways, but never saw herself make it all the way across. At the same time, she reported a deep-set fear of heights and a feeling that she would die by falling from a high place. The mystery was solved for her when she happened across a picture of her dream bridge in *Life* magazine—it was the first catwalk thrown across the East River preparatory to building the Brooklyn Bridge in the 1870s. What made this especially meaningful to her was that seeing this story ended the recurring dreams and cured her of her phobia.[47]

Another person who has written about reincarnation dreams is Hans Holzer. Holzer reports that although reincarnation dreams may be realistic, the majority of them are too fragmentary and hazy; they leave the dreamer with the frustrating feeling of having been given some unusual glance at his or her own past without enough information to go to the nearest library and look it up. Like Lenz and Rogo, Holzer reports that reincarnation dreams have a habit of being in series—usually consisting of exact repetitions of one dream. More rarely these are partial repetitions of the original dream.

Holzer describes three recurrent dreams of a woman he calls "Karen G." When Mrs. G. was 21 she first dreamt of a woman in a long, black dress and a white apron. People full of hatred were shouting at her and tying her to a tree. They put brush under her feet and kept yelling, "Burn her, burn the witch!" She cried out that she was not a witch, and that if she were, they would never have a chance to burn her—hearing herself say this, suddenly she was the woman being burned. A second recurrent dream was of another woman, also dressed in a long dress. Somehow she knew this was in France, and that she was married or a man's mistress; in the dream, she eventually committed suicide. In the third dream she died when a volcano erupted. All three lives were cut short by a catastrophe.[48]

NOTES

1. Frederick Van Eeden, "A Study of Dreams." *Proceedings of the Society for Psychical Research.* (1913), vol. 26:431–461. Reprinted in *Altered States of Consciousness*, edited by Charles T. Tart, pp. 145–158. New York: John Wiley and Sons, 1969.

2. *Ibid.*, p. 153.

3. Oliver Fox, *Astral Projection*, pp. 34–35. New York: University Books, 1962.

4. Celia Green, *Lucid Dreams*, pp. 23–29. Oxford, England: Institute for Psychophysical Research, 1968.

5. *Ibid.*, p. 30.

6. Stephen LaBerge, *Lucid Dreaming*, pp. 109–116. New York: Ballantine, 1985.

7. *Ibid.*, pp. 19–20.

8. George Gillespie, "Lucid Dreams in Tibetan Buddhism." In *Conscious Mind, Sleeping Brain: Perspective on Lucid Dreaming*, edited by Jayne Gackenbach and Stephen LaBerge, pp. 27–35. New York: Plenum Press, 1988.

9. LaBerge, *op. cit.*, p. 77.

10. *Ibid.*, pp. 68–77.

11. *Ibid.*, pp. 78–95.

12. Van Eeden. *op cit.*, p. 151.

13. Green, *op cit.*, pp. 20–22.

14. Harvey J. Irwin, "Out-of-the-Body Experiences and Dream Lucidity: Empirical Perspectives." In *Conscious Mind, Sleeping Brain: Perspectives on Lucid Dreaming*, edited by Jayne Gackenbach and Stephen LaBerge, pp. 353–371. New York: Plenum Press, 1988.

15. LaBerge. *op. cit.*, p. 211.

16. Susan Blackmore, *Beyond the Body: An Investigation of Out–of–the–Body Experiences*, pp. 2–5. London: Heinemann, 1990. Pp. 2–5.

17. Susan Blackmore, "A Theory of Lucid Dreams and

OBEs.'' In *Conscious Mind, Sleeping Brain: Perspectives on Lucid Dreaming*, edited by Jayne Gackenbach and Stephen LaBerge, pp. 373–387. New York: Plenum Press, 1988.

18. Herbert Greenhouse, ''Two Parallel (Reciprocal) Dreams. 1. Three Dreams of the Same Murder.'' In *The New World of Dreams*, edited by Ralph L. Woods and Herbert B. Greenhouse, p. 87. New York: Macmillan, 1974.

19. David Ryback, with Letitia Sweitzer, *Dreams That Come True: Their Psychic and Transforming Powers*, pp. 65–68. New York: Doubleday, 1988.

20. Fox, *op cit.*, p. 47.

21. Montague Ullman and Stanley Krippner, with Alan Vaughan. *Dream Telepathy*, pp. 24–25. New York: Macmillan, 1973.

22. Louisa E. Rhine, *The Invisible Picture: A Study of Psychic Experiences*, p. 105. Jefferson, NC: McFarland, 1981.

23. *Ibid.*

24. Debra H. Weiner and JoMarie Haight, ''Charting Hidden Channels: Louisa E. Rhine's Case Collection Project.'' In *Case Studies in Parapsychology*, edited by K. Ramakrishna Rao, pp. 14–30. Jefferson, NC: McFarland, 1986.

25. Rhine, *op. cit.*, pp. 121–122.

26. Ian Stevenson, *Telepathic Impressions: A Review and a Report of 35 New Cases*, pp. 178–179. Charlottesville: University of Virginia, 1974.

27. Raymond Van Over, ''Introduction.'' In *Psychology and Extrasensory Perception*, edited by Raymond Van Over, pp. xx–xxi. New York: Mentor Books.

28. Sigmund Freud, ''Dreams and the Occult.'' In *Psychoanalysis and the Occult*, edited by George Devereux, pp. 91–109. New York: International Universities Press, 1953. Pp. 96–97.

29. Rhine, *op. cit.* p. 105.

30. Robert L. Van de Castle, ''Sleep and Dreams.'' In *Handbook of Parapsychology*, edited by Benjamin B. Wolman, pp. 473–499. New York: Van Nostrand Reinhold, 1986. Pp. 482–483.

31. Ian Stevenson, ''A Review and Analysis of Paranormal Experiences Connected with the Sinking of the Titanic.'' *Journal of the American Society for Psychical Research*, 1960, vol. 54; 1965, vol. 59.

32. J. C. Barker, ''Premonitions of the Aberfan Disaster.''

Journal of the Society for Psychical Research, 1967, vol. 44: 169–181.

33. Danah Zohar, *Through the Time Barrier: A Study in Precognition and Modern Physics*, pp. 4, 31. London: Heinemann, 1982.

34. John W. Dunne, *An Experiment with Time*. New York: Macmillan, 1927.

35. Nancy Sondow, "The Decline of Precognized Events with the Passage of Time." *Journal of the American Society for Psychical Research*, 1988, vol. 82:33–51.

36. Zohar, *op. cit.*, pp. 34–35.

37. Ian Stevenson, "An Example Illustrating the Criteria and Characteristics of Precognitive Dreams." *Journal of the American Society for Psychical Research*, 1961, vol. 55: 98–103.

38. Zohar, *op. cit.*, p. 34.

39. Weiner and Haight, *op. cit.*, p. 28.

40. Ullman, Krippner and Vaughan, *op cit.*, pp. 168–169.

41. Van de Castle, *op. cit.*, pp. 491–492.

42. *Ibid.*, p. 493.

43. *Ibid.*, p. 495.

44. C.G. Jung. *Memories, Dreams, Reflections*, p. 319. New York: Random House, 1961.

45. Ian Stevenson, *Children Who Remember Previous Lives: A Question of Reincarnation*. Charlottesville: University of Virginia Press, 1987.

46. Frederick Lenz, *Lifetimes: True Accounts of Reincarnation*, pp. 34–35. New York: Bobbs Merrill, 1979.

47. D. Scott Rogo, *The Search for Yesterday: A Critical Examination of the Evidence for Reincarnation*, pp. 28–32. Englewood Cliffs: Prentice-Hall, 1985.

48. Hans Holzer, *The Psychic Side of Dreams*, pp. 143–159. Garden City: Doubleday, 1976.

5

Dreams and Alchemy

Sometime between 1926 and 1928 Carl Jung, the pioneer of modern psychoanalysis, had a series of dreams in which he saw a previously unnoticed house annexed to his own. In each dream, he wondered how he could not have known about the existence of this annex when it had apparently always been there. Finally, he dreamed he entered the annex and found that it contained a wonderful library, full of large sixteenth-and seventeenth-century books, hand bound with pigskin, and illustrated with strange symbolic copper engravings.

Jung interpreted his own house as a symbol of his consciousness. He realized the annex represented something that belonged to him, but of which he was just now becoming conscious. He later learned the library represented alchemy, a subject about which he was ignorant at the time, but which he soon began to study. Within fifteen years he would assemble a library similar to the one in his dream.[1]

For years Jung had seen a need to find an historical precedence for his and his patients' inner experiences, to make analytical psychology more objective and free of the observer's personal bias. Between 1918 and 1926 he studied Gnostic writers and found they were concerned with the same inner landscape as he. Most accounts of these writers, however, were written by their opponents, and their remoteness in time made it difficult to apply their ideas to modern psychology. When he began to understand alchemy he found the continuity with the past that he had been looking for. In his own words: "Grounded in the natural philosophy of the middle ages, alchemy formed the bridge on the one hand into the past, to Gnosticism, and on the other into the future, to the modern psychology of the unconscious."[2]

With this treasure of symbols he was now able to understand certain dream motifs, which had previously puzzled him. His student, Marie-Louise von Franz, recalls an example in which one of Jung's patients had a dream of an eagle flying into the sky. In this dream, the eagle began to eat his own wings, then dropped back to earth. Jung was able to interpret the dream, on a personal level, as a reversal of a psychic situation. Upon discovering an engraving of an eagle eating his own wings in the alchemical text, the *Ripley Scroll*, he was able to see that the image was also "archetypal."[3]

Just as the human body has an anatomy that is the same in all people, despite their superficial racial differences, Jung saw that the human psyche has an anatomy—one that is collective and transcends cultural differences. And, just as the human body has a long evolutionary history that can be seen in its structure, he perceived that the psyche also carries its history in the form of primordial images, which he labeled "archetypes."

Archetypes, according to Jung, are the symbolic forms of our natural instincts. Manifesting in our dreams and fantasies, they are the patterns which transcend time and culture that can be seen in all mythology, art and literature. The archetypes are of unknown origin, are present in an individual's psyche at the moment of birth, and can make themselves known at any time. Jung felt they are the source of thoughtforms, or universal patterns and behavior established in humans long before the development of reflective consciousness; they can be the cause of panic, prejudice, inspiration or religious vision, but their appearance is always emotionally engaging, or numinous. He believed their study is as important for the analytical psychologist as the study of physical anatomy is for the surgeon.

One day a panicked professor came to see Jung. The professor thought he was going insane because he experienced a vision of a man on the sun and a woman on the moon. Jung, recognizing the vision as archetypal, calmly took a four-hundred-year-old alchemy book off his shelf, showed the professor a woodcut identical to his vision, and said: ''There's no reason for you to believe that you're insane; they knew about your vision four hundred years ago.'' The professor's panic subsided immediately.[4]

The correlation in this example is not unusual, and it shows how Jung used historic material in his practice. However, we still might ask—if all mythology is archetypal, why are alchemical allegories and images more important than other myths? In answer to this, Marie-Louise von Franz points out that when we study myth we have material that originated in the unconscious but has been censored by society, or the collective conscious. Alchemy, on the other hand, gives us a body of unconscious material with no preconceptions, because as the alchemists searched in their labs, they projected their unconscious onto the unknown phenomena before them.[5]

It may seem strange and overly subjective to us that alchemists, as the precursors of modern science, projected personal or archetypal symbols onto their chemical subject. Although they were looking for the truth about matter, just as modern scientists are, they were also looking for meaning in life, like modern philosophers, theologians, or psychologists. Alone in their laboratories, studying the unknown, observing the details of their chemical experiments without benefit of modern objective techniques, it was only natural that alchemists should project a psychological mystery onto the physical mystery before them.

In the following example, from an eighteenth-century manuscript by Hyle Jurain, we can see that a creation myth has been projected onto a chemical recipe:

> Take of common rainwater a good quantity, at least ten quarts, preserve it well sealed in glass vessels for at least ten days, then it will deposit matter and faeces on the bottom. Pour off the clear liquid and place in a wooden vessel that is fashioned round like a ball, cut it through the middle and fill the vessel a third full, and set it in the sun about midday in a secret or secluded spot.
>
> When this has been done, take a drop of the consecrated red wine and let it fall into the water, and you will instantly perceive a fog and thick darkness on top of the water, such as also was at the first creation. Then put in two drops, and you will see the light coming forth from the darkness; whereupon little by little put in every half of each quarter hour first three, then four, then five, then six drops, and then no more, and you will see with your own eyes one thing after another appearing by and by on top of the water, how God created all things in six days, and how it all came to pass, and such secrets as are not to be spoken aloud and I also have not the power to reveal. Fall on your knees before you undertake this operation. Let your eyes judge of it; for thus was the world created.[6]

In modern scientific terms Jurain created an experimental model to help him understand the creation of the universe, but this does not seem to have been his intent. It could just as well be described in hermetic terms as a manifestation of the universal truth: "As above, so below." In other words, by observing the details of a microcosm, in this case the liquid in his bowl, one can see patterns that parallel the macrocosm, or universe. The difference between Jurain's viewpoint and the modern chemist's is that Jurain freely interprets what he sees; in fact, he strives for a vision, or a picture of the unconscious.

Jung saw that the experiences recorded by the alchemists coincided with his experiences in analytical psychology, and that they gave him the necessary history of these experiences which he was looking for. More importantly, they taught him the unconscious can be seen as a "process." It was through alchemy that Jung saw the psyche is transformed or developed by the interrelationship between the conscious (ego) and the unconscious mind.[7]

From the beginning of its history, alchemy was focused on a goal. In medieval and Renaissance Europe it was called the "magnum opus" or the great work. The opus was a search for an elusive, transformative substance contained in all matter; this substance was called the philosopher's stone (lapis philosophorum). To find it alchemists had to determine the correct chemical procedure—a lengthy and difficult process of trial and error, with obscure symbolic texts as their only guide. (The word "gibberish" was originally a description of the writing of the medieval alchemist, Jabir, known in Latin as Geber).[8]

Once discovered, it was believed the philosopher's stone would have the power to transform base metal into gold. Taken as a medicine, it was a panacea. Some even believed it was an elixir of life that could bestow immortality. Paralleling this chemical transformation was a spiritual transformation of the alchemist himself that was as necessary to the process as any physical component. When the lapis was found the alchemist was said to simultaneously achieve spiritual perfection (gnosis), so that there was a mystical connection between the alchemist and the subject of his work. Jung saw that this process of transformation was identical to the psychological process he called "individuation"; he also saw that the alchemist's identification with his subject was what he termed "synchronicity."

Individuation can be described as the goal of the psyche itself, the state of wholeness to which the archetypal structure of the psyche leads. To Jung, it is the psychological reality synonymous to the goal of mystical philosophies and religions. Synchronicity is defined by Jung as meaningful coincidences between internal psychic reality and external material reality. When an individual experiences synchronicity an archetype has been activated. In Jungian terms, the alchemist, through a process of synchronicity with chemical experiments, was led to a state of psychic wholeness in which his ego consciousness was integrated with his total psychic self, sometimes called the Higher Self, or divinity within.

History of Alchemy

The word "alchemy" is of Greek-Arabic origin. "Al" is the Arabic definite article (the), which in Arabic is normally attached to the noun. "Chemy" most likely derives from the Greek "Kemia," which referred to Egypt (the land of Khem, from the hieroglyph Khmi, meaning black or fertile earth in contrast to desert).[9] In its name alone we can trace the history of this science.

As Egyptian religion evolved out of a shamanistic prehistoric past, it developed a complex body of magic formulas that were the beginning of what we would call geology, metallurgy, and chemistry. Among these were the techniques for separating gold, silver, copper, lead, iron, and tin from ore; the making of such alloys as bronze, from copper and tin (when this alloy was discovered it must have seemed like a type of gold made from base metal); dyeing; brewing; gilding; perfume-making, and chemical recipes and magic rituals for the embalming of the dead.

In these embalming rituals, designed to insure the rebirth of the deceased, the body was dismembered, reassembled, then chemically preserved. It was placed in a coffin (vessel), which represented the Mother Goddess (in this way it was returned to the womb). At the funeral wheat or barley was placed in the hands of the deceased, and watered so that it would sprout in harmony with the resurrection of the deceased.

The ancient Greek philosophers also had a curiosity about the physical world and a desire to find what was lasting in human life—that part of the individual that can transcend death. A philosopher was a scholar and a thinker who studied nature, and who sought to find truths about life and the universe; today we would call him a scientist. When Alexander the Great conquered Egypt, he brought Greek culture and philosophy into contact with Egyptian mystical religion and magic. One could say this mixture was the beginning of what we know as alchemy in the West.

The oldest known Western alchemical texts are from Hellenistic Egypt—particularly Alexandria—in the first century of the Christian era. For example, the *Codex Marcionus* in Venice contains a translated text said to be written by Isis to her son Horus, in which she tells him the secret of making gold and silver, a secret she coerced from angels by withholding her sexual favors.

Later, European alchemists themselves traced the origin of their craft to the mythic Egyptian author, Hermes Trismegistus (''thrice great Hermes''). The Hermetica, the texts ascribed to him, were actually written in Greek and Latin by Greek and Egyptian philosophers living in Roman Egypt and using a common pseudonym. They had always accepted as fact that Pythagoras and Plato studied with the Egyptian priests who had secret knowledge passed on to them in a collection of books written by the god Thoth (who became Hermes to the Greeks). The Egyptian books themselves, like the *Book of the Dead*, were written in hieroglyphics decipherable only to the priests. The philosophers could only imagine their contents, thus inviting projection, and did not question the assumption that they were the basis of their Greek tradition.[10]

Modern scholars regard Zosimos of Panopolis, Egypt, in the fourth century, as the oldest known authentic alchemist. His works are known from an encyclopedia-like compendium of alchemical texts, collected in the seventh and eighth centuries in Byzantium. His writing describes the ennobling of base metals into gold by first killing them and then resurrecting them (a process similar to Egyptian embalming). His method depends on the production of a series of colors: black, white, yellow and red, which are obtained through the materials' "divine" or sulfur water (divine and sulfur are the same word in Greek). Zosimos also mentions that the transformation depends on a magical substance called the powder (Xērion) which was translated into Arabic and then into Latin as "elixir," and finally as the philosopher's stone. Zosimos himself credits Maria "The Jewess" as the source of his knowledge.[11]

Chinese Alchemy

Alchemy in China stems from an ancient oral medical tradition that was first written down in A.D. 320. The Chinese were primarily concerned with the search for immortality, which they believed would be accomplished by ingesting a magical drug called the "elixir of life" or "drinkable gold." About this time, alchemy also became associated with Taoism and its mystical meditative practices.

The most famous alchemical text is the *Tan Chin Yao*

Chueh ("Great Secrets of Alchemy"), by Sun Ssu Miao, written in the sixteenth century. It contains formulas for the elixir using mercury and sulfur.[12] After this time most alchemists abandoned their labs in favor of perfecting Taoist techniques of meditation and breath control. These techniques demanded the retention of sexual energy (*ching*) at the base of the spine (the first crucible). By applying heat—created by deep breathing—the energy rose up the spine to the solar plexus (the second crucible) and down again. After many cycles it was enhanced by the higher energy (*ch'i*) of the second crucible, and the process began again, but this time included the third crucible in the head. There the highest energy (*shen*) would mingle with the others. After being purified in this manner these energies would be used to create a child within. This divine embryo caused an ambrosia, to be formed in the mouth which brought immortality.[13] Immortality could be taken literally, or defined as the attainment of enlightenment—freedom from the earthly cycles of death and rebirth, and the attainment of a higher timeless state of supernormal power.

Indian Alchemy

Indian alchemy is a living discipline with a continuous history of over 3,000 years. It can be traced to the science of Ayurveda ("wisdom of life") which practiced the dissection of corpses before 1000 B.C. By the twelfth century A.D., Ayurvedic physicians developed medicines which included opium and cannabis, as well as minerals and metals.[14] Indian alchemical texts contain the familiar references to gold, mercury, and elixirs of long life, but they seem less interested in immortality, perhaps because Indian religion already offered an approach to immortality.

As in China, Indian alchemy is associated with mystical meditation and sexual practices, known in India and Tibet as Tantra, which strives for enlightenment or wholeness through identification with the divine couple, Shakti and Shiva. This is accomplished, by the individual, through meditation on the divine couple combined with sexual restraint, or by a couple greatly prolonging sexual intercourse and withholding orgasm until they attain the state of original bliss. (Similarly, Isis used sexual restraint to gain knowledge in the previously mentioned Egyptian text, the *Codex Marcionus*).

It is impossible to determine the extent of the links between these geographically separate alchemies, or how independent they are as archetypal manifestations in their separate cultures. Alexander's empire extended to India in 325 B.C., leaving a Greek state called Gandhara, where Greek and Indian alchemy could mix. India and China always maintained contact. Buddhism spread from India to China, carrying with it Greek sculptural traditions; and silk from China traveled the trade routes, through India, all the way to Rome and Celtic areas.

Arabic Alchemy

By the fourth century A.D. Greco-Egyptian alchemy had absorbed and replaced much of the disintegrating mystery religions, and had integrated elements from Neoplatonism, Gnosticism, Christianity, and Hermetic philosophy. Through the early Middle Ages alchemy was absent from western Europe, but the knowledge was maintained in Byzantium, and added to in the Arabic countries.

The Arabian army, under Amribn al-Ass, conquered Egypt by A.D. 642, and for the first time Arabs came into contact with a large group of working alchemists. In the fifteenth century the Nestorians, in Byzantium, broke from the Orthodox Church, and emigrated east where they taught Hellenistic philosophy and translated Greek texts, including

alchemical ones, into their language (Syriae). By the eighth
and ninth centuries Syriae texts had been translated into
Arabic.[15] Meanwhile, by the mid-eighth century, the Islamic Empire under the Umayyad rules had spread east to
the Indus River, where there was ample opportunity to
share influences with Indian alchemists. Wherever they encountered it, Arabs were quick to learn the philosophical
science, and all great alchemists from this period are Arabic.

Jabir ibn Hayyan, the eighth-century alchemist, developed a theory which became common to all subsequent
alchemical texts. He said that all metals seemed to be com-
prised of "earthy smoke," which would become what he
called sulfur, and of "water vapor," which was also on its
way to becoming a single substance that he called mercury.
Sulfur and mercury became a masculine and feminine po-
larity in alchemy, similar to yang and yin in Chinese philosophy.

Although Jabir's references to mercury and sulfur are
symbolic, the discovery of the actual liquid metal, mercury,
circa 300 B.C., coincides with the beginning of alchemy and
seems to be crucial to the development of alchemy in both
the East and West. The original process of gold-plating involved dissolving gold in mercury to form an amalgam,
which was painted on the heated base metal. The heat was
then increased until the mercury vaporized, leaving the gold
on the surface.[16] (Scholars believe that some early alchemical texts actually describe the production of imitation gold
that could be made in this way, or by making a type of
paint which mixes gold with sulfur.)

Al-Razi, the ninth-century Arabic alchemist, introduced
the necessity of accurate weights and measures, and recorded in detail his laboratory apparatus—much of which
is still used by modern chemists. The Arabs were the per-
fecters, if not the inventors, of distillation. Parallel to their

technical contributions, Mohammed ibn Umail (known in Latin as Senior) added much to the mystical side in his many writings.

European Alchemy

By the twelfth century alchemy began to filter into western Europe. Among the first to be acquainted with it were the Templars, who during the Crusades had adopted the teachings of the Druses (a mystical pagan sect within the Islamic world). Jewish and Islamic scholars were invited to the court of Frederic II in Sicily. The Knights of St. John opened communication with the East on the island of Rhodes, and Spain and southern France were becoming multicultural communities. In these areas Jewish and other scholars began to translate Arabic and Greek texts into Latin, which made them available to the rest of Europe.[17] (The first was the *Book of the Composition of Alchemy*, translated into Latin by the Englishman Robert of Chester in 1144.)

In 1357 a Frenchman, Nicholas Flamel, bought a rare, old gilded book, *The Book of Abraham the Jew*, filled with strange illustrations and instructions for the transformation of metals into gold. With the help of his wife, Pernelle, he began the difficult and lengthy process of carrying out the almost incomprehensible instructions. By Flamel's own account, after twenty-five years of struggle they were successful. The couple used their sudden wealth to endow fourteen hospitals, three chapels, and seven churches in Paris and others in Boulogne. They also helped the poor. In their will the couple left numerous houses as well as money for the benefit of the homeless. According to legend, having also discovered the secret of immortality, Flamels only faked their deaths and moved to India with enough gold to last many lifetimes. The couple was reported seen at the Paris Opera in 1761, and there are other accounts of their appearing throughout the centuries.[18]

Flamel's account, and other equally fantastic stories, helped to popularize alchemy in Europe (after the Flamels' death their property was so thoroughly searched for pieces of the philosopher's stone that their house was reduced to rubble). Despite this fanciful quality, the ideas in alchemy were in strict accord with the best philosophical and scientific thinking of their time. Many of the most brilliant minds in the late medieval and Renaissance periods were alchemists, including Arnold of Villanova (1240–1313), Roger Bacon (1214–1294), Albertus Magnus (1193–1280), and Paracelsus (1493–1531). Even men such as Robert Boyle (1627–1691), who was critical of alchemists and helped lay the foundations of modern chemistry, believed he had achieved alchemical transformations in his work.[19] As the philosopher René Descartes was interested in alchemy, as was Isaac Newton (1642–1727), who discovered the law of gravitation. Newton devoted a large percentage of his study to alchemy and philosophy. Throughout his life he considered science a form of worship or mystical quest.[20]

In 1422 a book called *Hieroglyphica* arrived in Florence where it caused a sensation. Allegedly, it was a Greek translation of an Egyptian work which explained the meaning of Egyptian hieroglyphics; in reality it only passed on a Greek misconception. Because the ancient Greeks were unable to read hieroglyphics, they assumed that it was not an ordinary language but a type of allegorical picture incorporating many aspects of their subject into one image, and invited the viewer's interpretation (or projection).

The *Hieroglyphica* was translated into Latin, French, German and Italian, and became known throughout Europe. It was a major influence in developing the Renaissance fashion for symbolic engravings called "emblems" or "hieroglyphicall figures," created by prominent artists—including Albrecht Dürer—and used to encapsulate various fields of knowledge, including alchemy.[21]

By the seventeenth century, interest in alchemy had peaked, and an unprecedented quantity of enigmatically illustrated alchemical books were published—including the many works of Michael Maier, Jacob Boehme, and even a book with pictures and no written text, the *Mutus Liber* ("Silent Book").

Paracelsus, one of the greatest alchemists and the founder of modern medicine, defined alchemy as the transformation of one natural substance into another—one fit for a new use. He was the first to create non-herbal medicines, which he considered the main physical goal of alchemy. However, he was equally strong in his belief that the true quest of the alchemist was his own spiritual transformation. The students of Paracelsus tended to split in two directions: developing the science of medication, which led to modern medicine and then chemistry; and abandoning the laboratory to search for spiritual gold within, a course which led to mystical philosophies like Rosicrucianism.

The spiritual quest had been part of alchemy since ancient times, but from Paracelsus on it became more and more the primary objective of alchemy. These alchemists wanted to separate themselves from those who were interested in alchemy only as a means to wealth. Solely materialistic alchemists were called "puffers" because of their impatient use of the bellows to keep the fire hot and speed up the process (most alchemical texts recommend slow heating at a moderate temperature).

Others sought riches and fame through fraudulent claims of successfully transforming base metal into gold, which they accomplished by trickery. These charlatans caused alchemy to fall into disrepute. Fraud, plus the discrediting of alchemy's underlying theories by scientific discoveries—

e.g., the components of water and air—influenced a growing view of alchemy as a pseudoscience. It received the death blow from Antoine Lavoisier in the eighteenth century, when he discovered that air contained an irreducible component which he labeled "oxygine." Lavoisier redefined the term "element" (see the quadrangle under Basic Concepts, p. 54.) and went on to develop modern chemical terminology.

In the nineteenth century, the symbolic, spiritual alchemical quest was revived along with interest in the occult; this led to the formation of such groups as the Hermetic Order of the Golden Dawn, and, in the beginning of the twentieth century, the Ordo Templis Orientis (Order of the Templars of the East). In the 1920s and 1930s, the insights of Jung and his associates made alchemy a respected area of psychological study. Parallel to this revival, a renewed interest in laboratory alchemy has resulted in the recent founding of schools and the production of alchemical products for use as cosmetics, beverages, perfumes, and herbal medicine.[22] Interest in alchemy was never eclipsed in India. Under its Indian name, Ayurveda, it is still taught in universities.

Basic Concepts of Alchemy

Jung describes the method of explanation in alchemical texts, as "the obscure by the more obscure, the unknown by the more unknown,"[23] and points out that rarely have any two authors the same opinion on the correct course of the process. However, most agree on the basic concepts and principal stages of the opus.

These basic concepts and stages seem to be framed by a mystical, mathematical system of number symbols derived from Pythagoras. The numbers 1, 2, 3 and 4 are particularly significant, as can be seen in the following quote from a sixteenth-century alchemical text, the *Rosarium Philosophorum:*

> Make a round circle out of the man and woman, and draw out of it a quadrangle and out of the quadrangle a triangle, make a round circle, and thou shalt have the Stone of the Philosophers.[24]

The Circle: Primal Unity

Aristotle's theories underlie the Hermetica, and therefore all successive alchemical literature. Aristotle hypothesized the existence of a single, invisible, indestructible substance from which all matter was created, and to which all matter would return. This substance was called "prima materia" ("first matter"). Not only was it invisible, it had no physical existence; yet, from it the original four elements were extracted and then used to create the entire material world. The alchemists believed it to be a living soul (anima mundi), and that it was hidden in all matter (synonymous with the Gnostic belief in a divine spark trapped in all matter).

The object of the opus, or great work, was to duplicate the process of creation and the final resolution in the microcosm of the laboratory. Starting with the prima materia, which could be found in any substance, the alchemist would subject it to a series of operations that would fragment it, recombine it, kill it and revive it. These processes were designed to release the anima mundi from the subject of the work, and capture it in a form known as the philosopher's stone (the substance which could make gold, or from which could be created the elixir of life).

The philosopher's stone is thought of as a tangible expression of the prima materia. It is described as a stone, a powder, a liquid, as invisible, or as a stone that is not a stone. The descriptions of the prima materia are even more confusing. Ruland's *Lexicon of Alchemy* lists 134 different names for it, many of which seem to contradict each other: fire or water, medicine or poison, etc. They seem to point to a substance that unifies all dualities and is beyond the confines of logic.

In Jungian terms, the prima materia refers to the unconscious. In its initial state before creation, the prima materia is called the "massa confusa," or the chaos on which the world of form was imposed. Likewise, the unconscious, when first encountered, seems confusing and illogical until the order of consciousness is imposed on it. The philosopher's stone has the power to bring whatever it is combined with back into a preformed state, so that its form may change or transform. This is also the goal of the psyche itself, which seeks to dissolve fixed aspects of the personality back into their undifferentiated state, so that they can transform into the higher state Jung called individuation.

Images of the prima materia appear spontaneously in the following dreams described by Jung. In each case the dreamer had no knowledge of alchemy, and Jung was careful not to influence him.

Dream #1:
By the seashore. The sea breaks into the land, flooding everything. Then the dreamer is sitting on a lonely island.[25]

Dream #2:
A snake describes a circle round the dreamer, who stands rooted to the ground like a tree . . . The veiled figure of a woman seated on a stair.[26]

In the first dream, the prima materia is symbolized by the sea, which is also a common symbol for the unconscious. In the second, it is the snake.

The snake eating its own tail (ouroboros) is probably the oldest known pictorial symbol in alchemy, first appearing in the eleventh century in the *Codex Marcionus*. The ouroboros symbolizes the circular process of the opus, from the prima materia back to the prima materia, and the underlying unity of all matter. It is also a symbol for the prima materia as the lapis, which is the elixir that renews life. The snake was a symbol of longevity to the ancients, because it rejuvenates itself when it sheds its skin. Others believed it had the power to re-grow a severed tail; perhaps this is the secret of how it can nourish itself—by eating its own tail, thereby recreating itself indefinitely. To the ancient Egyptians the snake's head and tail represented the point where death and resurrection met; therefore, it was carved on the walls of tombs.

The veiled woman is an image of the anima mundi, another aspect of the prima materia. Jung calls her the "anima"—the female element in every male psyche, complemented by the "animus"—the male element in the female psyche.

Duality and Triplicity

A fundamental duality of masculine and feminine forces permeates all alchemical material. In China, the initial underlying force, Tao (prima materia), splits into yin and yang, a feminine and masculine pair who through their interaction create the universe. In Tantra, the original world egg splits into Shakti and Shiva, the divine couple, whose mutual sexual attraction stems from their initial unity. All creation is an illusion caused by their sexual play. This same sexual duality can be seen in Western alchemy where it is depicted by various pairs of symbols: mercury and sulfur, white and red, volatile and fixed, moon and sun.

Returning to the *Codex Marcionus* ouroboros, we can see that it is distinctly shaded—the upper half, containing the head, is black, and the lower half is white. Therefore, this symbol of unity also depicts a duality. If we think of the white tail as a phallus entering the feminine black upper half, then its life-renewing power stems from the sexual generation of its two parts (similar to the Tantric divine couple).

In a tenth-century Arab text, *De Chemia*, by Mohammed ibn Umail describes a statue of Hermes Trismegistus presenting in his hands an engraved tablet revealing the secrets of alchemy. On the tablet are various symbols of duality, including several variations of the sun and moon, and the two birds described in the following quote from that text:

> Looked at schematically, the birds would be lying one over the over, each with its head to the tail of the other bird, one being winged and the other wingless. It was as though they wanted to fly together, or as though the wingless one was keeping the other back, that is the upper bird wanted to carry away the lower, but the lower bird held it back and prevented it from flying away. The two birds were bound together, were homogeneous and of the same substance and they were painted in one sphere as though the image of two things in one.[27]

In this image of a winged and a wingless bird swallowing each other's tails, we can see a more differentiated form of the ouroboros. The two halves have become separate beings which devour each other. In later alchemical texts they take the form of two serpents or dragons, representing the volatile (winged) and the fixed (wingless).

The alchemical opus demands that the prima materia (the ouroboros) be cooked so that the fixed and volatile separate.

They then are transformed into one another, in cycle after cycle, until they are purified.

> That which is volatile may be fixed of them by the means of policies but from hence that which is fixed may be made volatile, and again volatile fixed, and in this order the most precious secret is accomplished.[28]

Senior says that his wingless, fixed bird is red sulfur (masculine) and that the winged, volatile bird is the soul (feminine). We may consider the fixed as the liquid, which is being cooked, and the volatile as the vapor rising from the boiling substance. The vapor must be captured and condensed so that it can be revaporised in a continuous process called distillation. Alchemists would patiently distill a substance numerous times before it was purified enough for further operations.

Jung describes sulfur as an active, corrosive, evil-smelling substance; in folklore it is equated with the devil, who is described as leaving a sulfurous smell. However, in alchemy, sulfur is the lover of the bride, and is equated with the sun. These conflicting qualities successfully depict the driving, emotional, psychic life force called the libido.

Depression, as viewed by Jung, is a natural process of the psyche. He described it as an introverted psychic state in which the imagination is churned to bring out hidden fears and fantasies. If allowed its full course, it leads to an integration of this material—to calmness and understanding.

This is the natural process that psychoanalysis duplicates, and it is analogous to the alchemical cooking of the sulfur (libido) to extract the vapor (fantasies). It must be preformed numerous times to approach a state of psychic wholeness, and find the true creative purpose behind the libido's seeming demonic demands.[29]

In later alchemical literature the masculine and feminine become personified as a king and a queen, who are brother and sister, as well as lovers. (Some texts expand this personification to the alchemists themselves, by recommending as essential that the male alchemist take a female partner, called the soror mystica, or "mystical sister." The sixteenth-century *Rosarium Philosophorum* contains a series of twenty illustrations, which at the start depict the king standing on the sun and the queen on the moon (like the vision of the panicking professor mentioned earlier). In subsequent pictures the couple disrobe, enter a bath together and engage in sexual intercourse. This prolonged intercourse leads to a merging of their two bodies, until they leave the bath as a winged hermaphrodite, standing on the moon. The process is repeated, and once again they emerge as a winged hermaphrodite, this time surmounting a three-headed serpent.

The king and queen correspond to Jung's animus and anima, archetypes of masculine and feminine psychic forces in the unconscious. As mentioned earlier, the animus represents the male element in the psyche of a woman, and anima the female element in the psyche of a man. Both are sources of inner convictions and fantasies that can be unreasonable or destructive (sometimes the anima is referred to as a femme fatale and the animus as a Bluebeard). They can also be benevolent inner guides or beacons, leading one into the unconscious and to the Higher Self. They often appear in dreams as lovers or beckoning guides (as the veiled woman in Dream #2).

The integration of the ego with the unconscious can be symbolized as a marriage or union with the animus or the anima, which can lead to the hermaphrodite, an image of the Higher Self. With the introduction of the Higher Self, the alchemical couple now develop a third force, which completes the triangle mentioned earlier in the quote from the *Rosarium*. The theme is further expanded in the following quote from the *Rosarium*:

Philosophy hath three parts . . . Sol, Luna, and Mercury.[30]

In Jabir's eighth-century symbolism sulfur is masculine (spirit) and mercury is feminine (soul). Gnostics claimed there were three parts to an individual: body, spirit, and soul; alchemists later added salt (the body) to Jabir's couple. In the above quote, however, we can see that the gender of the chemical symbols can differ greatly from one text to another—particularly that of mercury. Here mercury is clearly the hermaphrodite or the Higher Self which is both masculine and feminine.

In mythology Mercury (Hermes in Greek), as messenger of the divine world, was able to take on any form; therefore, he was able to change his sex, making him a manifestation of the anima, animus, or both. Priests of Hermes in Cyprus wore artificial breasts and women's clothing, similar to the practice of Siberian and Eskimo shamans. This may be interpreted as the priests' attempt to identify with their anima, and thereby make contact with the unconscious, or as their identification with the hermaphroditic god. The word "hermaphrodite" itself is a combination of the name of Hermes with his sometime lover, Aphrodite, suggesting a sexual connection similar to the images in the *Rosarium*.

Mercury, as a symbol, is as quick and elusive as the god himself. In another quote from the *Rosarium*, we can see that even in the same text he changes meaning from one statement to another:

The Body is Venus and the Woman; The Spirit is Mercury and the Man; the Soul is Sol and Luna. The Body must melt into first matter which is mercury.[31]

Here the body refers to the physical, which is seen as feminine. Mercury is both the spirit—which in the sixteenth century referred to what we would call the mind—and prima materia, which is the One, or all three combined. The soul (self), being hermaphroditic, is seen to have a masculine and a feminine part symbolized by the two luminous bodies. By differentiating them, we see that four parts can be drawn out of our triangle.

The Quadrangle

As stated earlier, Aristotle's theory postulates that all matter is composed of four elements extracted from the prima materia: earth, air, fire, and water. These four elements are ubiquitous in the ancient world, being almost identical in Europe, Asia, Africa, and even the Americas (in China there were five: water, fire, wood, metal, and earth). The number 4 in general is associated with the world and physical reality, which has four directions, four dimensions and four seasons.

Aristotle carried the concept a step further, by introducing the four qualities: dry, moist, hot, and cold. Each element possesses two qualities: earth is dry and cold, water cold and wet, air wet and hot, and fire hot and dry. As can be seen, there is one quality shared by any two successive elements; therefore, each element can be transformed into another element that shares the same quality by manipulating the unshared quality. It was thought that a substance could be changed in this way from one element to another in a continuous circle. Aristotle's theory was the basis for the alchemical belief in the possibility of the transformation of one material into another.

Now returning to Jabir's theory, we can see that his two components comprising metals are actually a variation of the four elements. Earthy smoke is earth becoming fire, as its dryness becomes hot, and watery vapor is water becoming air, as its wetness becomes hot. When these two substances were imprisoned in the earth they became sulfur and mercury, which combined in differing proportions with varying amounts of impurities to make all metals. Only if they were pure and in correct balance would they make gold. Therefore, the alchemists thought they could make gold by removing the impurities from other metals.[32]

The discovery of oxygen and the composition of water in the eighteenth century discredited Aristotle's theory, and redefined the term "element." However, these elemental archetypes are still found in modern physics in a different form: fire can be thought of as energy, and its complement matter has three states: solid (earth), liquid (water) and gas (air).

In the following dream, described by Jung, we can see references to the four elements as well as duality and triplicity.

Dream #3:
In the square space. The dreamer is sitting opposite the unknown woman whose portrait he is supposed to be drawing. What he draws, however, is not a face but three-leaved clovers or distorted crosses in four different colors: red, yellow, green, and blue.[33]

In this dream, the four elements can be seen first, in the symbol of the square space, which also relates to material reality, and the four directions. Then, they can be seen in the crosses, which evolve out of the three-leaved clovers, just as the three components and four elements merge with each other in alchemy. Last are the four colors: red, yellow, green and blue.

From the oldest Indo-European cosmology, which depicts the square Mount Meru in the center of the world, to the Hermetic societies of the nineteenth century, there have been numerous systems that relate four colors to the four elements. These systems are mostly based on the primary colors: red, yellow, and blue, with the addition and/or substitution of one of the following: white, black, or green. We can interpret the colors, which the dreamer draws out of his anima figure, as representing the elements, each assigned to a cross. If the dream continued, the dreamer possibly would assign each colored cross to one of the four directions of the square space—like an ancient world map. Jung uses this dream as an example of a "mandala"—a symbol of the total self and a means of entering one's true center. The term "mandala" itself is derived from the name of Hindu and Tantric circular, mystic diagrams which evolved from ancient world maps.

In alchemy there is another quadruple set of color symbols: the four stages, which can be traced to the oldest known alchemist, Zosimos. It outlines the process of the opus (also called a year because it had four stages or seasons), depicting each stage as a color. The stages and colors are sometimes paired with the four elements. The stages are, in order, the nigredo (the blackening), the albedo (the whitening), the citrinitas (the yellowing) and the rubedo (the reddening).

In the first stage, the nigredo, the initial substance which is placed in the alchemist's oven (athanor), is separated into its elements (the solutio, divisio, or separatio). The male and female parts are then reunited in the sealed retort or vessel (the coniunctio, matrimonium, or coitus), then the product of the union is killed (the mortificatio), reduced to ash (the calcinatio), and blackened (the putrefactio). In the putrefactio a substance is created that is "blacker than black," and the nigredo is complete.

The albedo is a process of whitening the black substance by washing (the baptisma, or ablutio). When the albedo is complete, the alchemist often starts over, reblackening the matter and again washing it white. After many cycles the matter is gradually purified, until the soul (anima mundi) is released from the death of the nigredo and is reunited with the body. This produces a temporary display of many colors (*omnes colores*) called the "peacock's tail." When the matter returns to white the albedo is complete and "the white that contains all colors" is formed. This is the lapis albus or tinctura alba, which can transform base metal into silver.

The albedo is called the dawn before the sunrise of the citrinitas, the yellow stage. The citrinitas is a result of raising the heat in the oven, and is a transitional stage leading to the rubedo. By the sixteenth century most texts omitted the citrinitas, or considered it part of the rubedo, reducing the stages from four to three.

In the final red stage, the rubedo, the sun of the citrinitas, who is also called the red king, is married to the white lunar queen of the albedo, in a final "great coniunctio," or "chymical wedding." In this way the hermaphroditic philosopher's stone, which has the highest power of transformation, is formed.[34]

In the following dream, which depicts a process of transformation and points to a condition of psychic wholeness, we can see symbolic color stages arising spontaneously from the unconscious.

Dream #4:
A death's head. The dreamer wants to kick it away, but cannot. The skull gradually changes into a red ball, then into a woman's head which emits light.[35]

Jung felt that the color stages accurately outlined the process of individuation. The nigredo represents the initial immersion in the unconscious, a process of self-reflection that happens naturally in depression—often described as a black mood. Often, when we first encounter the unconscious, we are confronted with the aspect that Jung calls the "shadow"—that part of our psychic energy that is repressed or neglected. Even beneficial forces, when repressed, become part of the shadow, and at first can appear as demons. As we observe and analyze these demons, or use active imagination to transform them, we are purified of their projections, entering a lighter (albedo) state of quiet and peace, then we go back to the nigredo and start again. This quiet state can be found over and over again, and eventually we learn to make it permanent.

The albedo's peace, however, is not individuation; there is a danger in the albedo of becoming overly analytical and losing spontaneity and drive. As Jung says, we are in need of the red, life-giving blood of the rubedo. The red sulfur demon from the nigredo, which is only a mask over our creative drive and joy of life, must be married with the white peaceful woman of the albedo to achieve the wholeness of individuation.

Great miracles appear in the hour of conjunction.[36]

Seven Metals, Seven Operations

To the ancients there were seven planets, each of which was equated to one of the seven days of the week. The word "planet" is derived from the Greek planētai (wanderers). The planets were called wanderers, because when viewed with the naked eye, they were the only luminous bodies in the night sky that appeared to move independently from the constellations. They include the sun and moon as well as the presently designated planets of Mercury, Venus, Mars, Jupiter, and Saturn.

Aristotle developed a model of the universe with the earth in the center and each planet on its own crystal sphere ascending away from the earth like layers of an onion. On the eighth sphere were the fixed stars. Mystics placed heaven beyond Aristotle's model, refined by Ptolemy, which was the accepted scientific theory for centuries. Copernicus challenged it in 1473 and put the sun in the center, but his model was not more accurate at predicting the movements of the planets until Kepler refined it in the sixteenth century by adding elliptical orbits.[37]

The ancient mystery religions viewed the planets as a ladder or stairway to heaven that was traveled by the soul after death. The ruling god, or later the archangel or archon, of each planet corresponded to an aspect of the personality: love, power, anger (this is the origin of the ''Seven Deadly Sins'' and the ''Seven Virtues''). The aspect had to be reconciled when the soul reached that planet in order not to impede its progress to the next level. The purer the soul, the greater its gnosis or its magic ability, the closer it progressed to heaven. Initiation rites in the mysteries often included an ascent of the ladder of the planets accomplished while in a trance. This mystic ladder or stairs often appears in dreams, as in Dream #2 mentioned earlier, and in alchemical texts, such as the *Mutus Liber*.

Alchemists in a series of correspondences equated each of the seven known metals to one of the planets and viewed them as a ladder of perfection from lead to gold (the order of the five in between differs from one author to another). This was not just a poetic metaphor; the alchemist felt that each metal was the living essence of that planet on earth. Just as plants and animals are alive, they believed that minerals are alive and reproduced in the earth through a type of sexual interaction. Each living metal, as it is purified in nature, progresses to a higher state until it becomes gold. The alchemists endeavored to copy and speed up this natural process in their labs, and simultaneously purify and refine their souls.

Metals as symbols can be seen in the following dream recorded by the Jungian analyst Edward F. Edinger. The dreamer was a middle-aged commercial artist who had no knowledge of alchemy.

Dream #5:
Four metal-clad figures descend toward me from the sky. They float down over an ancient Roman wall. Each suit is made of a different metal. One is bronze, another lead, another iron, and the fourth is made of platinum. The platinum-suited figure separates himself from the others and approaches. 'We are seeking metal,' he says. 'The metal we seek matches the material of our suits.' The figures remain suspended in the air by some unique method.[38]

The correlation between the seven planets and the seven metals is shown in the following chart. Their correlation and order of ascent, from the bottom up, is based on Martin Ruland's seventeenth-century *Lexicon of Alchemy*.

Metal	Planet
Gold	Sun
Silver	Moon
Quicksilver	Mercury
Copper	Venus
Iron	Mars
Tin	Jupiter
Lead	Saturn

In their work, alchemists developed numerous chemical operations, many of which had more than one name (as demonstrated in the previous description of the color stages). These were also seen as a ladder of ascent because of their order in the process of purifying the subject of the opus. Therefore, the principal ones were often placed in ascending lists of seven or twelve (twelve is another number of completion, related to the twelve signs of the zodiac, or the twelve months of the year).

Although the names, order and importance of the operations change from one alchemist to another, here is a progressive list of seven commonly mentioned operations:

> solutio, separatio, coniunctio, calcinatio, moritificatio, baptisma, and multiplicatio.

Solutio, or solution, literally means to turn a solid into a liquid. In the initial stage, the matter of the work is often liquefied for further operations. This is accomplished by a liquid solvent "swallowing" the coagulated (solid) substance. For example, gold or silver can be dissolved into mercury to form an amalgamate (this is the basis of the ancient method for extracting gold from ore). Psychologically, the solid can be thought of as the ego consciousness, consisting of fixed ideas, which at this stage is dissolved into the mercury of the unconscious.[39]

Separatio, or separation, is the breaking down of the subject into its elements.

> Reduce your stone to the four elements . . . and unite them into one and you will have the whole magistery.[40]

This is accomplished by various other operations: heating, evaporation, filtration, abstraction, depletion, dilation, or removal. The separation into elements is not meant to be literal; Ruland points out that it is only a separation of impurities from the subject.[41] Psychologically, it can be described as the analysis and classification of unconscious material.

Coniunctio, or conjunction, is the joining of two substances to make a third. To the alchemist it was a sexual union between the male and female elements of the subjects; it was necessary that they be "married alive" so that the union would be fruitful. The product could be described as the hermaphrodite or as a child. In the early stages the male and female were not yet purified, so it was necessary for their product to be put through further operations. The great coniunctio, at the end of the work after purification, produced the lapis as its product. Psychologically it can be described as a marriage of the ego with the anima or animus, which must reach the purification of the albedo before it can lead to individuation.

Calcinatio, or calcination, is the chemically executed corrosion or intense heating of the matter, to drive off water, or other volatile constituents, and reduce it to a white ash (calx, or snow). The fire or corrosive agent is called "the dragon who drinks the water." The word "calx" means lime, and the process probably stems from the production of quick lime by heating limestone.[42] The *Rosarium* instructs, "sow your gold into white foliated earth, which by calcination is made fiery, subtle and airy."[43] The king (ego) who is killed in the next operation must be buried in this white ground (created by the emotions of the libido intensifying and burning themselves out). In this way the king, like the sacrifice of a fertility ritual, will multiply like grain as he is reborn.

Mortificatio is the killing of the product of the initial union; this could be the king mentioned above, or it could be the hermaphrodite. It has no modern chemical equivalent, because chemists no longer believe that minerals are alive. This murder is performed so that the matter can be resurrected in a new and exalted form. To be complete the body must decompose or rot—to become a black substance—in the second part of the operation called putrefactio.

The king can be equated to the ego, who must die so that the emerging self will not be blocked, and so that he will be able to be reborn with this new psychic center.

> I never saw anything that had life to grow and increase without putrefaction, and vain would the work of alchemy be, unless it were putrified.[44]

The *baptisma*, or purification, is a washing or distillation of the black putrefied body so that it is purified and made white (the albedo stage). Like the religious ritual of baptism, it is meant to be a rejuvenating immersion in the womb of primal energies—internally, a death of the old ego and the rebirth of the new self. This process must be repeated until its peace and well-being bond to the personality. This operation creates a new substance called mercural water, or the "mother of the stone."

Multiplicatio is an operation that is performed by the philosopher's stone itself once it has been created by the final coniunctio of the resurrected king and queen (in the rubedo stage). Now, like a seed that can produce more seeds—after it has sprouted from the earth and matured—the stone purifies whatever it touches and thereby multiplies its perfection. It can transform base metal into gold, and it is the elixir of life. Similarly, when individuation is achieved, this consciousness of the self is contagious, and the individuated person has a transformative, healing influence on others.

In making known to you all that I have seen and experienced, I am only following the maxim of Seneca, who said that he desired knowledge chiefly that he might impart it to others.[45]

NOTES

1. C. G. Jung, *Memories, Dreams, Reflections*, edited by Aniela Jaffé. Translated by Richard & Clara Winston, p. 202. New York: Vintage Books, c. 1963.

2. *Ibid.*, p. 201.

3. Marie-Louise Von Franz, *Alchemy: An Introduction to the Symbolism and the Psychology,* p. 14. Toronto, Canada: Inner City Books, 1980.

4. C. G. Jung, *Psychology and Alchemy.* Translated by R. F. C. Hull, p. 246. Princeton, New Jersey: Princeton University Press, 1968.

5. Von Franz. p. 22.

6. C. G. Jung, *Psychology and Alchemy*, p. 246.

7. Jung, *Memories, Dreams, Reflections*, p. 209.

8. Rosemary Ellen Guiley, *Harper's Encyclopedia of Mystical & Paranormal Experience*, p. 5. San Francisco, CA: Harper San Francisco, 1991.

9. Richard Grossinger, "Alchemy: Pre-Egyptian Legacy, Millennial Promise." In *The Alchemical Tradition in the Late Twentieth Century*, edited by Richard Grossinger, p. 246. Berkeley, CA: North Atlantic Books, 1983.

10. *Hermetica*, edited and translated by Walter Scott, vol. 1, p. 4. Boston: Shambala, 1985.

11. R. P. M., "Alchemy." In *The New Encyclopedia Britannica*, 30 vols., vol. 1, 15th Ed., p. 433. Chicago: Encyclopedia Britannica Inc., 1980.

12. *Ibid.*, p. 43.

13. Neil Powell, *Alchemy, the Ancient Science*, pp. 120–122. London: The Danbury Press, 1976.

14. Elemire Zohar, "Alchemy Out of India." *Gnosis* (Summer 1988): 48.

15. John Turkevich, "Alchemy." In *Academic American Encyclopedia.* 21 vols., vol. 1, p. 263. Danbury, CT: Grolier Inc., 1983.

16. Oppi Untracht, *Metal Techniques for Craftsmen*, p. 31. Garden City, N.Y.: Doubleday & Co., 1975.

17. Von Franz, *op. cit.*, p. 43.

18. Powell, *op. cit.*, pp. 40–51.

19. Herbert Butterfield, *The Origins of Modern Science 1300– 1800*, pp. 140–141. New York: The Free Press, 1965.

20. Timothy Ferris, *Coming of Age in the Milky Way,* p. 105. New York: William Morrow & Co., Inc., 1988.

21. Stanislas Klossowski De Rola, *The Golden Game: Alchemical Engravings of the Seventeenth Century*, pp. 8–19. New York: George Braziller Inc., 1988.

22. Guiley, *op. cit.*, p. 6.

23. Jung, *Psychology and Alchemy*, p. 227.

24. *The Rosary of the Philosophers*, edited by Adam McClean, p. 42. Magnum Opus Hermetic Source works #6; London: The Hermetic Research Trust, 1980.

25. Jung, *Psychology and Alchemy*, p. 48.

26. *Ibid.*, p. 108.

27. *Ibid.*, p. 109.

28. *The Rosary of the Philosophers*, p. 90.

29. Von Franz, *op. cit.*, pp. 126–128.

30. *Ibid.*

31. *The Rosary of the Philosophers*, p. 26.

32. Powell, *op. cit.*, pp. 26–33.

33. Jung, *Psychology and Alchemy*, p. 164.

34. *Ibid.*, pp. 227–232.

35. *Ibid.*, p. 83.

36. *The Rosary of the Philosophers*, p. 35.

37. Ferris, *op. cit.,* pp. 61–82.

38. Edward F. Edinger, *Anatomy of the Psyche: Alchemical Symbolism in Psychotherapy,* p. 3. La Salle, IL: Open Court, 1985.

39. *Ibid.*, pp. 47–49.

40. Quote from the *Tractatus Aurens*. In: Jung, *Psychology and Alchemy*, p. 128.

41. Martin Ruland, A *Lexicon of Alchemy*, translated by A. E. Waite, pp. 291–292. York Beach, Maine: Samuel Weiser, Inc., 1984. (originally published 1612).

42. Edinger, *op. cit.*, p. 17.

43. *Rosary of the Philosophers*, p. 70.

44. *Ibid.*, p. 40.

45. John Frederick Helvetius, "Golden Calf: Which the World Worships and Adores." In *The Hermetic Museum: Restored and Enlarged*, translated by Arthur Edward Waite, p. 300. York Beach, Maine: Samuel Weiser, Inc., 1973. (Latin original published 1678).

6

Working with Dreams

Humans have been paying close attention to their night visions since at least 3000 B.C. The Assyrians, Sumerians and Babylonians held dreams in a rather generic light; the effect of individual experience and personality was not considered a factor. Rather, dreams were thought to be the evil work of a league of demons ruled by An Za Qar, the god of dreams.

Ancient Greeks and Egyptians were less afraid of, but just as serious about, their dreams. It was the Egyptians who established "oneiromancy," the science of dream interpretation. These civilizations regarded their dreams as messages from the gods, and therefore as "real" as any waking event. Divine messages were deliberately invited through the technique of incubation, or the effort to dream with a specific goal or question in mind—a practice still used today. Incubation spread to the Greek and Roman cultures, where it reached the height of its popularity.

Incubation rituals took place in serapims, or dream temples, and cures for physical ailments were often the subject of the appeals. Records from the serapims indicate that such requests were often answered; some appellants were successfully healed of ailments as serious as blindness. But the healing power of dreaming gradually lost some of its divinity and became recognized as a tool for human hands. In the fourth century B.C., Hippocrates used dreams to perform the diagnosis and healing himself, although he did acknowledge that *some* dreams still came from the gods.

The first thorough system of dream analysis to be documented was authored by Artemidorus of Daldis, who lived in Asia Minor in the second century A.D. His *Oneirocritica* consisted of five books in which he offered his own personal theories on dreams as facts. Although his methods may have been unscientific, some of his statements represented a turning point in dream analysis and are still valid in modern dream interpretation.

The gods had no place in the *Oneirocritica*. Artemidorus stated that dreams are not divine messages at all but perfectly natural functions of the human brain. He also stated that dreams are precognitive visions—of the dreamer's future as well as the future of others. (The prophetic properties of dreams would also be discussed by Plato and, much later, by Carl Jung.) The analysis of dreams, according to Artemidorus, involves sorting through all possible interpretations until the correct one is discovered; he stressed reliance on intuition and personal experience to make this discovery. Again, this is in synch with the approach of most contemporary dreamwork.

The dreamwork of Eastern cultures also expressed attitudes still found in dreamwork today. The Chinese *Meng Shu* of the seventh century A.D. sees dreams as teaching tools; therefore the correct interpretation is necessary if the dreamer is to learn how to improve his or her life. The *Meng Shu*, while it encourages the dreamer to look "inside" for interpretations of his or her dreams, acknowledges the influence of the external world, including astrological forces. Dream incubation was widely practiced by artists in China, who would dream to receive inspiration for their paintings and music. (Incubation was also practiced by the American Plains Indians.) The Vedas, a collection of sacred Hindu writings, offers instructions for dream interpretation, including determining what time of night the dream occurred.[1]

Like many other intangible subjects, dreamwork lost popularity when the Renaissance brought with it a focus on science and reason. Regarded as occult, unscientific, and a waste of time, dream analysis was put to sleep, but in the late nineteenth century, was reawakened by Sigmund Freud.

Contemporary Dream Analysis

In *The Interpretation of Dreams* (1900), Freud proposed that dreams do indeed have significant, interpretable meanings. His theories were the first to make a connection between dreams and the unconscious, despite the doubts of his contemporaries.

Freud believed that only free association could reveal the true meaning of dreams, because they are never what they appear to be. He proposed that dreams usually represent unfulfilled wishes that, for whatever reason, are prohibited by the conscious mind. Demanding attention and recognition, these wishes show up in the unconscious mind, disguised as dream symbols. (In fact, according to Freud, everything in the unconscious originated in the conscious mind and was repressed.) However, he also noted:

> [I]n the case of adults, anyone with some experience in analyzing their dreams will find to his surprise that even those dreams which have an appearance of being transparently clear are seldom as simple as those of children, and that behind the obvious wish fulfillment some other meaning may lie concealed.[2]

The source of a dream, Freud believed, could be found in "day residue"—whatever had happened during the day, or perhaps the last couple of days, and not prior to that. Much of his theory focused on dreaming's connection to the past, on unveiling the cause of the dream. But he paid little attention to the dream's connection to the present and future—what the dream's purpose was, and how it might improve the dreamer's attitude and behavior.

Alfred Adler recognized that dreams take problems represented in the day residue and indirectly show the dreamer how to deal with them more positively. Their purpose, he believed, is personal growth. Adler also believed that, in general, the "attitude" of a dream is in synch with the dreamer's waking personality, a belief common to most contemporary methods of dream interpretation. But Adler also adopted Freud's mistaken theory that well-adjusted people do not dream, because they handle their problems successfully while awake.[3] Carl Jung also viewed dreams as tools for individuation—the attainment of one's "personal best" by leaving behind habitual, unproductive methods of problem-solving. He emphasized dreaming's role in finding wholeness of self, and how different aspects of the personality will appear in dreams based on what is needed to achieve that wholeness. Jung worked with the concepts of *animus* and *anima*, the male and female (respectively)— or yin and yang—halves in each individual, which must be balanced for happiness and wholeness. (Philosopher Emanuel Swedenborg first discussed animus as the rational mind and anima as the soul.) The animus is "male"—less emotional and more aggressive. The anima is "female"— softer, nurturing and more spiritual.

People often seek to balance the two through a member of the opposite sex, searching for those qualities that are weak or lacking in themselves. Jung found that the choice of a mate is often based on a person's mental image of his or her "other half." But true balance, he said, could only be achieved from the inside.

There is another duality of self, according to Jung, that makes itself apparent in dreams: the persona and the shadow. The persona represents the dreamer's "surface" self—brighter, simpler, perhaps the way we like to see ourselves and have others see us. The shadow self is darker—that is, harder to recognize, more complex, and representing aspects of ourselves that we would rather not see. Indeed, in dreams the shadow is often literally a dark shadow, or a faceless person.

All parts of a person show themselves in dreams, said Jung, indicating which parts need to be softened or strengthened. This is why dream analysis is so important to personal growth. He believed that the symbols in dreams are manifest—that, basically, they are what they appear to be. (The existential-phenomenological approach to dream analysis agrees.) Deciphering the meaning is not such cryptic work as Freud would have us think. However, Jung did stress that interpretive work needs to be done in order to fully understand what the dream symbols are trying to teach. (He claimed that much of his interpretation of patients' dreams was done intuitively.)

While Freud believed that all of the unconscious consists of formerly conscious thought which has been repressed, Jung believed that was only part of it. He proposed that there is a collective unconscious—that is, a primordial, instinctual knowledge woven into the blueprint of all humans.

Energy from this unconscious knowledge is symbolized by ageless, universally recognized images called archetypes. Jung called them "self-portraits of the instincts" and "primordial images." Archetypes can be found in our waking life as certain religious symbols, forces of nature, animals, people, shapes and actions. (Jung proposed that flying saucers are actually mandala symbols which appear at times of great societal and individual change.) They find their way into our dream life as well.

When an archetypal image appears in a dream, the dreamer is seeking knowledge that he or she already possesses, but which is buried deep in the mind. Archetypal dreams most often occur at times of crises or turning points in a person's life. They can also be a sign of psychological imbalance, since they are frequently found in severely neurotic and schizophrenic people. But those who have reached a level of great emotional and spiritual growth may also find archetypes frequently in their dreams.

An archetypal dream is more spiritual, profound, and abstract than a dream reflecting, for example, the previous day's activities. Although its meaning may not be understood by the dreamer, he or she understands that it is significant, even supernatural. Often, archetypal images are things not ordinarily found in the dreamer's everyday life, such as the Mythological Hero. The dreams contain "cosmic" situations and actions, such as dying, flying at tremendous speeds, and experiencing unlimited time or space. Images that appear repeatedly over time are considered archetypal. Numbers can also be considered archetypes (unless they refer to something specific in the dreamer's life, such as an age, or if they are an element of a precognitive dream, such as a date).

Although Jung disagreed with Freud's equating dreams with wish fulfillment, he did agree that dreams provide something missing from the conscious life of the dreamer. They are compensatory. But the missing elements they provide are not designed for ego fulfillment; they exist to provide what is genuinely needed. (A variation on compensation is complement; although it also functions to provide balance, it does so in a superficial, less psychologically significant way.)

In Jungian analysis, there are two ways of interpreting the compensatory nature of a dream: reductively (negatively, or analytically) and constructively (positively, or synthetically). In reductive interpretation, one looks back to the source of unpleasant images that have been repressed and therefore are limiting the dreamer's growth. Constructive compensation, on the other hand, points out the positive aspects of the dreamer's mental make-up that need to be enhanced.

It may be possible to interpret the same dream both ways—constructively or reductively. The decision depends on what seems to be necessary at the time to help the dreamer learn.

There are some dreams, however, that are not compensatory, according to Jung: traumatic, prospective, telepathic, and precognitive dreams. A traumatic dream is a recurring one that relives a physically painful or life-threatening event. A prospective, or guidance, dream lets the dreamer know that his or her present, conscious attitude is unsatisfactory. It may show what the result of this continued attitude will be, or it may suggest a more appropriate attitude and its consequences. A telepathic dream occurs simultaneously with, or immediately before or after, the dreamt-of event; often, this event may be rather mundane or insignificant. A precognitive dream "witnesses" a future event in specific detail and has some significance for people other than the dreamer. Regarding precognitive dreams, Jung put forth the interesting possibility that the *deja vu* experience may be caused by precognitively dreaming about a situation and then flashing back to the dream when the situation occurs in the present.

Different Techniques of Dream Interpretation

Interpretation in Psychoanalysis

If a person is unwilling to face certain aspects of himself or herself, or if a distorted outlook threatens to turn itself on the dream analysis, the growth experience will probably be thwarted. For this reason, dream analysis with the help of a therapist is preferable for some people. The therapist's challenge is to take into account the individual's bias and experience (through the use of free association, for example) and to avoid projecting his or her own bias and experience onto the interpretation.

The first dream remembered after starting analysis is important, as many of the elements that need work will make an appearance in this dream. Some therapists note that the first dream is very direct, almost blatant, in its message. In addition to identifying the problem, it may also suggest appropriate methods of therapy.

Not only do dreams influence therapy, therapy influences dreams. The therapist may begin to appear in the patient's dreams, either literally or figuratively,[4] and the dreamwork done in therapy may influence the dreams that follow. Dreams that occur in early analysis tend to be unpleasant ones, since therapy dredges up the sources of negative attitudes, which the patient may resist recognizing. Early in therapy the patient may not remember dreams at all, if he or she is unwilling to face what the dreams reveal.

The transference that occurs in any psychoanalysis—that is, projection of aroused emotions onto the therapist—may also occur in dreamwork with an analyst. However, this can be helpful in cases where the patient is unwilling to see any value in dreamwork. If the patient regards the therapist as the source of wisdom (even though the source of wisdom is really within the patient), and the therapist states that dreams are significant, the patient may begin to believe that it's true. Dreams where the therapist is represented either directly or symbolically will alert the therapist to the transference process, and provide clues as to how to proceed.[5]

The particular stage of therapy influences dream interpretation. Analyst Mary Ann Mattoon notes:

An explicit sexual image . . . may be interpreted as a wish for that experience if the dream occurs early in the therapy, when the dreamer's sexual impulses may still be under repression. Later . . . the same interpretation could result in arresting personality development.[6]

The therapist faces the difficult task of determining whether his or her interpretations are aimed in the right direction. Interpretation is a delicate task, as the wrong one may hinder further development. One therapist notes that if a dream is not dealt with adequately or is interpreted incorrectly, the patient may have difficulty remembering subsequent dreams.[7]

Having a patient interpret his or her own dreams under hypnosis and looking for agreement with the therapist's analysis is one possibility for verifying an interpretation. Jung also includes some suggestions for verification in his method of dream interpretation.

Jung's Steps in Dream Interpretation:
—First, keep in mind the right way to approach dream interpretation.
—The personalities of both the dreamer and the interpreter must be considered, as both will affect the interpretation. Assume nothing.
—While realizing that the content of a dream is manifest, not hidden, be aware that the dream does not directly tell the dreamer what to do.

The structure of the dream should be examined first; look for wholeness or lack of it. Next, consider the context of the dream, keeping in mind the conscious attitude of the dreamer and any possible external stimulus. Notice if the dream is one of a series with a common theme, and if there are any archetypes or image amplifications. (Before concluding that an image is archetypal, check for personal associations. It may not be as abstract as it seems.) Determine whether the images are subjective or objective.

After discovering what problem the dream represents, determine what may be the compensatory purpose of the dream. Then decide whether a constructive or reductive approach is in order. Does the dream compensate by modifying, confirming or opposing the dreamer's conscious attitude? Determine whether the dream is actually compensatory, or is instead perhaps telepathic, traumatic, prospective, or prophetic.

With all of the above considerations made, offer an interpretation of the dream, and then look to the dreamer for verification. The interpretation should "feel right" to and "act" for the dreamer—that is, there should be a "click" of recognition of the interpretation's accuracy and a subsequent positive change in the dreamer's life. The interpretation is likely to be wrong, however, if the same theme continues to be played out in subsequent dreams.[8]

Nonprofessional Dream Analysis

Of course, the only person who truly knows the meaning of a dream is the dreamer. As mentioned earlier, professional dream analysis is preferable in situations where distorted attitudes would negate the purpose of the dream— or even worsen the situation. In less serious cases, most dreamworkers agree that self-analysis and group dreamwork, when handled properly, is beneficial.

Most methods of dream analysis (many based on Jungian methods) agree that to benefit from a dream's interpretation, the biological and social sources as well as the psychological sources must be given due consideration. Is the stimulus a physical one, either external (such as a car horn honking) or internal (physical discomfort, for example)? Or is the stimulus emotional? Obvious emotional stimuli would include problems on the mind just prior to falling asleep. However, emotional stimuli can be external, too; a sound heard while sleeping can trigger a memory or mood. It is also important to keep in mind that dream symbolism can be very exaggerated—the mind's way of making its message loud and clear. Being aware of this should prevent unnecessary embarrassment or offense for either the dreamer or interpreter.

If there is an intense behavior or emotion in the dream that the dreamer feels is totally out of place or inappropriate, remember that this may be inversion taking place. Inversion occurs when a feeling is too intense to be dealt with consciously; it then shows up in a dream as an opposite but equally strong feeling. Look to the opposite of that emotion or behavior for possible meaning.

Questions that will stimulate the interpretation process include the following: "What symbols in the dream are important to me?" "How am I acting in the dream?" "Who or what is the adversary in the dream?" "What would I like to avoid in this dream?" "What relation does the dream have to what is happening in my life right now?" "Why did I need this dream?"[9]

Another Jungian method is to choose one of the symbols of the dream and focus on it during meditation. The symbol should not be allowed to alter, although it can expand itself, or amplify its essence. Do not try to evaluate the experience as it is happening; wait until the meditation is ended. Then write down or discuss the details, and try to recall if any sense of important meaning came to you during the meditation.[10]

Somewhat related to this method is the use of active imagination. Active imagination is that which is enhanced by intuition and a feeling of unconscious forces at work. The key is passivity. The "active imaginer" allows dream images to float to the surface while in a relaxed but conscious state. Scenarios should be allowed to evolve in an improvisational manner; they should not be manipulated. The main threat to active imagination is rigid thinking and moral barriers. The images—any images—must be allowed to surface without censorship, and to go wherever they may.

Often when individual dreams remain obscure, it is more helpful to consider a series of dreams. A theme may become apparent, or a ''myth-countermyth'' struggle may show itself. The myth-countermyth struggle occurs when a person's personal myth, or view of himself/herself and ''reality,'' has outlived its usefulness. Restructuring the personal myth may cause a crisis in the person's waking life. The dreams will mirror this crisis, showing a struggle between the old way of thinking and the new. The psyche may be trying to hang onto the old myth and producing dreams to fit; it may also be caricaturing that myth in order to demonstrate its uselessness. The dream series may also show a gradual, comfortable integration of the two myths. Dreams representing the old myth tend to make one feel hopeless and drained, while new-myth dreams are exhilarating. The dream that represents a synthesis of the two makes one feel calm and assured.[11]

While searching for a dream's meaning, it is vital to be aware of conscious attitudes that are unconstructive and threaten to bias the interpretation. If the dreamer's view of life is not a constructive one, it is likely that he or she will use this same negative view when interpreting dreams. Bias control must first be achieved; for example, the dreamer, after arriving at an interpretation, should not stop there, but should seek the opposite interpretation, perhaps by reversing the actions and personalities in the dream. What the dreamer should be looking for is the opposite of his or her usual attitude, but that interpretation should not be immediately accepted, either—just left open as a possibility. Attention should be paid to the most imaginative parts of the dream—things the dreamer wouldn't have thought in waking life.[12]

This practice of choosing an interpretation that offers a new attitude is recommended by many dreamworkers. Dreams show us what we need to learn. This is why interpretations that serve to over-inflate the ego, or shift the responsibility for problems onto others, should be rejected as incorrect.[13]

Many dreamworkers recommend sifting through possible interpretations until one of them "feels" right, intuitively. Take, for example, the "it clicks" method. If the meaning of a dream or an element in a dream remains unclear, the dreamer should run through all the possible associations. Eventually, one of the associations will inspire a surge of energy—an intuitive "yes." When it clicks, the dreamer will know he or she has found an answer, or at least is on the right track.[14]

Similar to this is the method of applying focusing techniques to dream analysis. In focusing, one seeks personal insight and problem-solving techniques through the body's physical reactions—"gut feelings." When insights are revealed there is a physical "felt shift," the body's way of indicating what's right and what's wrong.

If an interpretation is still elusive, it should not be forced. The dreamer should keep the dream in mind, discussing it from time to time, and compare it to subsequent dreams. Eventually an interpretation may arrive.

If an interpretation that "clicks" *is* found, if gut feelings affirm what the dream is trying to teach, it's important to apply that lesson in waking life. There should be a connection between the cerebral/spiritual and the physical. Jungian analyst Robert Johnson offers the following advice: "Go out and walk around the block in honor of your dream, if that is all you can think of. Light a candle. Do *something*.

If you consciously do some act—any act—in honor of your dream, it will register with your unconscious."[15]

Group Dream Work

People who try to interpret their dreams alone may find they are limited by their own attitudes and narrow range of experience. This is where group dreamwork is beneficial. The varied viewpoints and experiences of others will expand the number of possible interpretations. Again, some professionals feel that the amateur nature of group dreamwork is dangerous. However, dreamworkers such as Montague Ullman feel that "we have the ability to be a healing influence for one another through dreamwork."[16] Group dreamwork has also been used as a source of community togetherness.[17]

What is needed for successful group dreamwork, according to Ullman, is for the dreamer to feel safe in exploring and sharing this sensitive area of the mind (the safety factor) and to realize that meanings may be discovered with group help that would not have been realized alone (the discovery factor). Group dreamwork is problematic only when the interpreters try to control or do not respect the needs of the dreamer.

First, the group should discuss how everyone is feeling emotionally and why, then precede the interpretation session with relaxation and centering techniques, such as meditation. The next step is for everyone in the group to relate a dream without any immediate discussion following. (Alternatively, the group might focus on one person and one dream per session.) Be sure that equal time and attention are given to everyone, and that speakers are not interrupted.

Some dreamworkers recommend that dreams should be related in the present tense to better hold the attention of everyone in the group. If this advice is followed, the interpreters should note any shift into the past tense; it may indicate a particularly meaningful or intense point in the dream from which the speaker is trying to gain distance.[18]

If a dream journal is kept, the dream should be read directly from it. This will discourage the reader from editing out any element of a dream, either because it's puzzling or unpleasant. All details should be given consideration. If the speaker already has some insights into the dream, it is best to wait until all other interpretations are offered. If the speaker's interpretation is offered first, it may narrowly limit the group's interpretations.

After a dream is told, others in the group could take turns telling the dream as if it were their own, without the speaker getting involved. No assumptions about what is important to the speaker should be made at this point; all parts of the dream should receive equal attention. Members can then begin offering suggestions as to possible meanings of the various elements in the dream. Whenever comments are offered, they should be made as gently and considerately as possible. Also, interpreters should keep in mind that their analyses tell as much about themselves as they do about the speaker.

Expression of the dream artistically is often helpful—through painting, writing, music, etc., or through decoration of the dream journal itself. A dream could even be presented theatrically, with other group members playing parts in the dream and acting according to their interpretations.

Even when the group members are strangers to each other, without knowledge of each other's personal situations, Ullman says, they can often intuitively make accurate connections. This is a delicate art, and suggestions should be offered as gently and respectfully as possible, letting the speaker maintain control. Interpreters need to fight the impulse to jump in prematurely—to win the guessing game—or to lead the dreamer into giving details that will support their theories of the dream's meaning.

Once the group members have offered their interpretations, the speaker could talk about whether he or she has learned anything from the experience. Or a dialogue could be set up between the speaker and the other members, and the details of the speaker's life aired, expanding on the possible connections realized and offered by group members. The mood that prevailed upon falling asleep, recent events that have left emotional residue—these are details that aid the group in finding connections. Although the speaker may be questioned at this point, the questions should be open-ended, not prying or judgmental. If a question or suggestion is offered to the speaker and he or she does not seem to want to pursue it, the subject should not be pressed. The speaker must continue to feel safe and in control.

If random questioning still does not bring any enlightment to the speaker, the interpreters may try to connect some of the images sequentially and therein find the dream's meaning.

After the meeting, the speaker should continue to evaluate the dream, keeping all the new information in mind.

Improving Dream Recall

Of course, before dream analysis can be undertaken, dream recall must be successful. A notebook or tape recorder could be kept within easy reach, so that it is unnecessary to get out of bed. In fact, it is wise to limit movement as much as possible. Record the dream immediately upon waking, noting all details without trying to interpret them. (While elements of the dream may seem too bizarre to make any sense, upon rereading the dreams as a series, a pattern may become obvious.)

Some people may be uncomfortable with the idea of recording their dreams, in which case the practice will hinder rather than improve recall. There are also some dream-workers who feel that recording dreams tends to distance the dreamer from a dream's vitality and impact. As an alternative, after waking, try spending some time deliberately concentrating on your dream. Take only the most salient aspects, commit them to memory, and then free associate with them. If this produces any revelations, they could be recorded for future reference.

Certain rituals practiced before falling asleep will encourage the recall of dreams. The most common ritual is autosuggestion—telling yourself "I will remember my dreams," repeatedly, while falling asleep. Then there is the related incubation ritual, where a specific dream is requested or a question is posed. For example, consider a recent problem and ask for a dream that will offer answers to it.

Be aware, however, that the experiences and emotions of the day will affect the dream: positive thoughts usually induce positive problem-solving dreams, while a negative attitude could produce dreams that worsen the situation. Phrase the question in the most positive way possible. Used constructively, incubation can also increase waking intuition, and improve the dreamer's attitude and behavior the following day—acting as a rehearsal of sorts.[19]

The practice of meditation with active imagination prior to falling asleep is another exercise recommended for enhancing dream recall. Upon entering the meditative state, concentrate upon an archetypal dream image of the self, such as a circle or mandala, without trying to control it.[20]

If you awake during the night after a dream, record *something* from the dream, even a few words or details. Then, upon waking in the morning, reread or replay these words; they will probably jog the memory into full recall. Also, lying in the usual sleep position will sometimes stimulate recall.

If you would rather not have your sleep interrupted, try the "backward recall" technique. Before going to sleep, recall in reverse all the steps of your day. Then, upon waking, recall the previous night, again in reverse—for example, "I am awake, I am waking up, I am asleep, I am asleep and dreaming. Here is the dream . . ."

Sharing dreams has a positive influence on recall, so try group work—or even just discussing them with a friend. And if you are still having difficulty with recall, you may want to try a nutritional approach. Research indicates that B vitamins may play a part in the storage of dreams in memory. Try increasing the B-vitamin-rich foods in your diet or taking B-complex supplements.

Control of Dream Content

Perhaps one of best ways to benefit from dreaming is to take the bull by the horns and actually control the dream through lucidity (although there are critics who believe dream content is a message from the psyche and therefore should not be tampered with). Here, the approach is not to analyze the content after the fact, but to create or control the content as it is happening.

Functions of Lucid Dreaming

There are two ways of manipulating dream content: through control of the dream self, or through control of the other people and elements in the dream. While both methods may be effective, some dreamworkers suggest that control of the dream self is a more positive approach. If the dreamer means to apply the lessons learned in dream life to waking life, then achieving inner peace and happiness is a lesson well learned—and more far-reaching than the perhaps temporary satisfaction achieved through the manipulation of others.[21]

The lucid dream is a testing ground, where behaviors can be repeated over and over without any negative consequences, until the desired effect or attitude is achieved. Overcoming lack of confidence, stage fright, and general insecurities and anxieties can all be aided by practicing in lucid dreams. Take public speaking—pace of speech, tone of voice, facial expressions, and body language—can all be practiced without fear of recrimination.

Shedding some lucidity on a recurring nightmare is a good way to master it. The dreamer who controls a dream also controls the negative characters and elements within it, and thus has the ability to disarm them—whether they are murderous pursuers or doomed airplanes. The pursuer can be faced, talked to, and rendered harmless. The airplane can be shielded with a layer of protective white light that prevents any danger from befalling it.

When negative, unproductive emotions toward a person cannot be resolved in the waking world, perhaps because of the other person's unavailability—physical or otherwise—the lucid dream offers a solution. Anyone and anything are available in a lucid dream. A scenario that, for example, allows the dreamer to speak those final, unspoken words to a deceased loved one might be very therapeutic.

Lucid dreaming can help the dreamer learn complex new physical skills, or practice those skills that are being blocked during consciousness. The vivid detail of a lucid dream sheds light on the correct motor skills and attitude necessary to achieve the desired result. As LaBerge points out, "Remember that you cannot hurt yourself by straining muscles, getting overtired, or making an error of judgment, because your muscles aren't actually moving. You may be able to get the feeling of a new skill in your dream, and this will prepare you to learn it faster when you are awake."[22]

It has long been believed that the mind can harm the

body, that negative or stressful psychological states create or encourage physical ailments. Now even mainstream medicine is becoming increasingly accepting (despite the inability to definitively prove cause-and-effect) of the mind's ability to *heal* the body through visualization, biofeedback, hypnosis, meditation, etc. Lucid dreaming is yet another instrument in the psychosomatic medicine bag. In a lucid dream, a broken bone can be made whole—or the action that broke it in the first place can be undone. A tumor can be dissolved, blood pressure can be lowered, and pain can be erased. While these dream actions may not be immediately and fully paralleled in the conscious state, it is possible for the healing process to be initiated or accelerated.

Entering a Lucid Dream

Those who have never attempted lucid dreaming might try dream continuation for a few days as a warm-up exercise. When a dream seems to be fading, try to extend it until it seems to reach a natural ending (if it won't continue, it's possible that the dream has nothing more to say).

Before attempting to dream lucidly, it is helpful to perform relaxation exercises. LaBerge and Rheingold recommend several, including "pot-shaped breathing." Fully distend the abdomen while inhaling, and imagine healing energy being "inhaled" as light simultaneously; while exhaling, imagine this energy being distributed throughout the body.[23]

There are a variety of techniques for initiating a lucid dream, from a waking state (WILD—wake-initiated lucid dream) or from the unconscious state (DILD—dream-initiated lucid dream).

Incubation/Auto Suggestion. Tell yourself, "I am dreaming, I am dreaming," repeatedly while falling asleep. Counting along with this is also recommended. Also, try asking the question, "Am I dreaming?" several times throughout the day, in the hopes that you will continue the habit while sleeping. You may even try telling yourself throughout the day that your waking life is actually a dream—again, to start a habit that will be continued while sleeping. Or try a DILD method: tape yourself saying "This is a dream" and have it playing while you are asleep.

Use of Imagery. Witness the hypnagogic show that goes on in the "twilight" state just prior to sleep. Watch the images with a relaxed, passive attitude, and follow them as they become more vivid and complex, evolving into a true dream. Remind yourself all along that "this is a dream." Or, while falling asleep, concentrate upon a white dot between your eyes until a dream begins.

Use of Technology. Dream researcher Stephen LaBerge created a "light mask" to induce lucidity. The subject is first conditioned to realize that a flashing red light indicates the occurrence of a dream. The subject then falls asleep wearing the mask, which flashes red lights when rapid eye movement occurs.[24]

Maintaining Lucidity

Two problems often encountered while attempting dream control are awakening or slipping into non-lucidity shortly after lucidity is achieved. Experienced lucid dreamers suggest several techniques for overcoming these problems.

If you feel the clarity and reason of lucidity starting to fade, focus on an object in the dream—the ground is often recommended as a helpful focusing point. Talking "aloud" in the dream, repeating, "This is a dream," is also helpful. Or try concentrating on the senses other than sight—touch dream objects and listen to sounds and voices.

The "spinning" technique is a variation on this theme. As soon as lucidity starts fading, begin spinning around (in the dream world) while repeating that the next thing encountered will probably be part of the dream.[25]

If lucidity cannot be maintained and you awaken, lie perfectly still. This is the best way to fall asleep again and re-enter the dream.

Benefits of Dreamwork

Since dreams exist chiefly to point out those aspects of ourselves that need some work, the main benefit of dreamwork is self-growth—by eliminating negative attachments, mastering new skills, solving problems, or increasing intuition and imagination. Members of dream groups often report an increased sense of self-esteem and creativity by removing the psychological barriers pointed out in their dreams.[26] As already noted, lucid dreaming in particular can help the dreamer "rehearse" situations and even conquer medical problems.

In discussing his teaching of dreamwork, Montague Ullman said, "What delighted me was the way that dreamwork touched on and opened up dormant areas of interest, liberated creative energies, and, in some instances, found new directions for those energies."[27]

Although all schools of dream analysis warn against treating it as a parlor game, overall, dreamwork should still be enjoyable. If it isn't, if it becomes hard work, then let it go for a while, or consider working with an interpreter who can guide the process constructively.

Archetypes and Their Meanings

Listed below are some common archetypal dream images and their interpretations.[28] However, before interpreting an image as an archetype, before giving it a "universal" meaning, consider the possibility of any personal experiences and associations to which it may be connected. (See also the encyclopedia listings in Part Two.)

Characters and Animals

Archetypal Woman (beautiful, large, noble, ageless): represents spirituality, guidance rather than nurturing

Wise Old Man: guidance and rational wisdom gleaned from experience; dreamer is seeking wisdom from within

Wise Old Woman: guidance and feeling wisdom gleaned from experience

Child: creative forces

Trickster: human consciousness, wise and unwise simultaneously

Teacher: dreamer seeks to understand himself/herself and improve life

Leader/Mythological Hero: father figure, protection, rescue

Horse: primitive animal needs

Snake: male sex organ; healing; rebirth (ability to shed skin); energy arising from unconsciousness

Dog: masculinity, instincts

Cat: femininity; mystery; independence

Bird: freedom

Nature

Sun: masculine, life-giving

Moon: feminine, mysterious

Earth: mother figure, security, nurturing

Sea: unconsciousness, eternity

Fire: energy, destruction, sexuality

Rain: crying, suffering before release, cleansing

Strong tree: father figure

Island: isolation

Mountain: ambition, spiritual climb

Actions

Flying: desire to escape from responsibilities; expansion

Crossing a bridge/Climbing a mountain: entering a new stage of life

Eating: devouring, transformation

Dancing: symbolic unity; sexual intercourse; relationship

Swimming: dealing with life

Dying: end of an attachment or a stage of life

Objects

House: structure of self (if walls are collapsing or wiring is frayed and exposed, psychological health may be in danger)

Door: transition, choice

Window: eyesight, perception

Wall/Fence: restrictions, introversion

Fruit: sex organs, reproduction

Key: power, masculinity

Lock: potential, femininity

Mirror: soul

Stairs: gaining (up) or losing (down) consciousness

Shapes

Circle/Mandala: wholeness, harmony

Triangle: magic, spirituality

Square: solidity, establishment

Colors

Red: anger, intensity

Pink: innocence, love

Yellow: energy, anger

Green: life, fertility

Blue: rational

Purple: spirituality, arrogance

Brown: earth, primitive instincts

Black: shadow, power

Gray: neutral
White: purity, spirituality

Numbers
Odd numbers: masculine
Even numbers: feminine
Zero: the void from which everything arises and returns
  1: beginnings, individuality, masculinity, indivisibility
  2: duality, yin and yang, light and dark, femininity, receptivity
  3: magical, spiritual (e.g. the Holy Trinity, the Three Wise Men); the union of two opposites to create a third
  4: stability, wholeness, materialization, sensation
  5: human in star formation (two arms, two legs and head), or human physical form, physical life
  6: symmetry, spirit and body united, God and human united
  7: cycles in life, inner rhythms and energies
  8: generation, degeneration, and regeneration; death and rebirth, infinity
  9: completion of growth process (as in the nine months of pregnancy)
  10: a new beginning, reincarnation, karma

NOTES

  1. Stanley Krippner and Joseph Dillard, *Dreamworking*, pp. 14, 175. Buffalo: Bearly Limited, 1988.
  2. Sigmund Freud, *On Dreams*, translated by James Strachey, p. 38. New York: W. W. Norton, 1952.
  3. Krippner and Dillard, *op. cit.*, pp. 41–43.
  4. Mary Ann Mattoon, *Understanding Dreams*, p. 148. Dallas: Spring Publications, 1978.
  5. *Ibid.*, pp. 156–157.
  6. *Ibid.*, p. 156.

7. *Ibid.*, pp. 156–157.

8. *Ibid.*, pp. 48–49.

9. Strephon Kaplan-Williams, *The Jungian-Senoi Dreamwork Manual*, p. 97. Berkeley: Journey Press, 1980.

10. *Ibid.*, pp. 146–147.

11. Krippner and Dillard, *op. cit.*, pp. 126–130.

12. Eugene T. Gendlin, *Let Your Body Interpret Your Dreams*, pp. 71, 82. Wilmette: Chiron Publications, 1986.

13. Robert A. Johnson, *Inner Work*, pp. 94–95. San Francisco: Harper & Row, 1986.

14. *Ibid.*, p. 56.

15. *Ibid.*, p. 107.

16. Montague Ullman and Claire Limmer, eds., *The Variety of Dream Experience*, p. viii. New York: Continuum, 1988.

17. Jeremy Taylor, *Dream Work*, pp. 100–106. New York: Paulist Press, 1983.

18. *Ibid.*, pp. 80–81.

19. Krippner and Dillard, *op. cit.*, p. 176.

20. L.M. Savary, P.H. Berne and S.K. Williams, *Dreams and Spiritual Growth: A Christian Approach to Dreamwork*, pp. 155–156. Ramsey: Paulist Press, 1984.

21. Stephen LaBerge and Howard Rheingold, *Exploring the World of Lucid Dreaming*, pp. 117–118. New York: Ballantine Books, 1990.

22. *Ibid.*, p. 159.

23. *Ibid.*, pp. 117–118.

24. *Ibid.*, p. 72.

25. *Ibid.*, pp. 117–118.

26. Ullman and Limmer, *op cit.*, p. 71.

27. *Ibid.*, p. vii.

28. Kaplan-Williams, *op. cit.*, pp. 320–327; Tony Crisp, *Do You Dream?* pp. 285–288. New York: E.P. Dutton, 1972; Phoebe McDonald, *Dreams: Night Language of the Soul*, chapter 14, passim. New York: Continuum, 1987.

PART II

This section features an alphabetical listing of approximately six hundred of the most common images and symbols that appear in dreams, and interpretations of them. No symbol in a dream has a hard and fast meaning, especially one that applies to all persons. However, many of the most common dream symbols appear also in art, myth and fairy tale, and throughout history have acquired certain widespread, if not universal, meanings.

The explanations given for each symbol are drawn from these sources, as well as from alchemy, Jung's views on archetypes, and from contemporary dreamwork recorded in the literature. They are *suggested* interpretations, intended to stimulate the dreamer to finding the correct meaning. Ultimately, of course, the only person who can decipher a dream is the dreamer. Symbols, which may have universal meanings that apply to a dream, also may have personal meanings and associations unique to the dream and the dreamer. It is up to the individual to decide what applies.

This encyclopedic section can be augmented with a personal dream symbol diary, in which one may record notes on the personal associations discovered during one's own dreamwork.

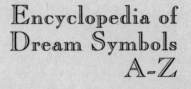

Encyclopedia of
Dream Symbols
A-Z

A

Abandonment. Feeling of being left behind; sense of betrayal; fear of being alone; losing touch with the purpose of life. Abandonment dreams may occur following separation or divorce, or the death of a loved one, especially a parent or spouse. These dreams mirror unresolved grief, anger, resentment and despair. Facing and working through these feelings are part of the recovery process; abandonment dreams may help make one aware of emotional blockages.

Academy. See **School.**

Accident. Dreams involving accidents commonly occur during stressful times, especially those involving a major upheaval in one's life, such as divorce or grief. Such dreams are most likely to occur during the first stage of recovery—shock and denial. Typical accident dreams are: losing control in a car or other vehicle, falling off a precipice, out of a boat or out of a window; being struck and injured; or being caught in a natural disaster.

Accidents also may mirror catastrophic events that have occurred in life. Or, they may reflect the making of others responsible for what happens in one's life.

See **Falling; valuables; disasters, natural.**

Abandonment

Acorn. Spiritual rebirth; growth; new life. A new phase in life.

See **Tree.**

Actor. Role-playing in life. Being an actor in a dream, or observing an actor (the equivalent to seeing oneself) may point out unfulfilled wishes or desires, or may demonstrate how one is acting out the expectations of others.

Air. Creativity; intellect; thoughts; mental effort. Note the quality of the air in the dream—whether it is crisp, clean and pure, and easy to breathe, or fogged, polluted, stifling, stagnant and difficult to breathe. .

Airplane. The intellect; ideas; freedom of thought; open-mindedness; the ability to rise above situations, life or prob-

Accident

lems. On the other hand, an airplane is a means of fast, but temporary, escape from life's troubles. Flying in an airplane is a symbol of the *sublimatio* phase of alchemy—the ascension of intellect.

Dreams involving commercial aircraft have more of a collective symbolism than those involving small, private aircraft. Being a passenger is a symbol of passivity, of allowing someone else or some other force to determine the journey. Being a pilot indicates having control.

Planes that do not or cannot take off indicate ideas that are having difficulty taking shape.

An airplane crash indicates one is soaring too high and needs to return to earth and become grounded. Plane crashes also are a metaphor for stressful periods in life.

See **Flying.**

Alcohol. A creative or destructive force, depending on context. Alcohol might represent a releasing of inhibitions, social enjoyment, or "mingling with the crowd." Too much alcohol, or its abuse, may symbolize destructive or addictive forces in one's life.

Alley. A symbol related to life's journey or transitional stages in life. The alley is a type of path, a common motif that appears in dreams when one is undergoing a major change of course in life, or a life-review.

Alleys have a dark aspect: they are narrow and constricting, almost tunnel-like, and often seem lonely and sinister. They are off the main roads, and may indicate that a sidetracking has taken place. In a more positive aspect, alleys can represent shortcuts. Notice whether the alley is dark and seems dangerous, has a dead end, or seems more like a convenience.

See **Path**.

Almond. Like all nuts, almonds generally symbolize hidden wisdom. Because of its shape—called a mandorla or a *vesica piscis*, the almond specifically symbolizes the feminine principle, including sweetness and charm, fertility and pregnancy. The mandorla shape also is often used in connection with the Virgin Mary.

Almonds have a spiritual meaning, because they are sweetness (spiritual) concealed by a hard shell that is difficult to open (the material).

Other meaning: In a Christian context, divine approval.

Altar. A place where sacrifices are made; a spiritual center. In a dream, an altar may symbolize the letting go of something, or the need to let go. It also symbolizes renewal, for through sacrifice comes change and new beginnings.

Altars also may represent a consuming force. For example, an "altar of love" may require the sacrifice of freedom or individuality.

Other meaning: Thanksgiving.

Anchor

Amber. See **Jewels.**

Ambush. A symbol that appears during stressful periods in life, when one is likely to suffer emotional upheaval, and unresolved grief or anger, such as during a divorce or loss. Being ambushed in a dream indicates one may be at an emotional impasse and needs to work through the block.

Amethyst. See **Jewels.**

Amputation. The cutting off or removal of something no longer desirable, necessary or healthful. An amputation is forceful, often done under emergency conditions. It may indicate a serious or crisis situation that needs to be addressed.

See **Operation.**

Angel

Ancestors. To dream of being reunited with one's ancestors indicates that a healing process is taking place. Ancestors may be represented by totem animals.

Ancestors also may represent attributes from the dreamer's past.

Anchor. Safety; stability; security. Anchors secure boats, which in dreams are vehicles for navigating the waters of the unconscious. An anchored boat is at rest, secure in a harbor, at a dock, or in shallow water near shore—symbolizing a respite from traveling in the unconscious.

Losing an anchor: fear and feeling adrift in the unconscious.

Angel. Literally, a messenger of God—an intermediary between God and humankind who has the power to intervene in mundane affairs. Angels in dreams sometimes appear to guide or inform. They are messengers from the unconscious or from the Higher Self, bringing something to conscious attention. Figures in white, especially flowing robes, might be interpreted as angels. Dark angels, personified by dark or black persons or persons dressed in dark clothing, perhaps embody a shadow element.

Animals. One's primitive, physical, sexual and instinctual natures; the impulses which reside in the unconscious; the less conscious part of the shadow; spiritual growth. Animals may correspond to physical, sexual, sensual, emotional and spiritual needs that the conscious mind needs to address. They also symbolize stages of psychic growth and development.

In dreams, as in fairy tales and myths, animals often represent archetypal forces. Animals are close to their instincts and always behave according to their true natures; their positive and negative qualities remain constant. Thus, animals which are domesticated and docile are symbols of those qualities; and animals renowned for their craftiness, stealth or fierceness are representative of those. In addition, one's personal associations with animals—likes, dislikes, fears and so on—must be considered.

Common dream animals are birds, which are a universal symbol of soul and spirit; and snakes, a symbol of transformation and renewal. See **Birds; Snake.** Animals which exist close to or under the ground, such as lizards and rodents, as well as water-dwellers such as fish and turtles, represent the unconscious and instinct. They can also represent the origin of things and rebirth. See **Water.**

The self sometimes appears in dreams as an animal. Jung found that the most common images are elephants (often representing the highest true Self), horses, bears, bulls, white and black birds, fish and snakes. Less common images are snails, tortoises, spiders and beetles.

The forces that animals represent sometimes erupt from

the unconscious with tremendous power and wildness. Frightening animals are a common motif in dreams, to fight one may indicate an inner battle between the conscious mind and the deeper instinctual nature. To dream of being pursued by a frightening animal may indicate that something has become separated from consciousness and needs to be reintegrated. The pursuit dream is either calling attention to this need or is a signal that the reintegration process is struggling to take place. The more dangerous the animal, the more urgent the need to address reintegration. The type of animal may provide clues to what has become alienated.

Being devoured by an animal is a widespread archetypal motif in legend, myth and fairy tale; it symbolizes a descent into the underworld, the sinking of the consciousness into the unconscious. Such a descent precedes a spiritual renewal.

Fabulous animals are powerful instruments of psychological projection, for they are primordial and belong to the deepest realms of unconsciousness. They often symbolize the *prima materia*, the matrix or vessel from which arises all life, and thus represent the beginning stages of individuation. See **Dragon; Monster.**

Fabulous animals and animals with mythical associations may represent transcendence, higher stages of spiritual consciousness or the highest manifestation of the Self. Spiritual or psychic growth, or the need for it, may be represented by animals with extra legs, wings or unusual powers; animals associated with various deities, religious figures or spiritual systems; or by animals which transform themselves into deities or humans. Such animals typically appear as helpers or guides in a dream.

During pregnancy, dreams of newborn animals—especially puppies, kittens and seals—and small furry mammals are common among both men and women. They symbolize the vulnerability of the newborn, in anticipation of the birthing of the baby.

Chthonic associations. Psychoanalyst James Hillman rejects instinctual symbolisms of animals in favor of symbolisms as gods or as carriers of soul, which demand the respect of the dreamer. He cites the history of art and religion, in which gods appear in animal forms, animals are what gods desire in sacrifice, and that relation with animals is similar to the relation with gods in terms of sensitivity and ritual. Thus, dream animals are carriers of the soul, taking the dreamer through the underworld of the unconscious. And, because animals in myth are widely believed to embody the souls of the human dead, dream animals present specific soul qualities and behaviors. The dreamer should pay attention to what the animal does in the dream.

The underworld journey is especially symbolized by animals associated with chthonic deities, such as dogs to Hecate, pigs to Demeter and pregnant cows to Tellus. Dream animals lead, chase, drive and guide the dreamer into the underworld. Preparation for such a psychic journey is sometimes the sacrifice of an animal in a dream, including putting a pet to sleep. Unspecific, black horned animals often were sacrificed to the chthonic deities in ancient times.

See **individual listing for animals;** see also **Horns; Insects.**

Anointing. To be consecrated or made pure or holy; to be initiated or conferred with authority. Anointing is done with water or oil, which symbolize the primal water. In a dream, anointing may symbolize navigating a spiritual rite of passage.

Annulment. A denial that something intimate, such as a sexual encounter or an emotional confession, ever took place.

Ant. Diligence, industriousness, organization. Ants are a symbol of collective action or behavior in which individuality is lost. They are stockpilers and tireless laborers; hence, they are associated with foresight and perseverance. They possess enormous strength, and are able to bear loads many times their size. Ants also are tiny, fragile and seemingly insignificant.

See **Animals; Insects.**

Antlers. A mark of supernatural power, especially of the shaman. Antlers also represent power over nature and fertility.

Other meanings: 1) Trophy of the hunt. 2) A matter sharp and difficult to deal with.

See **Animals.**

Anvil. Earth; matter; the receptive, passive feminine force—a counterpart to the generative, active masculine force of the hammer. Anvils are tools for forging—not only things, but in mythology, the cosmos. Thunder gods make lightning (creativity, inspiration and illumination) with hammer and anvil.

Other meaning: Stability.

Apple. Fertility; love; immortality. Apples represent bounteous nature, the Mother Goddess. They are a token of love and desire. In mythology, apples are the fruit of the underworld (the unconscious in dreams). Golden apples, the food of gods, bestow immortality.

The round shape of the apple symbolizes totality and wholeness. The red color is desire and ripeness.

In Christianity, the apple is a symbol of the Fall, and thus of lust and earthly desires.

See **Fruits; Vegetables.**

Anvil

Apron. A symbol of work. Although aprons may be associated with traditionally masculine work, such as carpentry, they usually are feminine symbols of the mother, motherhood, the home, hearth and domestic work.

Apron strings generally have a negative symbolism of being tied to one's mother, the home or domesticity.

Aquamarine. See **Jewels.**

Argument. See **Quarrel.**

Armor. Protection against others and the world. Armor protects one from harm, prevents others from getting close, and prevents others from seeing one's true self.

Arrow. Irrevocable penetration. To be shot by an arrow in a dream is to be forcibly injected. The arrow is a masculine, phallic symbol. It represents truth, power, inspiration and illumination (see **Lightning**), and the fertilizing force of creativity. It symbolizes the rays of the sun.

The arrow also represents union. A heart pierced by an arrow has associations with love, and with the mystical conjunction of opposites in alchemy.

To be wounded by an arrow may be symbolic of a spiritual initiation (see **Wound**).

Broken arrows represent broken vows or broken plans.

As weapons, arrows are associated with war, violence, aggression and the hunt. They represent the element of air.

Other meanings: 1) Movement toward a goal. 2) Sense of purpose.

Art. Creativity, beauty, inspiration. Art also represents the expression of the contents of the unconscious, or the release of creative potential.

Artichoke. Sexual feelings and sexuality. Artichokes are considered an aphrodisiac. In mythology, the artichoke is associated with Aphrodite.

See **Vegetables.**

Ash. A tree that represents solidity and stability, and which holds all things together. In Norse mythology, Ygdrasill, the World Tree that unites heaven, earth and the underworld, is an ash.

See **Tree**.

Ashes. The raw material of spiritual rebirth, of life rising anew after setbacks or devastation. The old has been burned away in the fire of *calcinatio*; ashes remain to fertilize new growth.

Other meaning: Triumph, victory over adversity: the phoenix rising anew from its own ashes.

See **Fire**.

Asp. See **Snake**.

Asparagus. A phallic symbol; sexuality. In mythology, asparagus is associated with Aphrodite. Plutarch reportedly stated that brides should wear veils of asparagus because it was rough-spined but pleasant to eat.

See **Vegetables**.

Attic. See **Home; House; Room**.

Automobile. An archetypal dream symbol that usually represents the ego, the vehicle one uses in getting around the world and in traveling through psychic life. Automobile dreams are common, and may be a warning that something is amiss: lack of control, too much control, traveling too fast or too slow, going down a street the wrong way, taking a dead-end street, needing repairs, having an accident.

A dented, dilapidated automobile might indicate low self-esteem. A big, impressive car that barrels over or through obstacles may indicate that one is running roughshod over others. The presence of a backseat driver, or sitting in the back seat and allowing someone else to drive, may indicate a forfeiture of control over one's life to another person.

An automobile that goes nowhere with its wheels spinning indicates a feeling of powerlessness over circumstances in one's life, or of being stuck in place.

Dreams of automobiles being out of control are symbols
of stress and anxiety. These occur during pregnancies (to
both men and women), and reflect a feeling of being emotionally overwhelmed. They also occur during major life
changes, such as marriage, separation, divorce, any kind of
significant loss, and during serious illness, especially cancer.

See **Vehicles.**

Axe. The liberating power of spiritual light. In mythology,
the axe is a symbol of sky gods and is associated with
thunder, rain and lightning, which in turn symbolize fecundity, fertility, inspiration and illumination. The double
axe has particular magical and mystical import, representing the union of sky god and earth goddess (i.e., opposites),
resulting in wholeness.

As a weapon, the axe also represents war, aggression and
violence; it separates and cleaves, symbolizing the alchemical process of *separatio.*

B

Baby. A rebirth of the Self; the emergence of something new into the consciousness; new possibilities; a stage of innocence and purity.

A baby wrapped in swaddling clothes may represent an emergence that is being restricted, confined or tied up before it is allowed to develop.

Dreams of babies are common during pregnancy, to both men and women. Forgetting a baby reflects anxieties about becoming a parent or being able to handle the responsibilities. Violence or injury to a baby, or birth of a deformed baby, reflects fears concerning birth defects.

Other meanings: 1) Vulnerability. 2) Helplessness. 3) Dependency.

Backyard. See **Yard.**

Bag. Something that holds emotions, secrets, repressions, hopes, dreams, desires, etc. In general, a bag denotes secrecy, regardless of its contents. Releasing the contents may have serious consequences, like the opening of Pandora's box.

Packing a bag might symbolize putting one's emotional life in order. Putting something away in a bag may symbolize reluctance to face up to a problem or situation.

Other meaning: A womb.

See **Box; Packing.**

Baby

Ball. Wholeness, completeness. A symbol of the fertile, nurturing Mother Goddess.

Other meanings: 1) Associations with childhood. 2) Something that is not being resolved or decided, the equivalent of a ball being tossed around. 3) Relaxation. 4) A game.

Baptism. An initiation, or death and rebirth, especially of a spiritual nature. Baptisms also may represent becoming aware of one's own "dirt" and removal of projections of the shadow.

Baptisms take place in different elements. A baptism by water represents an immersion in the unconscious and emotions. This is a cleansing and dissolving process. In myth, baptism by water is the creation of a new personality on a higher plane. In alchemy, it is the *solutio,* a rejuvenation of spirit, energy and viewpoint that transcends the ego. Bathing, showering, swimming, sprinkling and any immersion in water are common baptism dream symbols.

Baptism by wind represents a blowing away of chaff; air represents the involvement of the intellect.

Baptism by fire represents a purging or burning away of what is no longer needed. Baptism by blood is comparable to baptism by fire, since both blood and fire are symbols of intense purging. Blood has the additional dimension of redemption, as seen in Christ's sacrifice of his own blood to redeem humanity. Psychologically, baptisms by either fire or blood refer to enduring intense ordeals that tax the ego. Successful endurance of this ordeal results in a refinement. In alchemy, this type of baptism is the *calcinatio,* or burning away to ash.

Baptisms are associated with the number "8," an expression of wholeness. The Bible tells of how Noah's ark saved eight persons from the baptismal flood. Medieval baptismal fonts were built in octagonal shape. See **Numbers.**

Baptisms also are associated with the color red, for blood and for the Red Sea. The Biblical story of the Israelites' exodus and the drowning of the Egyptians in the Red Sea is a baptism in which enemies (sins) are drowned. To alchemists, the Red Sea represented the universal solvent and the prima materia from which the philosopher's stone (wholeness) could be formed.

See also **Blood; Fire; Water.**

Barley. Denotes fertility and the cycle of birth, death and rebirth.

See **Vegetables.**

Bath

Basement. See **Home; House; Room.**

Basket. A symbol of the Mother Goddess and the womb, and thus of fertility, abundance, fruitfulness and everlasting life through birth, death and resurrection. A basket may symbolize the plenty of home and hearth, or it may symbolize a spiritual rebirth.

Bat. An embodiment of one's fears or the unknown, or one's shadow. In folklore, bats are death omens. Thus, a bat might be a harbinger of the end of a cycle or a period in life.

Bath. A bath is a baptism representing voluntary death and rebirth or renewal. It is a preliminary to initiation into a new level of consciousness. In the psychic cleansing process, the old is scrubbed away in order to make way for new ideas, a change of mind or a change of heart.

In the classical world, the bath was believed to purify both soul and body of contamination, and thus cleanse both for communication with the gods. Dream incubants who went to the healing temples to be cured of illness were prepared to receive their healing dreams from the gods by first having a bath. To bathe in a dream may therefore symbolize the beginning of a healing process.

Other meaning: Getting rid of unwanted emotional or mental ''dirt'' such as prejudices, resentments and anger, and unwanted relationships.

See **Baptism.**

Bathroom. See **Home; House; Room.**

Battle. Warring instincts; inner conflict. Dreams of battles and fights are common and reflect turmoil over decisions and choices. To watch a battle rather than participate in it may indicate an unwillingness to accept responsibility for the matter in question.

See **Fight.**

Beans. A symbol of the ''vegetable soul,'' which connects humanity to its roots in the community, earth and collective unconscious. Beans are lowly food in the vegetable kingdom, and are often scorned.

However, beans have a widespread and ancient association with the underworld and souls of the dead, giving them an exalted status. Beans have been sacred food offered in rituals to feed and propitiate the dead. The Greeks considered beans to be symbols of transmigration of the soul and immortality. Beans also are believed to have magical properties, and have been used in exorcism rites to banish unwanted ghosts and spirits from homes. These underworld associations link beans in dreams to the unconscious.

Other meanings: 1) Fertility. 2) Phallus. 3) Erotic pleasure. 4) Wild, unpredictable humor.

See **Vegetables.**

Battle

Bear. Resurrection, rebirth; initiation into a life passage. Because of its seasonal hibernations and awakenings every spring, the bear symbolizes the cycle of birth, death and rebirth, and is a companion of various female lunar deities, such as Artemis and Diana.

In alchemy, the bear has a similar meaning, representing the *nigredo,* the darkness that occurs before spiritual rebirth or a new phase in life.

The bear also is a figure in some hero myths, representing the solar, masculine principle.

Other meanings: 1) Raw power, primitive instinct. 2) Ferocity. 3) Fierce protectiveness. 4) In a Christian context, carnal appetite, evil, and the Devil.

See **Animals.**

Beard. A symbol of masculine strength, virility, wisdom, dignity and authority. A long beard represents the wisdom of the ages. A white beard represents spirituality or saintliness.

Bear

A bearded man in a dream may symbolize the onset of a healing process. The Greek god of healing, Aesclepius, was believed to appear in the dreams of sick persons in the form of a bearded man, among other guises.

Other meanings: 1) A disguise. 2) A cover-up.

See **Wise Old Man/Woman.**

Beaver. Industriousness; meticulous planning. Beavers are excellent engineers and build sound structures.

See **Animals.**

Bed/Bedroom. Sexual relations; sexual intimacy; marriage; the foundation of a relationship. The size of a bed, and whether it is made-up, neat or unkempt, offer clues to the state of affairs in a relationship. To replace a large bed with a smaller one may reflect an impending separation. To make a bed indicates the paying of attention to a relationship in order to improve it.

Something under the bed represents secrets, or issues pertaining to a relationship that have yet to come out in the open.

Other meanings: 1) Having to make do with situations one has created in life. 2) Accepting the consequences of one's actions.

Bee. Industriousness, organization, cleanliness and purity. Like the ant, the bee is a collective symbol in which individuality is submerged in the group.

In mythology, the bee has divine associations because of its honey, which is the food of gods. Bees are symbols of the soul and the sun, and are messengers to the heavens like birds. They are associated with the gift of prophecy; the priestesses at the temple of the Delphic oracles were called "Melissae," or "bees." The oracles and gods of prophecy were given offerings of honey and honey cakes.

In Christian symbolism, the bee represents Christ.

In medieval times, it was believed that bees never slept, and so they became symbols of vigilance, especially in Christianity. It also was believed that bees did not bear their own young but harvested them from flowers; thus bees became symbols of virginity and the Immaculate Conception.

Queen bees symbolize the Mother Goddess.

Bees also are associated with eloquence and poetry. Their hives are sometimes symbols of tombs and resurrection.

Other meanings: 1) Being too busy and over-committed. 2) Flitting about from one thing to another. 3) Drudgery work.

Beehive. See **Hive.**

Bile. Bitterness, rage, aggressive anger. Black bile represents depression.

Birds. The soul; higher states of consciousness; transcendence; the embodiment of immaterial things. Birds also symbolize freedom.

In mythology, birds are messengers from the gods, and the carriers of souls of the dead. Thus, dream birds might represent the opening up of the Higher Self or the attainment of enlightenment, or the process of going down into the underworld of the unconscious. Birds also are a widespread means of divination. Dream birds might point to important information overlooked by the dreamer.

In general, birds are solar symbols and thus represent the masculine principle. Large, high-flying birds are symbols of air and intellect. Forest birds have associations with the Tree of Life, the unconscious and the "vegetable soul" (see **Vegetables**). Water birds have associations with the unconscious and the feminine principle. Black birds symbolize death, as in death of the old Self. They also symbolize the fear of physical death that comes during serious or life-threatening illness.

Bird claws symbolize the destructive power of the Great Mother.

See **individual bird listings; Egg.**

Birth. Emergence of a new Self or a new aspect to one's life. Such a dream may involve giving birth, witnessing birth, assisting birth, or being born. A newborn who resembles someone known to the dreamer may point to a change in that relationship, or to the dreamer's acquisition of new characteristics observed in the other person. A baby born to one's family may represent changes in family relationships. See **Baby.**

Anxiety dreams involving birthing also occur to both

men and women during a woman's pregnancy. These dreams often involve the woman's birthing of kittens, puppies or other furry animals, grotesque or monstrous human infants, or human infants which can immediately walk and talk. Anxiety birthing dreams usually reflect fears about the outcome of pregnancy, an individual's ability to cope with the subsequent life change, or the impact of a child upon a relationship.

See **Bubble; Cave.**

Birthing. See **Birth.**

Biting. See **Mouth, Teeth.**

Black. See **Colors.**

Black birds. See **Birds.**

Blindness; blindfolds; blinders. Ignorance; failure to see the obvious, or the right path; narrow viewpoint or focus.

Other meanings: 1) Deception. 2) Being led astray. 3) Seeing something forbidden.

Blood. The emotions, the soul, the vital life-force. Blood is one's essence, and is connected to matters of the heart. It represent's one's ideals.

Blood also is a symbol of supreme sacrifice. Blood is sacred in all cultures.

To give blood means to engage one's emotions, to give of one's self from the deep core of one's being. To lose blood is to ''bleed'' emotionally. To receive blood is to receive emotional support that is vital to one's psychic existence. To make a blood oath is to pledge an unbreakable pact or forge an unbreakable bond. Bloody violence in a dream reflects emotional upheaval, or a feeling of being out of control or overwhelmed.

Menstrual blood is a symbol of wisdom, spiritual initiation and fertility.

Blood figures in baptisms (spiritual rebirths) and often has the same symbolism as fire.

See **Baptism; Fire; Wine.**

Blue. See **Colors.**

Boat. See **Ship.**

Body, body parts. The body is a container, both of physical health and of the soul. Dreams about bodies and body parts can provide information on matters pertaining either to one's physical or spiritual well-being.

In addition, the body itself may not be portrayed literally in a dream, but may be represented by two common dream metaphors for bodies, the house and the vehicle, especially the automobile. The structure of a house, and the parts of an automobile, can represent body parts and body functions.

See **individual listings for body parts; Automobile; House.**

Bog. A soggy wasteland that threatens to suck one down into the ooze of the unconscious. Bogs are treacherous territory, their boundaries uncharted, their depths waiting for a misstep. Yet, bogs may be likened to an alchemical cauldron of the vegetable soul: the black of the nigredo, the putrefaction that precedes the rebirth.

See **Vegetables; Water.**

Bones. Structure, especially of an internal and unseen nature. Notice whether the bones are strong or brittle, which may provide clues to inner strength. Animal bones may relate to instinct, especially the type associated with a specific animal.

See **Animals.**

Book. A source of wisdom and information. Books are a fundamental source of education by which we learn to make our way in the world. They expand our consciousness and give advice. In a dream, a book may represent something we need to learn, especially about our shadow side. It also can be a "book of life," a retrospective of one's life to date; stories about ourselves and others; a look at paths that were not taken; or perhaps even a look at a possible future.

The condition of a book adds additional shades of meaning in a dream. A tattered, worn or damaged book may represent something that is undesirable or obsolete, or something in one's life that has passed (or is in the process of passing) from the scene. A new book may have associations with beginnings. Books in excellent condition or in luxurious bindings have positive associations.

Hidden books may represent wisdom we are searching for and have yet to find. Or, they may symbolize secrets about ourselves and others. Locations where books are hidden, or where one searches for hidden books, can yield additional insight into the meaning of books in a dream.

Shutting a book and putting it away can signify the closing of a chapter or period in one's life. It also can indicate one's refusal or reluctance to acknowledge something, or even one's fear of learning something about one's self.

Box. Like the bag, the box symbolizes containment of the psyche, especially its secrets and repressions. Opening Pandora's box can release repressed contents of the unconscious.

Book

Boxes also protect truths.

Boxes are means of organizing one's life and one's emotional life. Packing boxes can represent putting one's life in order.

Other meaning: The womb.

Break-in. The forcible entry of someone or something, such as into a home, indicates the intrusion of new or strange elements or circumstances into one's life. Break-ins typically happen beyond one's control. Fear in the dream may indicate fear of what is taking place in waking life.

Breast. A desire to be nurtured; or, being nurtured by the feminine principle, the inner Mother, or the anima. Breasts also represent fertility, nourishment, and maternal protection and love. To be bare-breasted often symbolizes humility or a sense of exposure.

See **Food.**

Bride. The lost soul.

On a mundane level, brides may appear in prenuptial anxiety dreams.

Bridegroom. The Christ consciousness.

Bridge. Transition from one state to another. A support structure that prevents one from plunging into the depths of the unconscious or the unknown.

Brown. See **Colors.**

Bubble. Emerging from a bubble, especially an underwater bubble, is a symbol of birthing. When such a dream applies to a pregnancy, it usually indicates unresolved anxieties (see **Birth**). In a non-pregnancy situation, emergence from a bubble signifies the birth of a new self from the waters of the unconscious.

Bugs. See **Insects.**

Building. The Self. Different floors may represent different levels of awareness.
See **Home; House.**

Bulb. See **Seed.**

Burglary. See **Robbery; Valuables.**

Bus. A means of transportation and getting to your destination by a collective, safe and pre-planned route. Buses serve the needs of society. Their routes and schedules are decided by authority figures who determine how the greatest needs will be served. Thus, a bus does not provide the most direct and fastest means to a destination. Riding as a passenger on a bus may indicate that you have chosen a relatively safe, impersonal or unthreatening path or course of action and have surrendered a certain amount of control to collectivity. It is the opposite of forging your own path through wilderness, for example, and much less direct than driving your own car through traffic. See **Automobile.** Compare to **Airplane; Ship; Train.**

Buttons. Fasteners that hold one's clothing (social presentation or facade) together. Tight buttons might represent a social face held tightly together, perhaps out of fear of becoming undone; they might also represent constriction. Loose buttons or missing buttons, or the losing of buttons, might represent a social face in the process of change, one that is becoming undone.
   See **Clothing.**

Butterfly. Metamorphosis, transformation, especially into something more beautiful.
   Other meaning: A symbol of the soul.

C

Cabbage. Boredom, inactivity, dullness, a state of vegetating. In folklore, the cabbage—a staple of peasants—is one of the lowliest of vegetables; in earlier times, its consumption was blamed for depression and dark moods. Galen claimed the cabbage caused a "heaviness of the soul." In modern times, the term "cabbage" is often used to describe a dullard.

Cabbages also symbolize the "vegetable soul," the deep unconscious that connects humanity to its earthy roots.

Other meanings: 1) Earthiness. 2) A connection to one's roots, home and community. 3) Solidity and orderliness, as seen in neat rows of cabbages in a patch. 4) An amiable fool.

See **Vegetables.**

Cafeteria. A collective, public place, institutional, where adequate but uninspired food (spiritual and emotional nourishment) is served. Food is in abundant quantities in cafeterias (some of which feature all-you-can-eat offers). Thus, someone who is in need of emotional or spiritual nourishment might dream of selecting from and eating enormous quantities of food in a cafeteria. As an institution, a cafeteria is depersonalized, however.

Cakes. A common food in rituals, such as sacrifices and offerings to the gods or spirits of the dead. The eating of cakes in a dream may relate to a spiritual initiation or passage.

See **Food**.

Cancer. Dreams of having cancer probably do not concern a real illness, but rather symbolize anxieties over a debilitating, consuming problem or situation that leaves one feeling ravaged.

Candles. Spiritual light; faith; the human soul. Candles have been used in rituals since about 3000 B.C. to repel evil spirits. Symbolically, candles push away the darkness of spirit with their own spiritual light. Especially in Christianity, candles represent divine light and the light of Christ's resurrection.

Candles also symbolize the human soul and the fragility of physical life. In folklore, naturally occurring phosphorescences, sometimes called "corpse candles," are held to be the wandering ghosts of the dead, or harbingers of death. Candles burned at funerals and wakes protect the dead from evil spirits, and help light the way of the soul to the afterworld.

In dreams candles are likely to represent light in a spiritual darkness or time of uncertainty. A candle being lit may represent the birth of something new, while a candle being extinguished may represent the passing of something old.

Cannibalism. Consuming the flesh of another person is to absorb his or her life force or vital power. The dreamer should identify the attributes or characteristics of the victim that he or she wishes to possess, or take into spirit. Eating is a symbolic form of taking spiritual nourishment.

Cap. See **Hat**.

Car. See **Automobile.**

Carnelian. See **Jewels.**

Carrot. Novelty; ornamentation; the surreal. Carrots also are symbols of the ''vegetable soul.'' See **Vegetables.**

Castration. Fear of sexual inadequacy; fear of being emasculated; fear of manhood with its attendant responsibilities; repression of deep emotions.

Fear of emasculation also may reflect a conflict between animus (the masculine) and anima (the feminine), with the latter struggling for greater recognition.

Castration also may relate to feelings of guilt, sin or repulsiveness concerning sex.

Other meanings: 1) Fear of impotence in old age. 2) Loss of vital energy. 3) Competition with a woman in some arena of life.

Cat. An archetypal image of the feminine principle and the anima, especially aspects of mystery, independence, stealth and power. Cats are symbols of the Goddess, and represent in particular her chthonic and lunar aspects. In myth, the cat is the companion to Bast, the Egyptian goddess of marriage.

Cats also are a symbol of sex, sexuality and sensuality. Black cats represent bad luck, bad omens and death (symbolic).

See **Animals.**

Cave. A womb; the unconscious. In mythology, caves are a symbol of the Great Mother's womb that brings forth all life; in dreams, this includes the Self. Emerging from a cave represents birthing of a new Self. Retreating into a cave represents going down into the unconscious, where one

Cat

connects with earthy emotions and instincts. Living in a cave represents an incubation of a new Self.

Caves also occur in pregnancy dreams, and symbolize the pregnancy and birthing.

Cedar. Immortality; strength; durability. The Cedar of Lebanon is particularly associated with the sublime because of its great height. In medieval times, the cedar was a symbol for the Virgin Mary.

See **Tree.**

Celebrities. See **Famous people.**

Ceremonial disasters. See **Disasters, ceremonial.**

Ceremony. See **Initiation.**

Chanting. Chanting utilizes the mystical power of sound to bring body and spirit into attunement. Chanting a word or phrase may be a means of calling one's attention to a matter that needs addressing (reattunement). Chanting by protesters is a way of calling attention to a problem.

Chains. Chains can have either positive or negative associations. Negative associations include bondage, slavery, and imprisonment—to places, people, jobs, situations, beliefs, dreams, addictions, etc. Positive associations are anchoring, binding, and communication.

On the material plane, chains generally are a symbol of marriage, blood relatives and comrades-in-arms. On the spiritual plane, chains symbolize the marriage of heaven and earth. They are a form of the spiral, a lunar symbol of the Mother Goddess and of the eternal cycle of renewal.

Other meaning: 1) a succession of events that are linked together in some fashion.

Chair. Support and provision of rest. Chairs also are one's seat or place in the world, an everyday version of a throne. As such, they represent power and authority. A chair being held for you by someone else represents entrusting your power to another.

Sitting on a chair can represent the act of repressing of something.

Chemistry. Transformation, especially of an alchemical nature. Participating in versus watching chemistry experiments or procedures indicates the degree of self-responsibility one has assumed in the matter to which the dream relates.

Notice characteristics such as whether the procedure/experiment is risky or safe; whether the chemist knows what he or she is doing; what the purpose is; and what the processes are. Combining solid ingredients into a bowl symbolizes an earthy grounding, or matters pertaining to the mundane or the physical. Combining liquids, or dissolving solids into liquid, brings in the elements of emotions and the unconscious. Vaporizing or burning by fire symbolizes an intense purification process.

Cherry. The feminine principle and female sexuality; fertility. Cherries also are the sweetness of character that comes from good works. In Christianity, the cherry is called the Fruit of Paradise.

Other meaning: A forbidden fruit signifying lust and desire.

See **Fruits; Vegetables.**

Child/children. Innocence, naiveté, purity, simplicity. Children often represent one's inner child in a dream, and can bear both positive and negative meanings.

Positive meanings include unrealized potential, the process or need for growth, the acquisition and development of skills, the fruits of relationships and of the future. Other positive meanings are the ability to experience awe, wonder and curiosity, to freely express emotion, to trust, to explore and to fantasize.

Negative meanings include immaturity, infantilism and self-centeredness.

The inner child may have emotional or psychological wounds, which can manifest in dreams as physical injuries, personality traits, or in activities. To dream of wounded children, especially of saving them, symbolizes a need to heal one's own emotional or physical wounds. This symbol also relates to feeling a loss of one's cultural roots, and occurs in dreams of women who are going through menopause.

To dream of your own children may not concern them literally, but may symbolize a part of the Self. Children symbolize events in the past, or in the dreamer's own childhood. The age of a child should be considered. For example, a three-year-old child may represent something that

Child/Children

took place in the dreamer's life three years earlier, or else at age three. Childhood memories often are repressed, and children in a dream may relate to repressed and traumatic memories.

Parents who have suffered the death of a child often dream of finding lost children, or reviving a dead, dying or fragile child. These dreams usually occur immediately following the death, and continue until the loss is accepted.

Childbearing. One's literal fertility; also, creativity. Being able or not able to have children in a dream also occurs to women who are going through menopause, and reflects un-resolved emotions or anxieties about this life change. For women, childbearing may relate directly to self-esteem and self-worth.

See **Birth**.

Chimney. Access to the spirit world or heaven; a means of communicating with the spirit world. Coming down a chimney represents the gifts bestowed by heaven on earth, i.e., the spiritual descending to manifest on the physical plane. Going up a chimney represents escape to heaven. In dreams, chimneys may symbolize the manifestation or ger-mination (depending on direction of movement down or up) of new ideas.

Church. The established order for morals and ethics. Churches in dreams also carry potent personal associations.

Circle. A universal archetypal symbol of wholeness, com-pletion, totality and perfection. The circle is the unmanifest; God without beginning or end, timeless and eternal. It is the symbol of the Mother Goddess and the never-ending cycle of birth, death and rebirth. It is the radiant spiritual illumination of the sun rolling through the heavens. It is the feminine psyche, the encircling waters of the uncon-scious.

Circles form mandalas, symbols of wholeness. A circle within a dot in the center represents cyclic perfection. A circle with a square is an alchemical symbol of *conjunctio,* or integration of heaven and earth, masculine and feminine, spirit and matter. Circles also have a magical potency and are universal protection against evil.

Circles are associated with the number 10, a symbol of completion and perfection (see **Numbers**). If a circle in a dream is divided into parts, consider other number symbolisms.

Objects shaped like circles, such as balls or wheels, or containing circles, should be examined in terms of circle symbolisms.

Circling. To go round and round in a circle in a dream, whether on foot or in a vehicle, indicates feelings of being stalled. A secondary meaning relates to protection and security (see **Circle**). To draw a circle is to define limits and boundaries.

City. A collective place that depends upon the collective observance of certain rules, laws and behavior standards in order to function. Generally, cities are symbols of the masculine/active principle, since their skylines bristle with thrusting buildings and the best technology (a product of intellect). Cities also have their feminine/passive aspect as repositories of a society's greatest cultural expressions, in their museums, performing arts and artists-in-residence.

The meaning of a city in a dream depends a great deal upon one's own personal associations with "city." Is a city a desirable place to be or an undesirable place, and why?

Cities have both positive and negative associations. Positive associations include enterprise, challenge, activity, vitality, opportunity, creativity, fun, accomplishment. Negative associations are overcrowding, stress, confusion, oppression, conformity, authoritarianism, crime, inner decay.

Class. See **School**.

Climbing. Making an effort to overcome obstacles, to work toward intellectual achievement, or to make a spiritual transformation. Hills and mountains often represent life's obstacles in dreams, and the difficulty or ease with which we climb them—or go around them—can be barometers of our sense of pace, accomplishment and frustration.

Mountains also are abodes of the gods in mythology. Thus climbing mountains in dreams can represent an ascension toward spiritual enlightenment. Likewise, climbing stairs can represent gaining access to the world of spirit.

Climbing towers represents intellectual growth or accomplishment.

See **Mountain; Stairs; Tower.**

Cloak. A garment that disguises, hides secrets, hides one's true nature, or renders one invisible.

See **Clothing.**

Clock. Deadlines, running out of time; an acute awareness of the passing of time. Clock dreams often occur when one is faced with serious or life-threatening illness, or is close to someone who is in such a situation. Trying to stop a clock, or a clock breaking, can represent a fear of death. Clocks gone out of control symbolize unresolved fears and anxieties.

Other meaning: 1) A woman's biological clock, that is, her time remaining to conceive and bear children.

Closet. Something being hidden away or hidden from view, such as talents, potentials or problems. Closets can be orderly storerooms, or places where everything one wishes to ignore are kept. Questions to consider about dream closets are: Is the closet secret or locked? Where is it (see **House**)? What are the contents? Is there fear or anticipation associated with opening the closet? If the closet is opened, do things spill out in disarray? Are there frightening things inside that surprise the dreamer?

See **Box.**

Clothing

Clothing. One's social presentation or facade; the appearance we wish to make upon the world. Clothes hide shortcomings, flaws and faults, or advertise assets. They also represent professions. Clothes can make us appear to be something other than what we are.

The type and condition of garments in a dream may make a statement about one's self-image. A change of clothing indicates a change of direction, a new phase of life, or a reckoning with one's self. Shining clothing, such as the raiment of angels, indicates a conquering of the material. Clothing soiled with excrement indicates a raw creative power from which the alchemical gold or the sun of spiritual illumination emerges.

Clothing dreams also sometimes occur as premonitions of death of someone close to the dreamer. In such dreams, the one who is about to die typically appears in new clothing. This symbol is of the ultimate *coagulatio*, the acquisition of an immortal body.

See **Costume; Excrement; Rags.**

Clouds. Clouds have a double meaning. They represent confusion, a state of complete unhappiness, or something being obscured from understanding. In alchemical terms, clouds represent the *nigredo*—especially if they are black—which is the psychological darkening that brings a period of unhappy self-reflection prior to an emergence of a new consciousness.

Clouds also symbolize the unknown, unknowable and bewildering aspect of the Godhead, the light of which cannot be comprehended unless one is first stripped of every idea and intellectual conception.

Other meaning: 1) In Christian symbolism, clouds are produced by the Devil, who seeks to cover the earth in confusion and unconsciousness.

Club. Weapon generally used to beat someone or something into submission. Clubs may symbolize the use of unnecessary force or brutality in some matter in life.

Cock. As the herald of the dawn, the cock represents awakening to spiritual illumination (the sun). In ushering in the goodness of the sun, the cock banishes all evil spirits; hence the widespread folk belief that various supernatural creatures and spirits must return to their dwelling places by cock's crow.

The cock also represents vigilance (it does not fail each day to greet the dawn) and activity and renewal and resurrection (the dawn brings the world to new life.) The cock was said to be present at the birth of Jesus Christ. Medieval church builders placed models of a cock atop steeples and domes.

In a pagan sense, the cock's symbolic renewal comes as an embodiment of the corn-spirit, which traditionally was sacrificed at harvest time to ensure a bountiful crop the following season.

In the classical healing temples of the Greek god Aesclepius, sacrifices of cocks were made in thanks for healing. Thus the cock can in certain dreams signify that a healing process has taken place.

The cock can be both a symbol of good luck and bad luck, depending on local lore.

Other meanings: 1) Fertility. 2) Prognostication, or divining the future.

Cockroach. Furtiveness, hiding in order to survive. Cockroaches are associated with food (spiritual nourishment), especially its decay and rotting (an alchemical state of the dying away of the old in preparation for the new). They also are associated with dirt, as in one's psychological "dirt," that is, repressions or projections of the Shadow.

See **Insects.**

Cocoon. A womb of spiritual rebirth. Cocoons also represent protected places where one feels secure. They may be associated with fears of leaving relationships, jobs, places or situations.

Coffin. Death of the old; a womb of spiritual rebirth or resurrection. Coffins also can represent an unawakened or "dead" state of consciousness.

Collar. In a positive aspect, a collar is a symbol of authority, office or status. In a negative aspect, it represents constraint, bondage and slavery. A tight collar possibly symbolizes feelings of constraint, restriction or suffocation in a relationship, job or situation.

See **Clothing.**

Colors. The most ancient and universal of symbols. Colors represent the forces of light and darkness, the opposites of masculine and feminine, and various attributes. Colors are vibrations of light. Edgar Cayce (1877-1945), the noted American psychic who gave medical diagnoses in trance, observed that vibration is movement, and movement is activity that is either positive or negative. Thus, colors may have an impact upon all levels of consciousness and upon the physical form.

The essential division between the forces of light and dark is expressed in white, the combination of all colors of the spectrum, and black, the absence of color. In Chinese philosophy, the polar opposites of creation *yang* (masculine) and *yin* (feminine) also are represented respectively by white (the active principle) and black (the passive principle). In alchemy, the union of opposites is expressed by the colors red (the physical) and white (the spirit). The primary colors, red, yellow and blue, express primary emotions and forces. Other colors, which are combinations of the primary colors, represent qualities and attributes through natural associations, such as green, the color of vegetation, which is associated with harmony and tranquility.

Specific color meanings are:

Black. The dark aspect of God, nature, or the Self; the shadow. Black represents the repressed part of the Self, the areas seeking expression and most in need of attention. This dark side can be represented in dreams by black people, people dressed in black, black animals or monsters, and destructive forces of nature such as storms, tornadoes, hurricanes and so on.

As the color of mourning, black also occurs in dreams involving unresolved emotions over loss from death, divorce, accident or other upheaval. If one is suffering from life-threatening or terminal illness, black may symbolize one's fears about physical death. These fears also are expressed in dreams following the death of someone close, especially a parent, when one faces one's own mortality.

Black also represents passive forces, the feminine principle, the unconscious and processes in the unconscious, and the germination of light that occurs in darkness of an unenlightened state. It is the womb of the Great Mother, where all things are born; the descent into hell, or the unconscious; the caves and dark grottoes of the earth; and the inner planes. Black is the measurement of time.

In alchemy, black is the *nigredo*, the initial stage of the Great Work, and also the destructive aspect of the unconscious. The *nigredo* is the darkness that precedes spiritual light. It is the decay, destruction and death that sweeps away the old order/old self to make way for the new order/ new self. Psychologically, the *nigredo* is depression and dissolution, or the self-reflection that is induced by conflict and depression. When the *nigredo* is at its worst, a birth of a new Self occurs in the unconscious.

Black also is associated with *coagulatio*, the intrusion of reality, or the Saturnine grounding in the earth, during which one evaluates situations.

Blue. The color of spirit, the spiritual, the heavenly, the numinous, inspiration, devotion, religious feeling, godliness, contemplation, and inspiration. The images of various Hindu gods, usually attributes of Vishnu, have blue skin to denote their divine nature. Mountains, the abodes of the gods and the symbols of the spiritual ascent often are shown as blue.

As the color of water and the sky, blue has associations with the unconscious and feminine characteristics—it is the color of the cloak of the Blessed Virgin Mary, the Queen of Heaven.

The Egyptians associated blue with truth.

In yoga, blue governs the throat chakra, and is associated

with communication, creativity, self-expression and the search for truth.

Other meanings: 1) Enhanced productivity and sense of well-being. 2) Clear thinking.

Brown. The color of the earth, and earthy qualities. Also, renunciation of the world, spiritual death and degradation.

Gold. The sun, divine light, illumination, the highest state of glory. In alchemy, gold represents the attainment of the Philosopher's Stone. It also symbolizes the celestial.

Gold is the color of the masculine principle of the cosmos.

Gray. Mourning, humility, neutrality, penitence. In Christian symbolism, gray is the death of the body in order to gain immortality of the spirit. Expressed other way, it is the transformation from material to spiritual.

In Kabbalistic symbolism, gray represents wisdom; hence, wise figures are clothed in gray.

Green. A color with diverse meanings, both beneficent and destructive. Green is not a primary color, but is a bridge or transition from one primary color to another. It can be either warm or cool. Its significance in a dream depends upon the context.

In its beneficent aspect, green is the color of growth, hope, renewal, freshness, lushness, health, youth, vigor, harmony and refreshment. It is the root metaphor of the natural world, and of the way the world is perceived; it holds the secret of all life. Green is the blood of the vegetable world (see **Vegetables**), and thus is part of the fertilizing moisture that flows from the Great Goddess, the maternal consciousness of the cosmos. Green is the color of the soul, the World Soul, and the anima. Jung related it to sensation. Green also is the color of passion, from the amorous love of the Aphrodite to the ecstasy of Dionysius.

In color therapy, green refreshes and invigorates, and is used as an antidote for fatigue and insomnia.

In alchemy, it is the sulphurous, dissolving Green Lion, which is the beginning of the Great Work; some alchemists said it represented the prima materia.

In its destructive aspect, green is the color of rot, mold, slime, overripeness, decay and death. It is the color of all deities and supernatural beings associated with the underworld and the souls of the dead, and thus is sometimes the color of bad luck and premonitions of death. It is a symbol of suffocation and choking, as in an overgrowth of brush or a dense jungle, or of things neglected and gone wild and out of control, as in weeds taking over a garden. Green also is the color of envy, as in the jealousy of Aphrodite, and of bitterness and unripeness.

Other meanings: 1) Naiveté. 2) Innocence. 3) Inexperience.

See also **Evergreens.**

Indigo. Advanced spiritual qualities or wisdom, psychic faculties, intuition.

Orange. Pride and ambition, flames, egoism, cruelty, ferocity, luxury. As the color of fire, orange can represent the purifying power of flame, the burning away of impurities.

Pink. The flesh, sensuality, emotions, the material. The Gnostics considered pink the color of resurrection. Pink also is associated with the heart center and love from the heart.

Purple. The color of the gods, royalty, imperial power, pomp, pride, justice, truth. In Christian symbolism, God, humility and penitence.

Red. Blood, life, the life-force, the body, wounds (initiation) and death (transformation). Red is also the color of animal life, and the animal nature in man. It is the color of lust, passion, materialism and fertility.

Red also is associated with fire. It is the color of activity, energy, courage, will power, war and ferocity.

In medieval Christian art, red represents love and charity,

and is used in conjunction with martyrdom. In alchemy, it is the sulphuric stage in the creation of the Philosopher's Stone, and represents sublimation, suffering and love.

Silver. The color of the moon, which gives it associations with magic, the Goddess, psychic nature, emotions and intuition. Opposite gold, silver is the feminine aspect of duality of the cosmic reality. In alchemy, silver is Luna, ''the affections purified.''

Violet. Sanctity, religious devotion, knowledge, sorrow, temperance, grief, old age, mourning. In Christian symbolism, love and truth or passion and suffering, sacerdotal rule and authority. Violet also represents power, as well as nostalgia and memories.

White. Purity, holiness, sacredness, redemption, mystical illumination, timelessness, ecstasy, innocence, joy, light and life. White is transcendent perfection, the brilliance of the Godhead.

White signifies marriage (the union of opposites to form a whole) and death (transformation and renewal).

In the alchemical process of the Philosopher's Stone, white marks the second stage, the beginning of the ascent up from darkness.

Yellow. The sun, illumination, light, intellect and generosity. Like orange, yellow is a color of fire, and thus has associations with the purifying power of flames. Yellow is a point of departure in spiritual ascension, as opposed to the arrival state expressed by gold.

Column. Strength and support. Are the columns in the dream solid or cracked? What are they supporting? For example, are they supporting a bridge (transition), a house or a building (the Self)?

Composer. See **Music**.

Contamination. Something or someone that is upsetting.

Contamination dreams sometimes occur to individuals who are suffering life-threatening illness, especially cancer.

Corn. A totemic member of the vegetable kingdom that is closely bound to the mysteries of death and rebirth, the seasonal dying and reflowering of the earth. Corn is used in funerary rites, and symbolizes abundance in the underworld (the unconscious). It also symbolizes fertility, growth and abundance in the physical world, and is associated with the sun.

Other meanings: 1) Well-being. 2) Happiness.

See **Vegetables.**

Correspondence. Communication with one's self. Correspondence delivers a message about a matter requiring the dreamer's attention, or provides information useful in making a decision.

Costume. Disguise or facade. Costumes can represent how you wish others to see you or what you really want to be. They also can represent what you fear you appear to be.

Other meanings: The inability to see yourself or others clearly or truthfully.

See **Clothing.**

Couch. Often a symbol of a healing or therapeutic process. In the classical world, sick persons retreated to temples in order to incubate healing dreams sent by the gods. They would sleep on a *kline*, or couch, which sometimes was placed near a statue of the resident healing deity. The term *kline* is the derivative of the modern term "clinic." In establishing the foundation of psychotherapy, Sigmund Freud reintroduced the couch as a therapeutic tool in facilitating trust, relaxation and openness. While few therapists today

Correspondence

have patients recline on a couch, its long associations with healing remain imbedded in the collective unconscious.

Court. A place where justice is meted out by authority figures, and where social order is kept. Courts also may symbolize cause and effect, that is, reaping what one sows. They may be portents of what might happen if one holds to, or takes, a certain course of action.

Courtyard. A symbol of the feminine principle; a womb-like enclosure.

Other meaning: A place of tranquility and pleasure.

Cow. The maternal instinct, motherhood, fertility, nurturing, the giving and renewing of life. Cows are universal symbols of the Mother Goddess, and have associations with the moon (the unconscious) because of their horns. Cows also represent the plenty of mother earth.

By nature, cows are passive and peaceful, and go along with the herd. Cows in dreams may be associated with these attributes.

Other meanings: 1) Female sexual feelings. 2) Domesticity.

See **Animals.**

Coyote. A trickster figure; craftiness and slyness. Coyotes also are loners who fend for themselves in the wilderness, which in dreams would be the unconscious.

See **Animals.**

Crab. Indirect, sideways movement or behavior; scuttling; unreliable or dishonest behavior. As denizens of water, crabs are associated with emotions and the unconscious. The hard shell of the crab represents one's armor against emotional vulnerability. Other meanings: 1) Bad moods or irritable behavior. 2) A tendency to hold onto things, especially too long or in a manner that is painful to one's self or others.

See **Animals.**

Cradle. A new spiritual life or a beginning of a new phase in life. Rocking a cradle symbolizes nurturing the birth.

Crevice. An opening into the unconscious. A danger for the unwary.

Crocodile. Guardian of the gates to the underworld, which in dreams is the unconscious. The ancient Egyptians asso-

Cradle

ciated crocodiles with the souls of the dead. In a dream, a crocodile may also symbolize the guardian of any kind of threshold, such as an emotional or psychological barrier.

To be swallowed by a crocodile—or a whale or any large creature of the deep—is to be taken into the underworld, or the unconscious. Dreams of such symbolism may relate to a spiritual initiation, or a need to be immersed in the unconscious.

In myth, the crocodile swallows the moon and then sheds insincere tears. Thus, the crocodile can symbolize hypocrisy and insincerity.

Because the crocodile lives in both water and mud, it also is a symbol of fecundity (life-giving waters of the Mother Goddess) and vegetation (and thus the "vegetable soul" of humankind). See **Vegetables.**

Cross

Other meanings: 1) Animal power. 2) Viciousness.
See **Animals.**

Cross. One of the oldest and most universal of sacred symbols. The cross symbolizes the interpenetration of earth and heaven, matter and spirit, masculine and feminine; in terms of a dream, it can represent where the conscious meets the unconscious. The cross is a midpoint, the equilibrium, the harmonious center. It is humanity at its peak expression on both the mundane and spiritual planes. The cross also is a symbol of fire and the sun, both masculine principles representing spirit and intellect, respectively.

The four arms of the cross—especially an equilateral cross—represent the four elements, the cardinal points and the four seasons. Thus the cross has the magical potency of the number four, which represents foundation and stability (see **Numbers**). The equilateral cross also forms a mandala, a symbol of wholeness and completeness. A cross within a circle is a mandala, and also has associations with the Mother Goddess (represented by the circle) and the ever-turning wheel of birth, death and rebirth.

In Christianity, a cross symbolizes suffering, sacrifice and a burden to bear; it also symbolizes victory over death and the triumph of the immortal soul, as well as blessings and protection from evil.

On a mundane level, a cross also may represent a crossroads where one must make choices.

Objects shaped like crosses, such as anchors, tees, forked trees, etc., should be considered as potential cross symbols in dreams. Jung interpreted the ace of clubs in playing cards as a cross.

See **Circle; Square.**

Crossroads. Choices, especially in relation to momentous decisions or turning points in life.

Spiritually, crossroads represent a conjunction of time and space, a place where various forces gather to manifest at once. Like the cross, they also are a union of opposites, and thus represent a completeness.

In folklore, crossroads are magical and somewhat dangerous places, because they are a doorway to the Otherworld, a place where the supernatural and the underworld (the unconscious) intrude into the manifest world. Witches, fairies and the chthonic deities are particularly associated with crossroads. A widespread custom called for burying suicides, criminals and the unbaptized at crossroads so that their souls would be confused and thus not threaten the living.

Crow. A messenger between heaven and earth, an omen of death, and prophet of the hidden truth or the unconscious.

Like the raven, the crow in alchemy represents the nigredo, the initial blackening of the Little Work that paves the way for the Great Work.

Because of its black·color, the crow is often associated with evil.

Crowd. Collective action, opinion, beliefs. Pressure, stress, confusion, chaos, emotions running out of control. The individual is at risk in crowds, especially angry ones. One can become lost in a crowd, carried along or manipulated by a crowd or trampled by a crowd.

Other meanings: Loss of individuality.

Crown. Authority; sovereignty; mastery over one's self and one's own "kingdom," i.e., inner or outer life. Crowns also signify victory, honor and righteousness. Their circular shape symbolizes the endless circle of time.

Wearing a crown can represent enlightenment, intuition and highest thinking, all associated with the crown chakra.

Crowns often are associated with father figures.

See **Father; Hat; King; Queen.**

Crutches. Support; something one leans upon. Crutches in dreams are substitutes for something that dysfunctions in life. They may represent too much reliance upon others, or dependencies upon substances such as alcohol, or upon material things or other values.

Because the foot is often a symbol of the soul, crutches also can symbolize moral "lameness."

Crystal. See **Jewels.**

Cube. The earth, the material world, the four elements, the foundation of the cosmos. Cubes represent wholeness, and also Truth, because the view is the same from every angle. Cubes also symbolize solidity and firmness, and in allegories represent the persistence of the virtues. Chariots and thrones often are represented as cubes.

In alchemy, the cube is the squaring of the circle, or completion and wholeness. It also represents salt, which in dreams is sometimes a symbol of bitterness.

Cup. A symbol of the receptive, passive feminine vessel; the womb. Cups symbolize plenty and immortality; they represent the mysteries of the Mother Goddess: birth, death and rebirth. In mythology, sacred cups are never-ending sources of food, refreshment and the magical elixir of life everlasting.

In alchemy, the cup represents the philosopher's stone. The Holy Grail is the sacred cup of Christianity, the cosmic center, the heart, the source of all life.

Cups are used in many rites of initiation. A cup in a dream may be associated with a spiritual initiation.

Cypress. As an evergreen, the cypress symbolizes long life and immortality. Planted as a border around cemeteries, it protects corpses from corruption and banishes evil spirits. Ancients regarded the cypress as a symbol of death, because the tree does not rejuvenate itself if cut down.

Other meanings: 1) Mourning. 2) Endurance and perseverance of virtue. 3) Phallus.

D

Daisy. Innocence, purity, freshness, the sun, intellectual light. Daisies also are associated with the Virgin Mary, and as such are symbols of immortality and salvation.

Dancing. Connection with, or need to connect with, one's emotions. Dancing represents freedom of movement, creative expression, gracefulness, and a carefree, uninhibited spirit. Dancing also is a form of ritual; ritual marks transitions and passages in life. Dancing in a dream might symbolize a release of creative energy or joy at making a transition from one phase to another.

Dancing also may relate to personal relationships and reflect one's feelings about them. To dance with someone can represent unity, including sexual union. To dance apart may indicate emotional distance or conditions preventing unity.

Darkness. Death, destruction, dissolution; also chaos, and primordial chaos. Darkness is the *nigredo* stage of alchemy, in which the old is destroyed and dissolved in order to make way for the new. Being lost in the dark or suffering a ''dark night of the soul'' can be symbols of a psychic reordering prior to the emergence of a new Self, or also of the passing of an old stage of life. Darkness is not inherently evil, but

Dancing

rather is the womb of spiritual rebirth; it precedes the light of spiritual illumination.

Darkness also represents the unconscious. Monsters in the dark may symbolize unexpressed or unresolved fears. Exploring darkness or fear of exploring darkness may relate to fears of the unknown, or some issue that has been avoided.

Other meaning: Depression, low spirits.

See **Light**.

Dates. Fertility. See **Vegetables**.

Dawn. Emergence into the light of understanding, peace, harmony, a new cycle, or a spiritual state. Darkness, turmoil and uncertainty are behind one.

See **Twilight**.

Dead, The. The appearance in a dream of a person who is dead is part of the grieving process. The appearance of the dead restored to youth and vigor, or to give comfort or assurances that they are all right, aid the acceptance of death and resolution of grief. Dreams in which the dead appear as angels—which may not occur until a year or more has passed from the time of death—indicate that the healing process is complete or near completion.

Repeated dreams about a dead person may indicate that something concerning one's relationship with or feelings about that person remains unresolved. This unfinished business must be brought into the consciousness.

Death. Usually, dreams involving death are not literal warnings of impending physical death, but represent the decay and destruction of a stage in life, an attachment or a neurosis. Death is transformation from one state to another; it is necessary so that rebirth and renewal can take place.

Dreams about death—including mortal wounds and terminal illness—often occur at life passages (especially midlife), which bring stress and upheaval. The death in the dream may be of one's self or a person who is close, but ultimately the symbolism refers to the dreamer's psychological state.

Other meaning: Angry, vengeful feelings toward others.

Decapitation. A split between mind and body. Decapitation may occur in dreams related to mid-life crises, menopause or life-threatening illness, when one feels betrayed by the body or alienated from it.

Decay. A rotting away of a part of life or a part of one's inner self, either from neglect, or as part of a transformation that involves the death of something old in order to make way for a spiritual rebirth. In alchemy, decay is the *nigredo*, the blackening phase in which the old is destroyed in order for the philosopher's stone (wholeness and enlightenment) to be created.

Deer. Swiftness, grace, gentleness. In Celtic folklore, deer are supernatural and are the divine messengers of the fairies. Fairies live beneath the earth in mounds and burrows in a place where time stands still. Thus, deer in a dream may be messengers from the unconscious.

See **Animals.**

Defecation. A bodily function which is not to be taken literally, but which symbolizes the production of something, typically, out of the center of one's being.

See **Excrement.**

Deluge. See **Flood.**

Demon. A source of torment or bedevilment. A representation of weaknesses, vices and sins.

See **Monster.**

Dentist. Dentists in dreams have close associations with the various symbolisms of teeth. Dentists repair teeth and improve the appearance and bite of teeth, and in a dream this function may relate to a specific need, such as for sharper teeth (aggression and assertiveness). See **Teeth.**

Dentists also symbolize personal associations. For many people, dentists represent pain, fear and a feeling of helplessness. Dentists are authority figures, next to whom one often feels childlike.

Desert. A stark and harsh wilderness where spiritual transformation can take place. Many spiritual traditions call for mystics to withdraw into the desert or mountains to meditate, contemplate and seek enlightenment by overcoming the darkness within. The Gospels tell how Jesus, following his baptism by John the Baptist, felt compelled to retreat to the desert wilderness for forty days. During this time, he fasted and wandered for forty days in the desert on his own spiritual odyssey. He was tempted by the Devil, and overcame the temptations by quoting the word of God. Similarly, the Israelites spent forty years in the wilderness, being tested by God.

Dessert. Reward. The treat that comes when we are finished with something, or have accomplished something. See **Food.**

Detour. A roundabout, indirect way to get to where one is going. Detours take one off the main road of life and postpone accomplishment or completion. Detours that meander and become maze-like may indicate confusion or a feeling of being lost. Perhaps one takes a detour in order to avoid a straight course.

Devouring. Being devoured alive, either by an animal, a monster or a shapeless thing, expresses fear.

Diamond. See **Jewels.**

Diary. A place where secrets are kept. See **Book.**

Dice. Fate. Dice may reflect on one's sense of control over life, especially feelings of powerlessness ("what happens depends on the roll of the dice").

Digestion. The absorption into the psyche of spiritual nourishment (symbolized by food). Digestion is part of the "vegetable soul," our connection to earthy roots. It is the alchemical process of *dissolutio*, the dissolution that is decay and death, from which comes rebirth.

Dirt, dirtiness. Lack of cleanliness, or impropriety. Dirt, dirtiness and being dirty can relate to attitudes towards one's behavior, beliefs or state of mind. Dirt dreams related to sex are not uncommon.

Being dirty also can occur in dreams related to physical illness: the afflicted part of the body may be unclean or dirty. On occasion, these dreams may be early warnings of a yet unnoticed condition.

Disasters, ceremonial. Dreams in which ceremonies, such as weddings, social affairs or business presentations, go awry reflect anxieties about upcoming ceremonies in life. Such dreams involve virtually any mishap that can spoil an event, such as failure to have everything ready, forgetting crucial items, unexpected and terrible food, breakdowns of equipment, etc.

Ceremonial disaster dreams are particularly common before weddings, and symbolize natural worries that marriage is the right decision, or that the ceremony will go smoothly as planned.

Use anxiety dreams to reexamine emotions and discuss them with others. Perhaps ceremonial disaster dreams reflect one's desire to have a more assertive role in planning.

Disasters, natural. A common motif of nightmares that express profound anxiety over one's ability to survive a major upheaval in life. Such nightmares occur during the inner turmoil of life passages, and also as a result of severe injury or illness, grief, divorce, or loss of job or self-esteem. Natural disasters might be floods, tidal waves, earthquakes, avalanches, fire, etc. Such nightmares can clarify what you need to work on and resolve.

See **individual listings for disasters.**

Discovery. Dreams involving discovery commonly mark

the third stage of recovery from an upheaval in life, such as grief, divorce, injury or loss of job. This third stage is characterized by hope and renewal, and the formation of a new identity that has fully adjusted to the changes. These are symbolized by dreams of discovery of new rooms in a home or house, valuables or treasures, new clothing, new automobiles, new skills, new lands, etc.

Disease. See **Illness.**

Discipline. Regimentation, order. Self-imposed discipline may symbolize a desire to accomplish, to get something done, or a compulsion. Collectively imposed discipline, such as the rules and laws of society, also represent order but can symbolize limitations, even punishment. Discipline imposed by an individual, an authority figure such as a parent, can also represent punishment.

Disinfectant. Desire to heal or cleanse something, such as the wounds of a bad experience; emotions, attitudes or fears; or relationships or situations.

Dismemberment. Precursor to spiritual rebirth. Many mystical and spiritual traditions, especially shamanism, have rites of dismemberment that are part of initiation. The old self must be rent asunder and a new self created. In mythology, dismembered gods become the fertilizer for rebirth of crops and nature. The Egyptian god Osiris, dismembered by his evil brother, Set, and then reassembled by his wife, Isis, reigns as lord of the underworld and god of rebirth in the afterlife.

Dismemberment may relate to a particularly forceful and dramatic change in life.

Other meaning: Sacrifice.

Diving. Plunging headlong into something, such as an experience or the unconscious. Diving into water symbolizes total immersion in the waters of the unconscious. Diving from a high place, such as a cliff, mountain or building, onto earth symbolizes a descent from intellect to matter, or things that concern the body or physical plane.

Diving is a forceful and sudden descent, and one may have little or no control over the consequences. It may represent the means by which the unconscious forces one to face a situation. It may also be part of a healing process.

Doctor. An authority figure that often represents one's Higher Self, especially in terms of the ability to heal oneself. Doctors in dreams also are associated with a desire to be healed, either physically, psychically or emotionally, or they are associated with the process of one's own healing.

Dog. Generally, dogs are companions, guardians and protectors in the emotional/instinctual realm. They have both positive and negative attributes. Positive attributes are loyalty, protection, companionship, unconditional love, courage, sacrifice. Negative attributes are pack-instinct, dirtiness, viciousness.

Dogs act instinctively, and in dreams a dog may show a right way or a right decision, despite what the conscious mind thinks. However, a pack of dogs in a dream may indicate actions out of control or blind obedience to something that is wrong.

Though domesticated for thousands of years, dogs still retain their wild instincts to defend, hunt and kill. These instincts are summoned when necessary for survival.

In myth, the dog is a guide to the underworld, or in terms of the dream, the unconscious. The dog—sometimes fabulous, as in the three-headed creature Cerberus—also stands guard over treasures and the gates to the underworld.

The dog is an attendant to Aesclepius, Greek god of healing, and to various chthonic deities, such as Anubis, an Egyptian god of the underworld; Hades, Greek lord of the underworld; Hecate, Greek goddess of magic; and Hermes, the Greek messenger god, bringer of dreams and guide of souls to the underworld. These associations connect the dog to death and rebirth, and to mantic and medicinal powers.

In Christian symbolism, the dog is a spiritual shepherd, guarding the flocks, also representing the virtues of watchfulness and fidelity, and faithfulness in marriage.

Dogs also represent an animal-like masculinity.

Doll. A toy. Aspects of one's self or others can be projected onto dolls for belittlement or manipulation. Dolls may represent the shadow. The type of doll, its features and characteristics, and what one does with it in a dream have significance.

Other meanings: 1) Childhood memories or associations. 2) Future growth.

Dolphin. God-like qualities, intelligence, divine light, and in Christianity, the resurrection and salvation of Christ. In myth, the dolphin is a psychopomp, guiding or carrying the souls of the dead to the afterworld. Thus, in a dream a dolphin may pertain to the unconscious.

In classical mythology, the dolphin also is a symbol of Dionysus, the god of liquids and dissolution, and thus the alchemical process of *solutio*. Positive aspects of Dionysus are a greater appreciation of joy and ecstasy; negative aspects include alcoholism.

See **Animals.**

Donkey. Stubbornness; stupidity.
See **Animals.**

Door. Opportunities and choices; also barriers. Doors may relate to inner processes and growth as well as to external activities.

Being faced with many doors symbolizes being presented with many choices—perhaps confusing ones. Closed doors indicate areas which may need to be explored. Locked doors may relate to fears about opening up to new areas in life. Revolving doors—especially if one is stuck in a revolving door or winds up where one starts—indicate being stuck in a pattern or not making a choice that will lead to a new direction. Glowing doors, golden doors and doors filled with light symbolize opportunities for spiritual growth. Trap doors to basements indicate openings (perhaps unexpected) to the unconscious. A door that closes or is closing symbolizes the end of something, such as a phase of life, or being shut out of opportunities.

Doors also represent states of mind and means of personal expression.

See **House.**

Doublets. Pairs of identical objects or figures which, when they appear in a dream, indicate the emergence of something into the consciousness. This in turn is closely related to healing.

See **Twins.**

Dove. The soul, the life spirit, the soul of the dead. The dove is also a symbol of the Great Mother and thus of fecundity and the renewal of life. White doves in particular represent the Holy Spirit, purity, innocence, reconciliation, peace and spiritual salvation. A pair of white doves symbolizes love. Dark doves are symbols of death and misfortune.

Dove

Dragon. A symbol of psychic transformation. Like the snake, the dragon represents primordial consciousness, the feminine, the womb, the unformed prima materia, the alchemical process from chaos to the philosopher's stone, and wisdom and knowledge.

The dragon also symbolizes the hero figure; accompanied by treasure or a cave and treasure, it signifies an ordeal in the life of the hero. Slaying the dragon represents the battle between the forces of light and darkness—i.e., conquering one's own inner darkness in order to master the self. Rescuing a maiden from a dragon is the preservation of purity from the forces of evil.

The dragon also is associated with sky gods, and brings fertilizing rain (the waters of the unconscious), thunder and lightning.

Other meanings: 1) One's inner fears. 2) The negative aspect of the Mother figure.

See **Monsters; Snake.**

Drawer. Containment, confinement, or repression. Putting something away or keeping it in abeyance. Unwillingness to acknowledge something, wanting to forget something. Drawers often are similar in meaning to prisons or confining rooms.

Dragon

Other meanings: 1) A safe place. 2) Organization if neat. 3) Lack of organization if messy.
See **Prison; Room.**

Dress. See **Clothing.**

Drinking. Quenching an emotional or spiritual thirst. Drinking water may symbolize a connection to the unconscious. Drinking alcohol to get drunk may relate to low self-esteem, or a desire for oblivion or forgetfulness.

Drunken drinking also may represent an ecstatic and Dionysian release, such as of repressed emotions.

See **Food.**

Driving. See **Automobile.**

Drowning. Being overwhelmed in an immersion in the waters of the unconscious. Drowning may symbolize a sense of the loss of one's identity or ego, or of being overwhelmed by emotions.

Drowning dreams often occur during severe depressions, such as following a marital separation, when a person feels unable to cope with emotions.

Drowning dreams also occur during pregnancy, especially the last trimester, and reflect anxieties about birthing.

Drum, drumming. Beating one's own way in the world, or calling attention to one's self. Drumming also symbolizes the rhythms of life, which may be fast, slow, regular or irregular.

Drunkenness. See **Drinking.**

Duck. The duck does double duty in dreams. As a bird, it represents spirit and the Higher Self because of its ability to fly into the heavens. The duck also resides in the water, which represents the unconscious. Its swimming along the surface of water symbolizes what is in the conscious mind. By diving beneath the surface, the duck becomes a symbol for probing material that is in the deep unconscious. Its resurfacing, especially with something in its bill, could indicate the drawing up of new or repressed material into consciousness where it can be dealt with. See **Birds; Water.**

Other meanings: 1) When floating on the surface, superficiality. 2) A symbol of the Great Mother.

Duel. Warring factions within oneself.
See **Fight.**

Dusk. See **Twilight.**

Dynamite. Explosive emotions or temper. Being injured by dynamite may relate to injuries to oneself in an emotionally explosive situation. Hurling dynamite indicates repressed anger toward an individual, a situation or oneself.

E

Eagle. Spiritual victory; the triumph of spirit over matter; the spiritual principle of humanity that is able to ascend to heaven. Eagles also are associated with the sun (illumination) and air (intellect). Since antiquity, the eagle has been associated with kings and royalty (father and authority figures).

As a member of the animal kingdom, the eagle is true to its nature. Its symbolisms include pride, triumph, fierceness, liberty, authority, and inspiration. Jung regarded it as a symbol of the father. In Christian symbolism, the eagle represents Christ, rebirth and baptism.

See **Birds.**

Ear. Receptivity, willingness to listen, not only to others but to one's inner self.

In mythology, the ear is associated with divine inspiration, the means by which one hears the gods. Along with the ear's association with the spiral (a symbol of the Mother Goddess), this makes it a symbol of birth. In dreams, this might relate to the beginning of a new project or phase in life.

Earth, The. The center of life; the Mother Goddess in her triple aspects of birth, life (nurturing) and death. The Earth also represents a cosmic center, and is a symbol of foundation, solidity and firmness. It is the feminine, passive principle of the universe.

The Earth represents the physical plane and materiality, and thus the physical body or physical expression of the dreamer. It may also relate in dreams to too much emphasis on material things, or insufficient attention to them.

In Freemasonry, earth is the element that represents the lowest level of spiritual development (earth-bound); one is purified by ascending through the other elements of water, air and fire.

The Earth also is a symbol of the inexhaustible bounty of nature.

Earthquake. An inner shakeup going on. Earthquakes, like other natural disasters, occur in dreams during times of emotional upheaval, when one feels there is no firm foundation or stability in life. Earthquakes especially represent the materiality of life, and thus may mirror anxieties in particular concerning changes of residence or finances wrought by divorce, loss or accident. Earthquakes also have associations with the feminine principle, and maternal nurturing.

Earthquakes occur in dreams of persons suffering a life-threatening illness, especially cancer, which threatens to rip the very foundation out from under life.

See **Disasters, Natural.**

East. The direction of the rising sun symbolizes new beginnings, the dawn of spiritual light, the mystical side of nature. Also, one's spiritual nature and inner life.

Eating. An attempt to put spiritual nourishment into the body. Overeating or not having enough to eat are symbols of need.

In alchemical terms, eating is the process of *coagulatio*,

Eating

a grounding process that turns something to earth (the body, the material plane). Eating might represent a need to be more body-conscious or grounded in the material reality.

Eclipse. Something being overshadowed or devoured in one's life.

In many cosmologies, eclipses of the sun and moon are blamed on sky monsters that eat the celestial bodies. Thus, an eclipse in a dream might relate to being devoured by one's inner monsters, or repressed material in the unconscious.

Eclipses of the sun (intellect, rational thought) might relate more to waking life, while eclipses of the moon (intuition, the unconscious) might relate more to the unconscious or the shadow.

The end of an eclipse signifies a new beginning.

Eel. A phallic symbol, representing carnality or the penis. Eels also symbolize sperm, especially if swimming in cloudy, milky or salty water.

Other meaning: Slippery dangers lurking in the waters of the unconscious.

Egg. Genesis; beginnings. The egg, properly fertilized with the creative force and incubated, germinates new life. In a dream, this might be a new project, a new phase in life, or a new sense of self.

The egg is also a universal symbol of fertility. In mythology, the egg represents the primordial cosmos, the life principle, the undifferentiated totality, wholeness and the womb of the Mother Goddess. This cosmic egg is often represented by an egg entwined by a snake or ouroborous.

In alchemy, the egg is the *prima materia* from which the philosopher's stone is created. Its white color lends it the association of perfection.

As food, the egg is spiritual nourishment.

Other meanings: 1) Hope. 2) Resurrection.

Electricity. Energy, especially creative. The inner driving force.

Elevator. A confined and mechanical means of rising into the realm of the intellect and spirit, or of descending into the realm of emotions and the unconscious. Elevators are restricted to a certain number and places of stops; thus they present perhaps a more secure but very limited means of accessing different levels of the psyche. One sees nothing along the way. Elevators are, however, swift and direct.

An elevator moving from one floor to another represents a transition between states of consciousness or identity.

See **Stairs.**

Eleventh hour. Time running out; final moments. Dreams in which a clock reads 11:00 A.M. or (and especially) 11:00 P.M. sometimes symbolize fear of physical death. In some cases of serious or terminal illness, eleventh-hour dreams may appear prior to actual death. However, the eleventh hour should not be read as an irrevocable death omen. Most likely, it reflects stress and pressure, and the feeling that one is running out of time to accomplish all goals.

See **Time.**

Embroidery. Details, embellishments. The finishing touches, especially those requiring careful attention.

Embryo. See **Egg.**

Emerald. See **Jewels.**

Entrance. A common dream motif symbolizing the beginning of a transition in life. Note the type of entrance, whether to a house (the Self), a cave (the unconscious), or a tunnel (a constricted approach to the unconscious). If the entrance is closed off or locked, it might indicate difficulties in making the transition, or decisions yet to be made that will affect the transition. If the entrance is open, the transition has begun and progress may be hastened.

Eruption. A violent breakthrough of the unconscious into consciousness. A spewing of repressions.

Escalator. A variation of the elevator.
See **Elevator; Stairs.**

Evergreens. Immortality; the eternal, undying soul. Evergreens have funerary associations, as they are planted in cemeteries.
See **Cypress; Yew.**

Excrement. The power of a person, the essence of one's being. In many cultures, excrement is highly valued, and is associated with gold and riches. It is the fertilizer of new growth and beginnings.

In alchemy, excrement is the *nigredo*, which in dreams parallels the darkness of the unconscious from which enlightenment arises.

Executive/executive ability. The capacity to take risks, make decisions, and take actions. Executive ability is often expressed in dreams in the form of administrators, officials, managers, pilots, sailors, guards, explorers, caretakers and riders. Dreams with these images might indicate willingness or avoidance in terms of taking responsibility in one's own life.

Explosion. Something out of control; a destructive, unpredictable life-ravaging force.

Research has shown that dreams involving explosions also occur when individuals suffer from epilepsy; the explosions seem to mirror the effects of seizures.

Eye. An archetypal symbol with numerous meanings. The eye is the soul, the heart center, a symbol of the consciousness that resides within the unconscious.

In mythology, the eye is sacred. It is a solar symbol that provides access to heavenly realms. It symbolizes wisdom, knowledge, light, enlightenment, protection and stability. The Eye of God is wholeness, completeness and sovereignty. The Eye of Horus is the all-seeing eye of the mind and illumination. The third eye is the eye that looks within to seek transcendent wisdom. In Western mythology, the right eye represents the sun (enlightenment, the spirit) and the left eye the moon (intuition, the unconscious).

Eyes represent the Mother Goddess, especially her as-

Eye

pects of fertility, birth, death and rebirth. Eyes and related shapes—circles and spirals—decorated ancient goddess temples. Many-eyed deities are all-seeing and protective. Single eyes are the evil eye, which represents the shadow.

In dreams, eyes may also indicate how one sees things. Eyes that are blind, half-shut, crossed or otherwise vision-impaired may symbolize an inaccurate or partial view of one's world. Glasses may symbolize an aid to seeing things clearly; however, if the lenses are colored, perspective is filtered or skewed.

Eyeglasses. See **Glasses.**

Facelift. A superficial alteration that does not affect a core essence. Things appear to be different, but remain essentially unchanged. An attempt to cover up or fix a problem.

See **Make-up; Mask.**

Falcon. Sharpness of insight, solar consciousness, freedom, aspiration, ascension through all planes of consciousness.

See **Eagle.**

Falling. Feeling out of control, or being emotionally overwhelmed. Falling is a common nightmare motif that occurs during times of great upheaval and stress in life. Falling also is common during the last trimester of pregnancy, and anticipates the birthing process.

Falling into water indicates a need to immerse one's self in a healing in the unconscious. Falling through space or air, or falling to the ground, indicates a need to be grounded, to come back to earth (compare to **Flying**).

Other meaning: Lack of support.

Famous people. Dreaming of famous people and celebrities usually pertains to associations with their accomplishments, failures, personalities, skills, talents, qualities, and faults.

See **Names.**

Fan. Folding-fans are associated with the changing phases of the moon, and hence represent the feminine principle's instinct, imagination and intuition.

Waving a fan can mean a warding off of evil forces.

Other meanings: 1) The spirit. 2) The power of the air to infuse new life into the dead (spiritual rebirth, or a resuscitation of emotion, ambition or situation in life).

Far-sightedness. See **Glasses.**

Farmer. A nurturer, one who tends to the cycle of spiritual rebirth and regeneration of the vegetable soul (see **Vegetables**). Consider whether the farmer in the dream is tilling the soil or planting (preparing the way for change), is tending to growing crops (nurturing change), or is harvesting crops (completing a process or transition). Applications of fertilizer or treatments with pesticides may symbolize characteristics of the change. Crops withered or otherwise in poor condition might point to something that needs attention.

Fat. See **Obesity.**

Father. A father figure in dreams often represents authority, discipline, tradition, morals, law and order, will power and ambition. In myth, fathers are consciousness, the air and fire elements of intellect and spirit, and the opposite of the feminine principle's powers of instinct.

A father figure may also literally represent one's own father, or the father of someone known to the dreamer. Consider the personality traits, attitudes and behaviors of the individual, to which the dream may be bringing to attention.

Fan

Feather. A symbol of truth, wisdom, and of the soul. Feathers have the power and symbolism of birds. They represent the heavens and access to the heavens (the Higher Self), and the element of air (intellect).

To acquire or be given feathers may represent accomplishment.

See **Birds.**

Feces. See **Excrement.**

Fence. Barrier; territorial boundary. Fences confine, limit, and protect. To be on the fence is to avoid making a decision.

Fennel. A sacred plant with various associations. In herbal lore, fennel is held to strengthen vision; thus it is a symbol of spiritual clear-sightedness. In classical mythology, fennel is associated with Hermes, the trickster god of wisdom, magic and travel. It is also a symbol of sacred fire, for Prometheus carried the fire of the sun to earth in a fennel stalk. As a fire symbol, fennel has associations with illumination, purification and the *calcinatio* of alchemy, in which impurities are burned away.

In lore, fennel also allegedly causes snakes to molt, and thus represents the cycle of death and rebirth.

See **Vegetables.**

Field. The feminine principle. If plowed, the womb, especially the fertile womb. If not plowed, virginity and purity. Fields also symbolize the bounty of nature, and the grounding of one in the element of earth.

See **Earth, The.**

Fig. Eroticism; fertility; abundance. The fig is sacred to Dionysus, the Greek god who represents the living force of nature. The fig leaf represents the male generative principle, while the fruit represents the female principle and the Mother Goddess.

Other meaning: In Christianity, a fig tree is often a symbol for the Tree of Knowledge in the Garden of Eden, and thus is also a symbol of lust.

See **Fruits; Vegetables.**

Fight. Unresolved inner tensions. The dream is the result of a conflict usually between our conscious and unconscious selves. There is a part of ourself that we are ignoring and so it must fight for our attention. Conflict is the constant condition of life and we cannot attend to each one, but the dream is telling us that something that has been repressed is draining our inner resources and requires our conscious intervention. Hopefully the dream will give some clues about how to resolve the tension.

See **Battle, Quarrel, War.**

Fingers. Expressions of emotions and intent. Fingers in various positions convey a wide range of meanings. A finger pointing at someone can be an accusation or an insult; also, it is a widespread belief in folklore that a pointing finger carries magical power to effect the intent—good or evil—of the one who is pointing. A finger raised to the lips connotes silence or conveys a warning. The third finger raised has been an insult—especially a sexual insult—since classical times. The first and fourth finger raised is a gesture of protection against the evil eye, but is an insult if pointed at another person. The fingers clenched and the thumb thrust between the index and the middle finger also is a gesture of protection against the evil eye. Wagging fingers are accusatory or scolding. Beckoning fingers invite. Fingers raised upward with palms together (the benediction) are a symbol of spiritual power.

Fingers have been part of healing charms since antiquity. Healing deities cured by touch; consequently, the fingers are ascribed great regenerative, creative and medicinal powers.

Fire. Purification, transformation, transcendence, and illumination. Fire burns away all impurities, and reduces the old to ashes, from which arise the phoenix (new spiritual life), and in which is found the philosopher's stone (wholeness).

Fire

The alchemical process begins and ends with fire (*calcinatio*). Fire purges the blackness of the *nigredo* to white. The process is likened to a spiritual purgatory that can end with redemption.

Fire also represents passion, fecundity and sexual power. Like lightning, it impregnates, fuses and changes things from one state to another. Fire once was the chief method of sacrifice to the gods, and thus was considered the link between the mundane and the divine.

In ritual and in myth, fire often is equated with blood. Baptisms in both fire and blood signify an intense psy-

chological ordeal, which, if navigated successfully, will
end in refinement. Psychologically, fire dries up the watery
excesses of the unconscious.

Other meanings: 1) Handling fire may symbolize invul-
nerability to a situation. 2) Being consumed by fire may
symbolize vulnerability and loss rather than transformation.
3) Burning may symbolize punishment for sins and wrong-
doing, as in the fires of hell. 4) Ordeals by fire are a test
of purity, or a spiritual initiation. 5) Fire is a symbol of
divine wrath.

Fish, fishing. A fish is the content of the unconscious,
which in turn is symbolized by water. According to Jung,
fish especially represent the nourishing influences of the
unconscious contents, which require inputs of energy to
maintain vitality. Because of its ability to penetrate the
depths of its watery domain, the fish in a dream can represent penetration into one's own unconscious, in search of
truth. To fish is also a symbol of reaching down into one's
own psychic and spiritual depths.

Eating fish (see **Food**) is the taking in of spiritual nourishment.

Other meanings: 1) A symbol of fecundity because of
the large number of eggs fish produce. 2) A phallic symbol
because of its shape. 3) A symbol of the Mother Goddess,
because of its fecundity and its association with water. 4)
A symbol of Christ, and thus redemption and renewal.

Flames. See **Fire**.

Floating. A state of passivity and calm in the waters of
the unconscious; respite. Floating dreams also are common
during pregnancy.

Other meanings: 1) Hopefulness. 2) Buoyancy.

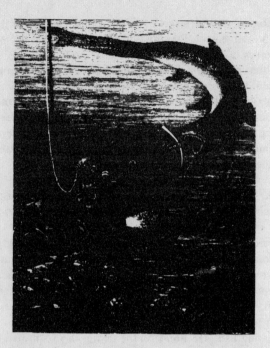

Fish

Flood. The destructive, overwhelming aspects of the unconscious; feeling out of control. Being consumed by a
flood often symbolizes the overwhelming emotions that accompany periods of great stress and upheaval in life.

A flood also symbolizes the end of an old phase in life,
in preparation for a new phase. In mythology, the flood
is a universal symbol for the death of the world (old
order) so that a new world can be born; it brings a spiritual
cleansing. The consuming waters carry both the power of
destruction and death and the power of fertilization and
birth.

See **Water; Waves.**

Flowers. Generally, flowers symbolize beauty, transience, the enjoyment of life and the receptive, feminine principle. Flowers also are an archetypal symbol of the soul or the mystic center, with petals forming rays that radiate outward. The alchemists called meteors, another symbol of the soul, "celestial flowers."

The opening of flower buds symbolizes potential and manifestation.

Individual flowers have their own symbolic meanings, uniquely related to their shapes and colors.

Other meanings: 1) Fragility, especially in relation to childhood. 2) Growth and flourishing.

See **individual listings for flowers.**

Fly. Dirt and dirtiness; associations with feeling unclean. The fly also is associated with sin, pestilence and corruption.

See **Insects.**

Flying. Dreams of flying are common, and usually symbolize inspiration and the ability to transcend ordinary reality. Flying means one is not stuck or limited. Problems and issues can be overcome by flying over them. A flying dream signals capability or readiness to act and make changes.

A dream in which one flies under one's own power may have more significance than a dream in which one flies in a public conveyance, such as an airplane or a helicopter. Gliders might indicate a particular freedom of movement. Fantastical flight, such as on a magic carpet or in a flying car, might indicate a wish for magical solutions.

Other meaning: Desire to escape from one's earthly problems.

Fog. Not being able to see a situation clearly. Feeling confused, lost, disoriented, uncertain. Since air is a symbol of intellect and rational thought, fog may also symbolize unclear thinking.

Other meaning: The primal substance of the world, the undifferentiated *prima materia*.

Food. We become what we eat. Cannibals hoped to increase their valor by eating their courageous opponents. Life is a process of digesting many experiences, so dreaming about food might indicate that certain experiences were being neglected or had not been assimilated properly. The dream is trying to compensate for our feeling of being undernourished, and it could be pointing to a physical, intellectual or spiritual need. The particular type of food in the dream might give some clue as to the particular need.

See **Eating, Indigestion; Vegetables.**

Foot. Mobility, balance, freedom of movement. Feet are essential to the support of the body; they are the foundation upon which one stands in the world. They represent taking steps in a direction in life, whether it be right or wrong.

The foot is a phallic symbol. Also, Jung saw it as confirmation of humankind's direct relationship with the earth. Thus, the foot grounds us to the material plane.

In addition, feet are a symbol of humility and reverence, from the practice of washing and kissing feet.

Bare feet signify a carefree attitude, or freedom from convention. Feet in painful shoes signify constrictions and limitations.

Footprints: Leaving one's mark. In mythology, footprints are signs of the way of the gods, of their divine visitations upon earth.

Footwear: Freedom from the bondage of slavery; liberation. In modern times, status symbols.

Forest. An archetypal symbol of the unconscious. Forests are vast, dark and mysterious, and harbor the unknown. It is easy to lose one's way in the forest.

The forest is the vegetative aspect of the unconscious: growth, life, primitive instinct, Mother Nature. Unlike the ocean, another great archetypal symbol of the unconscious, the forest has friendly aspects. It can offer protection and shelter; it can be smaller, more finite, more knowable. The ocean, on the other hand, is always wide open, uncertain, dangerous and without apparent limits.

See **Ocean; Vegetables.**

Fountain. The source of eternal life; the fecundating waters of life; the power of purification. Fountains are associated with the life-giving powers of the Mother Goddess. They also represent deep secrets and hidden sources within the unconscious.

Fox. Slyness; cunning; craftiness; deceit. In medieval times, the fox was a common symbol for the Devil, baseness and trickery on the part of enemies.

See **Animals.**

Frog. A symbol of fertility and eroticism. The frog's associations with water and rain make it a lunar animal (the moon is considered ruler of rains, tides and all waters), and therefore a companion to the Mother Goddess. In this regard, the frog represents resurrection and the ongoing cycle of birth, death and rebirth. It also represents forces in the waters of the unconscious.

See **Animals; Moon.**

Fruits. Generally, fruits are transcendental symbols. They represent the abundance of nature (and thus of the Mother

Goddess), fertility, prosperity, immortality, self-knowledge, and spiritual essence.

First fruits are the best and are those which are sacrificed. Christ is a first fruit. First fruits also are offered in rites to the dead, and thus have links to the underworld, or the unconscious.

Forbidden fruits, such as apples, cherries and grapes, are symbols of temptation, earthly desires and sin.

Other meaning: The source of All.

See **individual entries for fruits;** also **Vegetables.**

G

Games. Depending on context, games in dreams can represent playfulness, relaxation or competition. They may relate to a specific situation or relationship, or to the broader picture of life. Factors that should be taken into consideration include the type of game being played (one-on-one or group sports); one's attitude toward the game (enthusiasm, reluctance to play, enjoyment, anxiety); one's skill; and the outcome (win or lose).

Garbage. The raw material of spiritual transformation. The stink and rot of detritus and garbage is, in an alchemical sense, part of the great work—the decay that must occur before rebirth can take place; the darkness of the soul that precedes the light of spiritual illumination. From the refuse of life comes fertilizing power for change and new growth.

Garden. The soul; paradise on earth and in heaven. Gardens—especially those filled with flowers—symbolize the ideal, blissful state of being, an attainment of spiritual enlightenment. The fertility and bounty of the garden indicate the state of the soul. A garden in bloom and beauty means spiritual growth has taken place or is occurring. Withering or dead flowers in a garden mean there are spiritual matters in need of attention.

Gardens also symbolize a refuge, a place where one can be safe and at peace.

Gardens filled with vegetables and fruits rather than flowers symbolize the vegetable soul of humanity—its roots to the earth and the unconscious.

Gardens appearing in the dreams of terminally ill persons represent heaven and are a symbol of transition from earthly life to the afterlife. In Greek myth, the Elysian Fields—a garden for the souls of the dead—are planted with vines and roses to symbolize immortality.

Other meaning: An enclosed garden represents virginity or the Virgin Mary.

See **Flowers; Vegetables.**

Gardener. One who tends to the psyche on a vegetative level, that is, in terms of the vegetable soul (see **Vegetables**). The gardener is a caretaker, facilitating growth, removing decay and debris, keeping out unwanted growth such as weeds. This figure represents work taking place on a deep level of the unconscious.

Garnet. See **Jewels.**

Gate. The threshold of passage, such as from one phase of life to another, from the old to the new, or from one spiritual level to another. Gates also symbolize entry to levels of consciousness, such as to the unconscious (often represented by a gate to inner earth) or the Higher Self (a gate to the sky, heaven or bright light). Gates indicate the opening or closing of communication between levels of consciousness.

In mythology, gates between the worlds are guarded by various animals or fabulous monsters, such as the three-headed dog, Cerberus, who guards the gate of Hades. The purpose of such beings is to prevent the uninitiated from entering. Similarly, gates in dreams may be guarded by animals or monsters. Dogs, dragons and winged beasts are common guards, and may symbolize challenges associated with the transition.

See **Door.**

Gatherings. See **Groups.**

Gems. See **Jewels.**

Ghost. The spirit or essence of life.

Other meanings: 1) Something that belongs in the past. 2) Something that can be perceived only by certain persons, and otherwise goes unnoticed. 3) Memories.

Giant. Overpowering, primordial force; forces that are out of control. Giants often represent obstacles that appear insurmountable or larger than life; they also may represent any aspect of life, or a situation, that seems to be out of hand. Typically, they represent the dark side or the unconscious. Giants can be either beneficent or malevolent; in mythology they are usually portrayed as forces of nature (matter, the body) which are the enemies of the gods (spirit, intellect).

Gift. A blessing bestowed upon one. What is the gift, who is giving it, and why?

Glasses. A function of the ego that enables one to see the world, or see it better. Glasses correct near-sightedness (not being able to see things on a grand scale) or far-sightedness (not being able to see what is in front of you). Colored glasses indicate emotional qualities.

See **Eye; Colors.**

Globe. A symbol of wholeness; self-containment. It also represents the world, or the potential that lies beyond one's own environment. Globes also symbolize sovereignty and dominion. In a dream, this might mean rule over one's own world.

Gloves. Law and order; authority; chivalry; civility.

Gloves in dreams have different shades of meaning, depending upon other factors present. Generally, gloves protect and provide warmth; they also prevent direct contact with a person, object or substance. White gloves signify purity, purity of heart, and dignity. Work gloves may be associated with fear of "getting dirty," or with an unpleasant task at hand. Children's gloves or mittens may be associated with something from childhood. Kid, suede or fine leather gloves may be associated with the need to treat something gently.

Taking gloves off may represent aggressive behavior.

See **Clothing.**

Goat. Fertility; vitality; creative energy; unbridled sexual powers. In Greek myth, the goat is sacred to Dionysus, and thus is associated with the ecstasy of nature. In Christian symbolism, the goat is particularly associated with lust and sin, and demonic powers.

See **Animals.**

Gold. See **Colors.**

Goose. Fertility; love; marital fidelity. The goose's laying of eggs gives it the symbolism of primal creator and the Mother Goddess.

Geese also are symbols of agricultural domesticity and humankind's ties to the earth (matter, the body, the physical plane).

Grains

Like other birds—the swan in particular—the goose is a messenger from the spirit world.

See **Birds; Swan.**

Grains. In general, the cycle of birth, death and rebirth; fertility; abundance; prosperity.

See **Corn; Rice; Vegetables; Wheat.**

Grandmother. A caretaker figure or guardian. In her good aspect, the grandmother is associated with warmth, nurturing and happy feelings, perhaps reminiscent of childhood. In her negative or shadow aspect, she may be evil, malevolent and hurtful.

In myth, the Grandmother or Great Mother figure represents the goddess of individual fate. Thus, in a dream such a figure may symbolize an important change or transition, or a momentous event about to happen.

Any woman with white hair in a dream usually is a grandmother figure.

A grandmother figure may also represent a real person. Consider the personality traits, attitudes and behavior of the individual, and how they might apply to the dream's message.

Grapes. Wisdom; truth. Also, fertility, abundance, life and the cycle of renewal of life. In classical myth, grapes and wine are associated with Dionysus and Bacchus, gods of vegetation and nature who preside over eternal life and the ecstasies of life. In dreams, grapes may represent one's harvesting of the bounties of life, or reaping the intoxicating fruits of one's labors.

Wine grapes are associated with sacrifice and the blood of Christ.

See **Fruits; Wine.**

Grass. Submission to others, or allowing oneself to be walked on. Being taken for granted.

Other meaning: Ability to bend and be flexible.

Grave. The past that is "dead and buried." Also, thoughts of death, and the dying of something to the world. Spiritual withdrawal.

In alchemy, the grave is a symbol of the *nigredo*, the blackening phase that represents the death and destruction of the old in order to make way for new spiritual growth.

See **Death.**

Green. See **Color.**

Grocery store. A place where one can get all the food (spiritual nourishment) one wants or needs.

Grotesqueness. Dreams involving grotesque human beings often are symbols of anxieties. For example, prior to a wedding, a person may dream that his or her partner suddenly appears grotesque. This may reflect natural anxieties that a person has made the right choice in marriage. Prior to birth, the prospective mother or father may dream of a monstrous birth, which reflects natural concerns that the baby will be born without defect.

Grotesqueness also symbolizes a repressed or unexplored facet of the dreamer's own personality. Such a dream acts as a mirror, forcing the dreamer to look inward.

Groups. Racial, ethnic, national and cultural groups in dreams often represent qualities, attributes and character-

Gymnastics

istics the dreamer associates with those groups. Collective associations can be personified by a single individual in a dream.

Other meanings: 1) Groups of people symbolize collective opinion, action or influence. 2) Groups can symbolize the collective unconscious.

Gymnastics. Exuberance, liberation, freedom, emotional expression. A sense of being a child or child-like; a return to the freedom of childhood. Gymnastics is a holistic experience, connecting body and emotions.

See **Dancing.**

H

Hair. Strength, vitality, the life-force; virility. Hair also represents thought, mind and intellect.

Hair in various states and lengths carries different meanings. Loose hair is freedom, while bound hair is submission. Long hair on men is strength, as in the story of Samson and Delilah. Long hair on women, if loose, may be virginity or whoredom. Long wild hair, or hair entangled with serpents, is a symbol of the destructive power of the Mother Goddess. Disheveled hair is a symbol of grief. Hair standing on end symbolizes fear, or divine possession. To cut hair is to renounce physical powers or civilization, as in the tonsures of monks; it is also the loss of virility and strength, as in Delilah's shearing of Samson's hair.

Body hair represents bestiality, or animal-like powers or characteristics.

The color of hair may also have significance.

See **Colors.**

Hallway. A connection or route to the unconscious; a means of exploring the psyche (symbolized by a house).

Dark, constricting hallways are symbols of the physical birthing process, and often occur in dreams during pregnancy, especially the last trimester. On a spiritual level, hallways may represent the birthing or emergence of a new aspect of the Self.

Other meaning: Narrow, limited choices.
See **House; Maze; Tunnel.**

Hammer. The masculine, creative/destructive force of nature. In mythology, gods of thunder and lightning forged their lightning bolts with hammers and anvils. The hammer is the most important of three possessions of the mighty Norse thunder god, Thor, who hurls his hammer to smash the skulls of enemies. The Greco-Roman thunder god, Vulcan (Hephaestos) is the architect and artist of all work on Olympus, the abode of the gods. In addition to creating thunder and lightning, he forges chariots, golden horseshoes, brass houses and other objects owned by the gods.

The creative power of the hammer also has feminine aspects, in that thunder and lightning bring life-giving rain. The double hammer is similar to the Tau cross, a symbol of regeneration and the Tree of Life.

Other meanings: 1) Justice and vengeance. 2) A practical working tool used both to build and to tear apart or crush. 3) A forcible means of insertion. A hammer, or hammering, in a dream could symbolize an effort to make something fit or to acknowledge (integrate) something.

See **Cross; Lightning; Thunder.**

Hands. Perhaps the most expressive part of the body, especially of emotions and actions. There is little thought or feeling that cannot be expressed solely with the hands.

In occultism, the hand is often a symbol of strength, authority and power, a meaning perhaps dating from the ancient Egyptians, whose glyph for the hand also related to pillar and palm. An eye associated with a hand—in a dream, this might be represented by a hand pointing to an eye—means clairvoyance, or a wise, all-seeing vision. Hands in various gestures, such as fist clenched with thumb protruding through the index and middle fingers, are ancient

Hands

and universal amulets against evil and the evil eye. See
Fingers.

The hand of God, or divine power or intervention, is
often represented by a hand of light reaching down through
clouds. The gods of antiquity healed by touch; thus, the
hand is considered to possess great healing and regenerative
power.

Generally, the right hand is the hand of power that gives,
transfers and confers, while the left hand is the hand of
receptivity and submission. The left hand also is associated
with dishonesty and cheating. In alchemy, the right hand
signifies the masculine principle and rational, conscious

thought, and the left hand signifies the feminine principle and intuitive, unconscious thought. Thus clasped hands in alchemy symbolize the mystic marriage of opposites to create wholeness and completeness, also the communication between the conscious and unconscious. On a mundane level, clasped hands symbolize bonds between persons, e.g., marriage and fidelity.

Other meanings of hand positions include:

Shaking, offering, and clasped: friendship, devotion, forgiveness.

Open or palms turned up: receptivity, especially in terms of prayer and divine blessings.

Raised: worship, amazement.

Raised with palms out: blessing, favor, healing.

Raised or folded: submission, surrender.

Raised to mouth: silence, caution, warning.

Raised to head: thought.

Outstretched: welcoming, protection.

Outstretched with palms raised outward: warding off.

Closed: unwillingness, secrets.

Clenched: aggression.

Caressing: love, concern, tenderness.

Laying on of hands: healing, transfer of power or authority, benediction.

Clapping: approval.

The condition of hands also carries symbolic meaning. Soft hands may represent gentleness to or care of one's physical self. Rough hands may indicate neglect, or inconsiderate treatment of others. Excessively hairy hands have bestial associations. See **Animals**. Dirty hands symbolize hard work, or an unpleasant task or matter. Clean hands represent purity. Washing one's hands represents letting go or getting rid of something. See **Washing.**

Empty hands symbolize lack, loneliness, failure or emptiness, while full hands symbolize bounty, plenty and success.

Hands also symbolize one's creativity and action in the material world—one's deeds and accomplishments.

See **Gloves; Left hand; Right hand.**

Harbor. A safe port from emotions (water). A resting place for reassessment.

Hare. Fertility, rebirth and the female principle. Because of its female attributes and its nocturnal habits, the hare has an almost universal association with the moon. In turn, the moon is associated with the Goddess and intuition. Thus, the hare can symbolize transformation and leaps of intuition.

The magician pulling a rabbit out of a hat is an association that can be traced to Africa, where the hare is a trickster animal, and to ancient Egypt where it represented the transformation and trickster aspects of Thoth/Hermes/Mercury.

The March Hare symbolizes madness.

See **Animals.**

Hat. One's mental outlook, attitudes or opinions. Hats cover or enclose an individual's reality. The act of changing hats in a dream represents new thoughts or opinions—a change of consciousness.

As an article of clothing, hats also can be interpreted as representative of how one dresses the ego or personality. It could also signify an attitude or idea that fits comfortably with one's current state of mind.

Other meanings: 1) A collection of ideas into a single source. 2) A mandala.

Hawk. Like the eagle, the high-flying hawk is a symbol of royalty (and thus authority, sovereignty and power) and the sun (illumination). Like all birds, it is a messenger to the gods.

Other meanings: 1) Predation. 2) Sharp vision. 3) Transcendence. 4) Freedom.

See **Birds; Eagle.**

Head. The base of the spirit and the vital force. It symbolizes wisdom, genius and rational thought, and is a symbol of the world, the cosmos and Oneness.

Heads represent fertility, and when associated with pillars or poles, are phallic symbols. Winged heads signify supernatural wisdom. To lose one's head or to be beheaded in a dream may symbolize a loss of reason.

A two-headed person or beast symbolizes the duality of nature and the union of opposites. A three-headed person or beast has various meanings, such as the triple nature of the Mother Goddess (Virgin, Matron and Crone); the eternal cycle of birth, death and rebirth; past, present, and future; and heaven, earth, and the underworld.

Other meanings: 1) Cleverness. 2) Common sense. 3) Attitudes.

Heart. Love, especially of a mystical or spiritual nature; the mystic center; the temple of God. The heart has been widely believed since ancient times to be the seat of the soul, the seat of intelligence, and the locus of all emotion and of will.

The sun (illumination) is a symbol of the heart, and, conversely, in alchemy the heart is the sun within the person.

A heart surmounted by flames, a cross, a crown or a fleur-de-lis symbolizes love as the center of illumination and happiness. A flaming inverted heart symbolizes transcendent wisdom, and religious devotion.

Hearts also may be associated with the keeping of secrets, or with the vital life-force (see **Blood**), or with bonds to others. A bleeding heart symbolizes emotional wounds. Heart surgery indicates an emotional healing process taking

Heart

place, or the need to address an emotional issue.

Other meanings: 1) Romantic love. 2) Friendship. 3) Courage or resolve.

Hearth. Home; safety; security; the family unit; domestic affairs and duties. The protection and nurturing of mother and the Mother Goddess.

In mythology, the hearth is akin to the navel: a sacred center. It is especially an omphalos, or center of the earth. The hearth also represents one's inner spiritual center.

Heel. See **Foot.**

Hell. A common dream symbol of the *calcinatio* phase of alchemy, in which impurities are burned away. In a dream hell, the dreamer is being subjected to his or her own fire, from which there is no light and no escape until the *calcinatio* is complete.

Other meanings: 1) Lack of growth. 2) Being trapped by one's own boundaries.

See **Fire.**

Helmet. Strength and protection, especially in the context of a warrior or a hero's journey. In mythology, magical helmets confer supernormal powers to the wearer, such as invincibility or invisibility. Helmet decorations, such as shapes, feathers or horns, have additional symbolic meanings.

See **Hat.**

Hen. Maternal care and nurturing; the safety of a nest.

Other meanings: 1) Picking at or being picked at in an irritating fashion. 2) Gossip, meddling.

See **Animals.**

Hill. An obstacle to any goal. Consider the steepness of a hill and whether it can be traversed by a path, or must be navigated by hacking out a new path. Hills of brushy growth, woods and forest represent uncharted lands of the unconscious.

Conversely, a hill also may represent a small ambition, something to be achieved by climbing.

See **Mountain.**

Hive. Collective industry and enterprise; an ordered community. Individuality is submerged in the collective society in a hive.

Beehives in particular are symbols of the womb, motherhood and the feminine earth soul, and of immortality, because of their tomb-like shape.

Hole. An opening to other worlds, particularly the unconscious. Falling into a hole symbolizes a sudden drop into the unconscious to face matters needing conscious attention. Holes can also access heaven (the Higher Self).

Universally, holes are symbols of the vulva, and thus are ascribed powerful fertilizing and healing properties. A holed stone is believed to be a fertility talisman, and crawling through the hole of a megalith is believed to bring both fertility and healing of illness.

Holes also symbolize an inner emptiness, or errors or pitfalls in one's life.

Holocaust. Often a symbol of a whole burnt offering; a sacrifice that is totally consumed by flames.

See **Fire**.

Holly. Health and happiness. Also, a symbol of Christ, because of its thorns and red berries.

Since holly is a primary decoration of the Christmas season, its appearance in a dream may relate to things associated with Christmas—childhood, emotions, certain events, home and family, special memories.

Home. Security, shelter and safety. The home represents protection from the ills and troubles encountered in the world. At home, one can let down one's guard and behave as one chooses. One may have child-like feelings of a desire to be nurtured.

Leaving home symbolizes independence, striking out on one's own, assuming risks and responsibilities. Staying at home may represent a withdrawal from the world, a reluctance to face up to problems and difficult situations. However, escape is only temporary, for one must leave home again at some point. Discovering new rooms at home indicates growth or new aspects of personality that are opening up.

See **House; Room.**

Homeland. Dreams of returning to a homeland often occur to immigrants undergoing the stresses of adjusting to life in a new country. Like the home, the homeland symbolizes safety and security. It is the place where surroundings are familiar and life is predictable. Depending on the culture, it is either the "motherland" or the "fatherland," and, like mother or father, a parental figure that promises well-being.

Honey. Sweetness; eloquence; the divine word; food for the gods. Honey is also a symbol of wisdom, purity and immortality (see **Hive**).

Honey is associated with prophecy. The classical gods and supernatural beings of prophecy, and the great oracles, were propitiated with honey and honey cakes. Not to offer honey meant one risked hearing lies in return.

Honey in a dream may also relate to behavior or words. Too much honey implies insincerity.

Hood. Withdrawal; passing away. Hooded figures are associated with Death in mythology. Thus a hood may symbolize death of an old phase of life, or the passing of influences.

Other meaning: Something that is hidden from view.

Horns. A dilemma; aggression.

In mythology, horns are attributes of the Mother Goddess and are associated with the crescent moon. Thus, they represent fertility, and the increase and wane of life. Horns also represent the masculine principle, virility and the vital lifeforce. Horns are associated with numerous gods, especially of vegetation and nature. A single horn is a phallic symbol. The horn of plenty symbolizes abundance, especially of nature.

Horns also are symbols of sovereign and supernatural power when worn on helmets and headdresses. They are

Horse

amulets against the forces of evil. In Christianity, horns are
the sign of the Devil.

Horse. An archetypal symbol usually representing the human body in dreams. In mythology and folklore, the horse
signifies mankind's base animal nature, instinct, nonhuman
psyche and the unconscious. Thus, the horse symbolizes the
instinctive, animal life within the body. Dreams in which a
horse suffers injury or destroys itself may be an early warning of life-threatening disease. Jung and others relate cases
of patients dreaming of horses leaping to their deaths off
cliffs and out of high house windows. The patients subsequently were found to have cancer. This early warning
symbolism finds corroboration in folklore. According to
German and English lore, to dream of a white horse is an
omen of death (the Celtic goddess, Epona, whose associations included death and graves, sometimes takes the form
of a white mare). In legends and folktale, magical or clairvoyant horses must give timely warnings to their masters.

In ancient mythologies, the horse is a solar symbol, and
represents the dynamic power of the sun moving through

the heavens. In Greek myth, horses draw Phaethon's sun chariot through the sky. See **Sun**. The Greeks and Romans also related the horse to thunder, wind, war, water, fertility, and death and burial customs. The horses whipped up out of the depths of the ocean by Poseidon may be seen as wild creatures rising up from the unconscious mind. Wild horses or black horses in a dream may symbolize uncontrollable or unruly instinctive drives. See **Water**.

The Bible (Jeremiah 5:8) and Renaissance art portray the horse as a symbol of lust.

The horse as beast of burden bears close relationship to the mother archetype, a symbol for life at its origin. Jung said the horse is ''the mother within us,'' our intuitive and magical nature. See **Mother**. In myth, fairy tale and legend, horses often are ascribed clairvoyant and divination powers.

The magical power of flight turns the horse into a vehicle for consciousness. In Greek myth, the winged horse, Pegasus, aids Bellerophon in his heroic trials, including the slaying of the monster Chimaera, a symbol of animal nature and perversion. However, when Bellerophon seeks to fly to Olympus to take his place among the gods, Pegasus throws him off; there are limits to the ascent of human consciousness. In Islamic myth, the winged mare, Buraq, flies the Muslim prophet, Muhammad, through the celestial spheres. In various shamanic cultures, the horse carries the shaman on his mystical ascent to heaven. The shamanic horse also is a symbol of death or the carrier of souls of the dead to the underworld. In Teutonic mythology, Odin's eight-legged shamanic horse, Sleipnir, which is half horse and half god, takes Odin on a mission to the underworld.

Horseshoe. Good luck and protection against evil, misfortune, bewitchment and illness. The horseshoe is an aspect of the magical nature attributed to horses in myth and folktale.

Horse's hoof. A phallic symbol, representing creative energy, fertility and healing power.

Hospital. A symbol of life passages; a mother figure where birth and death occur; a place of spiritual recuperation and healing. Hospitals also may be symbols of physical health and thus point to health problems.

Other meanings: 1) Service to others. 2) Sterility. 3) Rules and regulations.

Hotel. Transience, a temporary state, a phase of activity or of life. Hotels are collective symbols and are impersonal. They represent a temporary resting place during spiritual or psychic transitions.

Hourglass. The passage of time and the transitoriness of life. Also, the impending death (end) of a cycle. Turning over an hourglass represents the end of a phase and the beginning of something new.

House. The total psyche, the dwelling place of the soul. The rooms in a house are compartments or layers of the psyche. The upstairs represents the head and mind and related such attributes as logic, will and self-control. The kitchen represents the alchemical process of transmutation; bedrooms are sexual matters; and basements are the unconscious. The exterior of a house is the persona, the appearance one presents to the world. The roof symbolizes the Higher Self or spirit. Doors are barriers to discovery and change, or protection from the unknown. Mysterious, closed rooms that seem to hold monsters or something terrifying may be alerting the dreamer of the need to face a problem or situation and resolve it.

The condition, cleanliness, furnishings and activity in rooms indicate various psychological states. Construction,

House

decoration, industry and maintenance of a house, or a room in a house, indicate a positive psychological state. Houses or rooms that are cold, empty, dirty, tightly locked and having no windows open to let in fresh air reflect a negative psychological state. The particular conditions of a house in a dream may contain clues for courses of action.

Finding new rooms in a house or moving to a bigger, nicer house reflect changes and growth occurring in the inner life. Building a house or entering a new house indicates the emergence of new ego space.

Empty rooms, or rooms filled with cobwebs, are symbols

Hunter

of emotional loss, such as separation or divorce, or one's children leaving home.

Other meaning: A mystical symbolism as the feminine aspect of the universe and as the repository of wisdom.

See **Home; Room**.

Hunter, hunting. Pursuit of material gain; striving for goals. Competition, aggression. Victory over one's animal nature.

The hunter and hunting also are symbols of impending death, or the end of an old phase of life. The Wild Hunt in mythology is a spectral procession of the denizens of the underworld, led by chthonic deities, giving the hunt associations with the unconscious. Herne the Hunter is a spectral huntsman of the wood (the unconscious), and various spectral hunting hounds also populate myth and folktale.

Other meaning: The search to satisfy insatiable desires.

Hurricane. See **Storm**.

I

Ice. Frozen emotions (the waters of the unconscious). Ice represents the absence of love (a cold heart) and rigidity. It is the hard barrier between the conscious and unconscious; it must melt for communication between the two to take place.

Ice, especially as icicles, also symbolizes repressed sexuality.

Thawing ice indicates a release or movement of feeling, or resolution of fears or inhibitions.

Skiing, skating or walking on ice indicates superficial acknowledgment of an emotional block. Thick ice means a great deal of work needs to be done on an emotional issue. Thin ice signifies an impending potential emotional breakthrough. Falling through ice is an immersion in the unconscious, and a release of emotion.

See **Snow; Water.**

Iceberg. A small protrusion of the unconscious into the conscious; a much larger matter or issue lies below in the unconscious, awaiting discovery.

Identification. Driver's licenses, passports and other forms of identification symbolize who you are in the world. Loss of identification indicates confusion or negative feelings concerning self-image or self-esteem; fear of a change in

Illness

identity, or a loss of connection to one's familial, cultural or religious roots. The same may be said for the inability to travel or act because of lack of identification. Acquiring new identification, especially a passport, parallels feelings of new or renewed self-confidence. Purses and wallets also may be forms of identification, but are not as universal as passports.

Illness. Although dreams of illness may depict or portend an actual situation, more commonly they are directing attention to the body as the container of the soul. Psychosomatics tells us of the relations between the mind and the body, especially how mental disturbance can give rise to physical symptoms. For instance, it is often in the gut that emotions are felt. A respiratory problem in a dream may reflect upon our spiritual well-being.

Dreams during an illness may point to areas of unconscious conflict or stress that are contributing to the illness.

See **Body, body parts.**

Immersion. See **Baptism.**

Immobility. Inability or unwillingness to resolve a situation. Inflexibility, impassiveness. Immobility also can symbolize a vegetative state.
See **Paralysis; Vegetables.**

Imprisonment. See **Prison.**

Indigestion. Indigestion, and also nausea, symbolize the inability to accept something; an adverse reaction of one's gut instincts (intuition). Indigestion in dreams also may be due to genuine indigestion experienced during sleep.
See **Vomiting.**

Infidelity. Dreams in which you or your partner have extra-marital relationships typically mirror anxieties concerning sex, commitment and health of relationships in life. Such dreams occur prior to marriage, or during times of stress when one feels estranged from a partner, or fears infidelity. These dream images point to a need to confront feelings and issues and resolve them.
Not all dreams of infidelity have overt sexual meaning.
See **Sex and sexuality.**

Initiation. Entry into a new phase of life, which could concern anything of significance to the individual, such as a change of job, home or relationship, or a spiritual transformation. Initiations are characterized by a ''descent into hell,'' an overcoming of inner darkness that must take place before rebirth can occur. Initiation dreams may reflect various stages of the process of change, such as struggle and turmoil, the battle with obstacles, or the end result of the new.
Initiation dreams often are marked by rites and ceremo-

nies; the bestowal of a gift; acquisition of an object with symbolic meaning; dismemberment, death and destruction (which represent the passing of the old life); birth; descent into the underground; ascent into the sky or heaven; lightning strikes; a change of wardrobe or clothing; transit across a bridge; and wounds and bites caused by such animals as a snake (a symbol of wisdom and renewal).

Persons who appear in initiation dreams are likely to represent archetypes, such as the wise old man or wise old woman; mother or father; hero or heroine; or healer. These figures are forces coming into play in the transition from one phase to another.

Initiation dreams may be confirmation of a change that has already taken place in life, or may be indications of a change taking place within the consciousness.

Insects. Fear, revulsion and dirt. Collectively, humankind reviles insects, and fears their ability to penetrate our lives either singly or en masse. Insect dreams are "pay attention" dreams. Things or places which are infested with insects indicate areas of the psyche that have been neglected. Such areas do not wither, but become twisted—bug-infested, so to speak, a projection of our fear or revulsion toward that inner part which is not being expressed or acknowledged.

In dreams, insects often are associated with emotional and sexual matters.

Insects also are like the many little worries that can pester us. Or, they may be busily trying to help us sort out the details when our affairs become hopelessly complex.

Insects may be eating away at our foundations, or indicate a corruption behind a facade.

Swarms of insects are at once fascinating and repulsive. As children, we were often captivated by insect behavior. They may remind us of the many subliminal promptings of our unconscious mental activities and instincts that we may perceive as a collective threat to our personal identity.

The bug-eyed monsters of science fiction reinforce the image of the insect as a totally alien life form. They signify that our psyches, in the dream state, may wander into realms far beyond human understanding.

In some mythologies and in Darwinism, insects are the primordial creatures, and can signify the beginnings of things.

Jackal. Scavenging animal associated with death, such as represented by the jackal-headed Egyptian god of death, Anubis. The jackal is a psychopomp that leads souls to the land of the dead. In a dream, it may be a symbol of transformation; specifically, the death of the old that precedes birth of the new.

Jackals are creatures of the night, and as such represent the dark forces of the unconscious. They represent animal traits, and may be a symbol of dark and destructive forces and a scavenging nature.

See **Animals.**

Jade. See **Jewels.**

Jail. See **Prison.**

Jaguar. A chthonic animal associated in myth with the underworld and the powers of the moon, and thus with the Mother Goddess. Natives of Central America regard the jaguar as a psychopomp, a guider of souls, or as a messenger god of the forest spirits. Jaguars also can be a shape assumed by some shamans.

A jaguar in a dream may represent certain animal qualities or attributes, such as speed, stealth, power, sleekness, predation, and various characteristics of the cat family.

See **Animals; Cat.**

Jar. A feminine symbol that can represent either death (the grave, the urn) or birth (the womb). A jar may also represent a receptacle (and thus the receiving of or containment of) feminine qualities and attributes.

Other meaning: Storage.

See **Cup.**

Jaws. Jaws, especially of a monster or large animal, represent the gates to the underworld, to being devoured by the unconscious. Jaws may be likened to gates, passage points that must be negotiated in a trial or transformation.

Other meaning: Something overwhelming in life that threatens to consume.

Jewels. Spiritual truths and wisdom; the reflection of divine light. The searching for jewels represents a spiritual quest. To possess jewels is to possess knowledge and enlightenment. The cutting of jewels represents refinement of the soul-in-the-rough through knowledge and wisdom.

Jewels in caves guarded by dragons or serpents represent intuitive wisdom buried deep within the unconscious. Jewels in crowns and necklaces represent the wisdom of the Higher Self. Jewels worn by royalty, especially women, and jewels kept hidden in secret rooms represent superior wisdom.

In occult lore, jewels are ascribed various protective, curative and magical properties.

In their negative aspect, jewels symbolize the material, greed for riches, and profane love.

Symbolic meanings of some specific jewels are:

Amber. A symbol of the sun (spiritual illumination and intellect) and immortality.

Amethyst. An ancient remedy for drunkenness, and thus

a symbol of sobriety, clear-headedness and peace of mind. Amethyst also is associated with enhanced psychic powers.

Aquamarine. Health, youthfulness.

Carnelian. Blood, the flesh or sexual desire; also, blood bonds, as in family ties and close friendships.

Crystal. Purity, clarity.

Diamond. Spirit, purity, clarity. Something that is inde-structible and of lasting value. Like the philosopher's stone of alchemy, the diamond also represents the union of op-posites—of spirit and matter—that results in a wholeness of consciousness.

Emerald. A symbol of the Mother Goddess, especially in her vegetation aspect; the renewal of the Earth; immor-tality. Emeralds also symbolize mystical wisdom. Accord-ing to lore, Hermes Trismegistus, the mythical author of the Hermetica, inscribed the axiom of Western occultism, ''That which is above is like that which is below,'' on an Emerald Tablet. According to Biblical lore, the emerald was one of four stones given by God to Solomon. In me-dieval times, it was believed that the Holy Grail was carved from an emerald that fell from Lucifer's crown as he was cast out of heaven by God.

Garnet. Devotion and loyalty.

Jade. The soul; also, the vital generative force of the universe. Green jade is associated with the vegetative force of nature.

Jet. Black amber, widely believed to protect against evil and harmful influences. It once was a symbol of mourning.

Lapis lazuli. A stone sacred to the Mother Goddess and also the Blessed Virgin Mary. The thrones of God and Ho-rus are said to be made of lapis lazuli. Because of these great sacred associations, lapis lazuli is believed to enhance spiritual qualities and inspiration, and bestow divine favor.

Malachite. A stone reputed to possess great magical and protective powers. Russian legend holds that drinking from a malachite cup enables one to understand the language of animals. The deep and variegated green color of malachite also lend associations with the vegetative force of nature.

Moonstone. The Greeks associated moonstone with the lunar goddesses Aphrodite and Selene; thus the stone represents the unconscious, intuition and emotion. Moonstone often is associated with romantic love and tenderness.

Onyx. Spiritual strength.

Opal. The ancient Romans believed opals bestowed the powers of foresight and prophecy. In medieval times, opals conferred invisibility, according to lore. Opals also are associated with prayer and religious devotion.

Pearl. The feminine principle. Pearls once were sacred to the Mother Goddess; ''pearls of wisdom'' were given out by Aphrodite Marina through her priestesses. As late as the Renaissance, it was believed that pearls were formed by an interaction between the sea and the moon, thus giving them associations with lunar forces of intuition, emotion and the unconscious.

Peridot. Thunderbolts, or spiritual illumination.

Ruby. Blood, passion, life and longevity.

Sapphire. Truth and the values of heaven, and thus protection against bewitchment, the evil eye, sorcery and all manner of negative influences. Pope Innocent III ordered all bishops to wear sapphire rings in order to resist ''inharmonious influences.''

Topaz. Friendship and faithfulness. Also, a symbol of the sun (illumination).

Turquoise. Good luck, success.

Zircon. Knowledge, high ideals, respect, honor.

Jewelry. See **Valuables.**

Job. One's role or duty. What one does to get by in the world, or to make a mark in the world, depending on context. Changing jobs or losing a job may symbolize a major transition phase in life that concerns self-definition and self-image.

Journey. Development of the soul; a spiritual quest; the search for truth and progress of life. Journeys may represent an initiatory experience, such as transition from one phase of life to another, or from one relationship or activity to another. The heroic journey, involving purification of the soul, typically is fraught with obstacles and dangers.

From a spiritual perspective, the true purpose of a journey is not transit from point A to point B, but self-discovery and enlightenment.

A journey across the sea is navigation of the waters of the unconscious. Mountainous terrain symbolizes intellect, while desert is the spirit. The presence or absence of paths, and whether they are clear or obstructed, may indicate sense of direction and purpose, and progress or lack thereof. A journey in which one wanders or becomes lost may indicate confusion or uncertainty about something in life. The mode of travel also has symbolic significance, such as travel by foot, by animal, by car, boat or airplane, etc. (see appropriate individual listings).

Juice. Like sap and blood, the life-force, especially of the vegetable soul.

See **Vegetables.**

K

Key. A solution to a problem; a means of accessing different layers of consciousness.

In mythology, keys are symbols of initiation into spiritual mysteries. They have the power to open knowledge and wisdom, to let in illumination and enlightenment. Keys are the emblems of the guardians both of heaven (the Higher Self) and of hell (the underworld or unconscious).

Keys also close and shut down: using keys in a dream to lock something may symbolize the locking away of secrets, the repression of emotions, and the repression of the shadow.

Other meaning: Happiness.

King. An archetypal symbol of authority, usually stern. The king is the undisputed ruler whose word is law, and who must be obeyed. Often in dreams, the king represents a powerful and authoritarian father. Such an image may be associated with rebellion and conflict. Kings also can represent any male figure in authority, such as an employer, a lover, a spouse, or a collective entity such as government. In wielding their power, kings can be just and wise, or cruel and tyrannical.

In mythology, the king literally embodies the health of his land. Thus, when a king is healthy, his nation prospers, and when he falls ill, the land wastes away. Certain fertility rites call for the sacrifice of the king, who refertilizes the land through the shedding of his blood.

A king and queen together represent perfect union.

Kiss. Reverence; good will; adoration; reconciliation. In lore, the kiss is sacred, an expression of the life-giving breath of the soul and a transfer of power. The kissing of objects, hands and feet are rituals of worship and reverence, and symbolizes spiritual union.

Kisses can awaken to new life (as in the fairy tale of Snow White), or can poison or betray (as in the kiss of Judas).

On a mundane level, the kiss is an expression of affection, passion and sexual attraction.

Kitchen. A place where spiritual nourishment is created. Dreams set in kitchens indicate the process of psychic transformation. Kitchens are alchemical places where food is transformed from its raw state into cooked and refined dishes for consumption. In dream language, a kitchen represents the process of growth to a new level of consciousness, which must then be integrated, or consumed. The kitchen itself is the equivalent of an alchemical vessel in which the transformation occurs.

See **House.**

Knife. Separation. Knives often occur in nightmares when one is under the stress of a literal separation, such as in a marriage or love relationship.

Knives also are symbols of the masculine principle of action, rational thought and intellect, but without the heavy symbolism of the sword. The knife is more a weapon or tool designed to cut, sever and separate. It has personal significance for the dreamer, for knives, unlike swords, are common implements in everyday life.

Knife

Serrated knives or kitchen knives are more feminine, with association to domesticity (nurturing) and food (spiritual sustenance).

Like the sword, the knife is an alchemical symbol of *separatio*.

Knight. A spiritual initiate, the quest of the soul on its journey to wholeness, facing trials and tribulations. A knight also is a guide of the soul.

In mythology, the colors of knights have different meanings. The Green Knight especially is an initiate, and also represents the powers of nature (see **Nature; Vegetables**). The White Knight represents purity, innocence and spiritual illumination. The Red Knight is the conqueror who has been baptized in blood (see **Baptism; Blood**). The Black Knight represents death (see **Death**), also evil, sin and expiation.

On a more mundane level, knights are romanticized figures representing high ideals, morals, ethics and chivalry; they slay dragons and rescue the endangered. Thus, knights in a dream may represent a dreamer's desire to be rescued by outside forces from a situation or circumstances.

Knot. A symbol of either constriction or freedom, depending on context.

Knots drawn tight bind things together, and thus symbolize continuity, connection, fate and unity. Knots in dreams may represent being bound to either desirable or undesirable things.

Knots loosened represent freedom, salvation and the solution to problems. Cutting a knot represents a quick solution to a problem, or a short path to spiritual realization.

Other meaning: A difficult problem that needs to be solved.

See **Maze; Necktie**.

L

Laboratory. A place of transformation and experimentation. In the laboratory, the scientist or magus explores formulas and takes risks in order to create something new. There is an understanding that most experiments will fail; yet, the scientist or magus is not disheartened, and perseveres.

See **Scientist.**

Labyrinth. See **Maze.**

Lack of preparation. See **Preparation, lack of.**

Ladder. Ladders unite heaven and earth, often representing ascent to spiritual heights or higher levels of consciousness previously unattainable. Rungs on a ladder correspond to separate events or markers in spiritual initiation. Jung described the climbing of ladders as the process of psychic transformation "with all its ups and downs."

A ladder also represents a rite of passage from one plane to another, usually a movement from darkness to light, or lower consciousness to higher consciousness.

On a more mundane level, ladders represent movement in career or social status.

Ladder

Lake. The unconscious, the feminine principle, a passive and collective receptacle of wisdom. In fairy tales and myths, lakes are the dwelling places of monsters and supernatural beings, and are places where the mysterious, dangerous or fatal can happen.

Lakes are associated with the souls of the dead, who either cross lakes to reach the afterworld, or go to live at the bottom of lakes after death.

Lakes also are sources of revelation: the future may be glimpsed on their still and shiny surfaces.

See **Water.**

Lamb. Gentleness; simplicity. White lambs symbolize purity and innocence. In ancient times, lambs were a common sacrificial animal. Thus, Christ is called the Lamb of God, because of his purity and his sacrifice for the sins of humankind. In Christian symbolism, lambs also represent faithfulness.

Other meanings: 1) Dullness. 2) A follower of the herd.

Lamp. Divine light, wisdom and guidance. The illumination of a problem or situation that needs to be resolved.

Lamps also symbolize birth (lighting a lamp) and death (extinguishing a lamp). In a dream, these acts may represent phases of life or influences that are either coming into being or passing away.

Lance. See **Spear.**

Lapis Lazuli. See **Jewels.**

Left hand, lefthandedness. The unconscious. Using the left hand in a dream, especially if you are right-handed, indicates a need to open up to the unconscious.

Lettuce. Fertility and rebirth; fragility. Lettuce has a long and distinguished history as a sacred plant. The Egyptians, from the time of the Middle Kingdom, regarded it as a symbol of fertility, its milky sap representing both mother's milk and semen. The ancient Greeks considered lettuce a symbol of the fragile nature of existence, and made it sacred to Adonis, whose myth is the story of seasonal growth and death of vegetation. Slain by a wild boar, Adonis was permitted by the gods to spend six months of every year on earth with his grieving lover, Aphrodite, and six months in the underworld. Within this context, lettuce represents impotence and lack of the vital force.

The moist, cool nature of lettuce links it to the moistness of the all-fertilizing Mother Goddess. In astrology, lettuce is linked to the moon, another feminine symbol.

See **Vegetables.**

Light. Truth, revelation, or illumination, especially as a result of supernatural or divine forces. Light is direct knowledge, a source of goodness. It banishes darkness (uncertainty, confusion) and evil.

Light also represents consciousness, and in a dream may pertain to something being brought into one's awareness.

Lightning. Inspiration, creativity, spiritual illumination. Lightning is both beneficial (spiritually or creatively transforming) and destructive. To be struck by lightning is to receive spiritual enlightenment, revelation or initiation. To be struck and killed by lightning is to be transported directly into heaven.

Like fire, lightning purifies through its destruction.

In its masculine aspect lightning is the tool of thunder and sky gods, and the terrible weapon of justice and vengeance. In classical mythology, the sky god, Jupiter (Jove), hurls lighting bolts at his enemies. Lightning is the descent of power from heaven to earth, a forceful, masculine power both destructive and fertilizing. In its feminine aspect, lightning is associated with regeneration and fecundity, for thunder and lightning storms bring fertilizing rain. Thus, lightning also is associated with other feminine symbols of fecundity and regeneration, such as the mon and the spiral.

See **Fire; Hammer; Moon; Spiral; Thunder.**

Lily. Purity, femininity and virginity. The lily of the valley peeking up through the snow represents the advent of new life in the Spring. The water lily, or lotus, having its roots in the mud and resting on the water, depicts a spiritual unfolding, or an emergence into consciousness. The lotus connotes the creation of order and beauty out of the chaos of the muddy waters.

Lion. Strength and courage; prowess; primitive or "animal" instincts. Lions often are associated with law, justice and military might, all authoritarian. They also represent the male principle.

Lockout. Being locked out of a house or building symbolizes a fear of being shut out of something in life, such as a relationship or a career opportunity. It also symbolizes fear of an imminent loss.

Loss of identification. See **Identification**.

Loss of valuables. See **Valuables**.

Lotus. See **Lily**.

Lover. A lover in a dream may represent a literal lover, but usually represents total involvement and passion—a consuming interest in something. This consuming interest may threaten balance and harmony, or other areas in life that require attention. On the other hand, a beneficial dream lover may represent a state of balance and harmony in life.

Lovers also may symbolize male or female principles—the animus and anima, which are brought to attention in a dream. Or, they may symbolize the dynamic tension between opposites, such as the intellect and the emotions, or the conscious and the unconscious.

In addition, lovers also may represent qualities or states of emotion, such as loving, giving, forgiving, passion or jealousy.

Lover

Other meaning: Addiction to ecstasy or physical pleasure.

M

Machinery. The inner workings of something. Machinery in a dream may represent introspection. However, because of the mechanical, cold nature of machinery, the introspection is likely to be somewhat distant or detached.

Machinery also may symbolize the state of one's affairs in life: things are going smoothly (as in the running of well-maintained, well-oiled machinery) or things are going poorly (breakdowns, failure to operate). To take machinery apart represents an attempt to find the inner core of something, or, if there is a problem, to find the source of the trouble. Machinery with missing parts means all the pieces to a solution, or the smooth operation of something in life, are not assembled.

Caretakers of machinery, or the operators of machinery, may represent the dreamer, or persons in the dreamer's life, or qualities or attributes that need to be brought to the dreamer's attention.

In addition, machinery may symbolize one's physical body, and thus may reflect one's attitude toward the body, or may point to health problems. For example, trouble in the "guts" of a machine may be a means of drawing the dreamer's attention to the stomach or intestines.

Other meanings: 1) Lack of emotion. 2) Mechanical, automatic behavior.

MAP 277

Madonna, The. The feminine principle, especially in its highest spiritual expression. The Madonna also represents the anima, the feminine unconscious. The Black Madonna represents the dark aspects of anima, which have the potential for great transforming power.

Magpie. Like other black birds, magpies are harbingers of death (transformation), or they forewarn of trouble. They also represent vanity and base instincts.

For the significance of black, see **Colors.**

Maize. See **Corn**.

Make-up. Putting on or taking off make-up in a dream pertains to one's social persona, the face presented to the world. Make-up can dramatically alter one's appearance; it may enhance, beautify, hide flaws, or deceive.

If one feels exposed without make-up in a dream, it may indicate the dreamer does not feel comfortable presenting himself or herself "as is" to the world. Make-up poorly applied, or that makes others in the dream stare or laugh, may be drawing attention to feelings of inadequacy or low self-esteem.

See **Clothing; Mask.**

Malachite. See **Jewels.**

Manhole. See **Sewer.**

Map. Directions for navigating through life or through a particular situation. A map that is not comprehensible indicates confusion. Maps that send one around in circles represent frustration and lack of sense of direction. Losing a map means losing one's way. Finding a new and unknown map represents finding a solution to a problem, or a new direction in life. Requiring a map before making decisions or embarking on a trip may represent a fear of taking risks; one must have the path ahead securely marked first. Maps to buried treasure, or to treasure in caves, represent an undertaking into the unconscious (see **Jewels**). Such journeys are part of the hero's quest toward wholeness.

Marching. Moving along at a steady pace; steady progress toward a goal. Marching with others represents a collective activity in which one is part of a unit, going along with collective will or the will of an authority figure. Marching alone, or departing from a marching group, means going off in one's own direction. Breaking stride may mean breaking with the expectations of others.

Marriage. A union of opposites, or a reconciliation of differences. Marriage also symbolizes the attainment of an undivided self, and the union of the material and the spirit.

Marriage may relate to a resolution of warring factions in waking life, to a union of opposing forces within the unconscious, the union of ego and anima, or to the conscious and the unconscious. According to Jung, the reconciliation of opposites in the psyche must occur if individuation is to take place.

In myth, the *hieros gamos* is the sacred, mystical marriage between heaven and earth, and is portrayed as the union of king and queen, bull and cow, and priest and priestess. In alchemy, marriage is represented by the union of sulphur and mercury (quicksilver), sun and moon, gold and silver, and king and queen. In Christian mysticism, marriage is symbolized by the union of the soul with Christ as divine bridegroom.

Marriage

A marriage requires a sacrifice on the part of both forces; each must give up something in order to create a whole. Thus, there is a ''death'' for each party in order for the birth of the union to occur.

On a more mundane level, a dream of marriage may relate to anticipation of, or anxiety about, an upcoming marriage. It also may relate to changes taking place in a marriage relationship that affect the harmony or balance, either positively or negatively. A dream of marital strife may reflect unresolved problems in marital life.

Mask. Concealment of one's real identity from the world; a facade; something to hide behind; or, something that protects the wearer.

Masks also symbolize a temporary, liberating spiritual transformation: in sacred ritual, liturgies, theater and folk art, they are objects of power that transform the wearer into an animal, an ancestor or a presumed image of a supernatural being. By donning a mask, the wearer allows himself/herself to become possessed by the spirit believed to live in the mask or the spirit that is represented by the mask. This enables him/her to invoke the powers of the spirit. In Jungian terms, a mask connects its wearer to archetypal powers residing within the collective unconscious. The mask is a mediator between the ego and archetype, the mundane and the supernatural, the sacred and the comic, the present and the past. In transpersonal psychology, masks help persons identify with archetypal forces and liberate suppressed parts of the Self, thus seeing themselves in new ways.

To discover the significance of a mask in a dream, consider the countenance of the mask (pleasant, frightening, etc.); the reasons for wearing it (to display, conceal, transform); the emotions associated with wearing it (pride, shame, exhilaration, fear); and the reactions of others to the mask.

Masochism. Dreams involving masochism are common during stressful periods in life, especially in the early stages following separation or divorce. The dreamer may be projecting self-blame for everything that went wrong, and thus feel deserving of self-inflicted punishment.

Mattress. See **Bed/Bedroom.**

Maze. A path to the underworld, or the unconscious; initiation into a life passage. In mythology, mazes are associated with the Mother Goddess, and represent initiation into the mysteries of life, death and rebirth.

Mazes also are symbols of mystical quests, and in dreams may represent spiritual attainment after trials and ordeals— a proving of the soul.

In mazes, one meets the supernatural—gods and goddesses who help or hinder progress, monsters that threaten safety. In dreams, these may be aspects of the Self, arising out of the depths of the unconscious to confront the dreamer.

Even the simplest maze is not easy to navigate; complex mazes can seem impossible to solve. Mazes thus may represent complex problems in life, the solutions of which seem elusive and hard to reach; the dreamer may be venturing down blind paths.

Other meanings: 1) Difficulty and danger. 2) Confusion. 3) Being on a path with limited choices.

See **Monster;** Compare to **Knot.**

Meat. The sensual and the sexual.

Meat may also represent animal powers.

See **Animals.**

Medicine, medication. The giving of medicine and medication is a powerful symbol in Western culture. Western medicine is largely allopathic, in that it relies on medicine and outside forces to effect healing and pays little attention to the potential healing powers within the patient. In contrast, other medicine systems, such as Chinese medicine and Ayurvedic medicine of India, take a more holistic approach of mind, body, spirit and environment. In Western culture, therefore, medicine is viewed as having the power to cure. Medicine in a dream may represent any external force desired to solve (i.e. "cure") a problem. It also may be a cue to look at a problem from another perspective. The solution may lie within, and the individual may have to use his or her own inner powers and resources to bring it about, rather than expect rescue by outside intervention.

Mending. Taking corrective action or fixing a problem, as in the "fabric" of one's life. The mending of clothing represents correcting perceived flaws in one's social façade. Mending requires patience and attention to detail.
   See **Clothing.**

Menstrual blood. See **Blood.**

Milk. Mother's nourishment; also, nourishment from the divine Great Mother. Milk also represents purity, simplicity, re-birth and the newborn.
   Other meanings: 1) Childhood and memories of childhood. 2) Semen.

Mill. Something being ground to bits; something being processed into another form. A mill represents a process of transformation: a raw material is treated and turned into a useful product. A food mill has associations with spiritual nourishment (See **Food**). A lumber or steel mill has associations with building something in life, such as creative ideas, one's psyche, etc. (See **House**).

Mine. A penetration into the earthy depths of the unconscious in order to bring out something of value. The unconscious is the reservoir of emotion, instinct and intuition, and is associated with the Mother Goddess. The earth is associated with the body and primitive drives.

Mirror. Mirrors symbolize self-knowledge, consciousness and truth, and they are associated with the search for self-realization. Although mirrors appear in dreams in a variety

Mirror

of different ways, they tend to represent related meanings.

When we look into a mirror, we tend to see what we don't like rather than what we like. Mirrors reveal us as we truly are. Consequently, a mirror in a dream reveals flaws and shortcomings—things we feel need correcting. In particular, looking into a mirror signals the need to reflect on one's inner self. Shattering a mirror is a way of symbolically ridding oneself of a poor self-image. A broken or cracked mirror reflects a distorted self-image.

Because of their shiny surface, mirrors are commonly used in divination to look into the future. Thus, a dream mirror may reveal the possible or likely outcome of events in motion. Or, it may reveal the dreamer's fears or hopes about the future. A fogged mirror may suggest feelings of uncertainty about the future.

Other meaning: In Christian symbolism, a spotless mirror is the symbol of the Virgin Mary.

Missing transportation. Missing an airplane, bus, boat, train, etc. is a common theme in frustration dreams. Usually, it symbolizes a sense of missed opportunity, especially from having waited too long. It represents the nagging "I should have . . ." or "I could have . . ." inner voice.

Missing transportation also can symbolize lack of preparation, lack of organization, or low self-esteem.

Mist. Confusion; inability to see things clearly.
See **Fog.**

Mixing. Stirring things up in life, for better or for worse, depending upon what one is mixing.

Mixing also can represent a synthesizing or an integrating process taking place. Trying to mix together incompatible elements or ingredients may symbolize that one is attempting something unfeasible. Mixing together explosive ingredients indicates that one is creating, or contributing to, a volatile situation.

From an alchemical perspective, mixing represents a stage in the process of the Great Work: after ingredients are broken down (the *nigredo* phase), they are recombined and then refined.

Mob. See **Crowd.**

Mole. This night creature represents a destructive force at work in the unconscious. Also, the powers of darkness (and therefore, of potential transformation).
See **Animals; Colors.**

Money. Value and worth—how one values life; and feelings of self-worth and self-esteem.

Money also symbolizes psychic energy—the inner resources one is willing or unwilling to invest in oneself, one's relationships, career, and so on.

Money

Dreams involving accumulation of money may demonstrate positive growth arising from wise investment of all the resources at an individual's disposal. On another level, a gain or loss of money could represent consequences from past acts.

The amount or denominations of money may have significance in terms of numbers.

See **Numbers; Identification.**

Monk. Spiritual wisdom, especially pertaining to the animus, or to a man in one's life. Monks, like nuns, symbolize withdrawal from the material world. The meaning of a monk in a dream also is likely to be colored by an individual's own religious experiences and attitudes toward religion and church teachings.

Monster. Monsters in dreams and nightmares are unnamed terrors: the embodiment of repressed emotions, anger, hostility and fear, or the unacknowledged shadow side of being. To be pursued by a monster in a dream is a signal from the unconscious of the need to confront something in life.

To look into a mirror and see a monster reflected back to be confronted by one's own shadow. Other people who become monsters may indicate that the dreamer is overlooking or ignoring some flaw or dark aspect of their character. Sometimes others who become monsters in dreams are vehicles for showing the dreamer's own shadow.

Supernatural monsters typically are repressed emotions, attacking from within.

Monsters are likely to occur in dreams during stressful times in life, such as crises and life passages, especially if the dreamer feels overwhelmed and unable to cope.

Moon. The moon is the Queen of Heaven, and thus is symbolic of the feminine principle. In mythology, it is associated with the Goddess.

In contrast with the harsh and steady light of the sun, the lunar light is much more subtle and changeable. Its many phases relate to the flow of the tides, the ebb and flow of blood, and of moisture in vegetation. Each month the moon dies and after three days is reborn. In dreams, the moon can represent intuition, change, and the ebb and flow of energies. It also can represent renewal.

In addition, the moon represents the dark and occult side of nature, and the unconscious part of our minds. It also relates to emotional, intuitive and psychic powers. In dreams, the moon also can symbolize things which are hidden, but which can be discovered by going within. Moon power is mind power.

The moon is associated with magic, witchcraft and sorcery. It can cast its own spell leading to lunacy and mania, especially at the full moon. In this aspect, the moon in dreams can represent things which seem magical or mysterious, or fears of losing one's rational ground.

Moonstone. See **Jewels.**

Morning. See **Dawn.**

Moth. Self-purification and self-sacrifice, after the manner in which moths commit self-immolation.

Mother. An archetype of the feminine principle: nourisher, protector, life-giver on one hand; destroyer, devourer and death-dealer on the other. The mother figure represents both the beginning and the end of the life cycle, as well as the constant renewal that marks the transition from one to the other. She is wisdom, wholeness, self-mastery and self-sufficiency. She is also dark and mysterious.

Mother figures come in various guises. The mother, nanny or nurse shelters and gives love, affection and approval. The empress or queen is a figure of authority and wisdom. The priestess is a keeper of secrets and mysteries of life. The huntress represents the forces that control or subdue animal instincts and passion. The witch or hag is a destroyer, a depriver or withholder of all the benefits the Good Mother bestows.

The Mother may also be represented by the moon (emotion, intuition, the creative force) and by spiders or webs, as the weaver and spinner of destiny.

Mountain. An archetypal symbol of the Self. To climb the mountain—a common motif in dreams, fairy tales and myths—is to ascend to the realm of spirit. The ascent itself is masculine in nature, and is associated with intellect and rational thought, and with heroes and warriors seeking truth and justice. The spirit at the summit is also masculine: the

Divine Masculine, the Father, God.

To descend the mountain is a feminine journey, a return to emotion, instinct and primitive nature. To enter inside the mountain, such as through a tunnel or especially a cave, is the descent to the unconscious, which also is a feminine realm and is associated with the Divine Feminine, the Mother, Goddess, the womb. In alchemical terms, the inner mountain is the vessel of transformation.

In dreams, it is significant to note the nature and characteristics of a mountain, and one's ascent or descent. Is the mountain forbidding and distant, a challenge, or an easy climb? What is the terrain? Is the mountain arid, lush, or snow-covered? Is there a path, or do you forge one? Are you confident where you are going, are you uncertain, or lost? Are there apparent dangers (your unconscious fears) along the way? Are guides present—human or animal? Human figures may represent aspects of the Self. Animals represent instinct; some, such as dogs, specifically are guides to the underworld, the realm of the unconscious. Do you carry tools or equipment (rational thought, masculine principle) to help you along?

See **Cave; Climbing; Snow; Volcano.** See also **specific animals and tools.** Compare to **Elevator; Ladder; Stairs.**

Mouse. A primitive aspect of the masculine principle. Also, mice represent chthonic or underground powers and forces. Their gnawing and swift, furtive movements may reflect qualities or attributes of someone in a dream.

Mouth. Breath, thus spirit and creativity. In its negative aspect, the mouth devours, and especially represents the devouring, destructive nature of the Mother Goddess.

Dreams involving the mouth also may relate to constructive or destructive words spoken to others; the ability or inability to keep silent; gossiping; spreading the truth, etc.

Moving. Reflection of a change in life, or of a desire or need to make a change. Moving can refer to changing attitudes or states of consciousness, or even physical changes that have occurred, or are occurring, in life. Moving house indicates a change in one's psyche (See **House**; see also **City**). Moving up to better circumstances represents improvement. Moving down to worse circumstances represents the need to work on something in life.

Mud. Fertilizing powers. The primeval ooze. Mud germinates new life, such as ideas and creativity. In alchemy, it can be compared to the *prima materia*, the "first matter" that can be shaped into the philosopher's stone.

Murder. Committing or witnessing a murder in a dream often represents the death of the old Self. It also might represent an angry liberation from someone or something. Having murderous feelings in a dream is an exaggeration of repressed anger, hostility and frustration.

Museum. One's past life, where memories are on display. Museums are collective places, representing the collective past of a family or a culture.

Mushroom. Something kept in the dark. Mushrooms live in the dense, moist parts of the forest, which in turn represents the dark, uncharted territories of the unconscious. Some mushrooms spring up suddenly after a rain (the waters of the unconscious). One must be careful with mushrooms, since some are poisonous.
See **Forest; Vegetables.**

Music. The emotions, the soul. Music has tremendous power to influence emotions, and the nature of the music reflects the nature and quality of emotions at play.

To compose music is to open up new emotional areas in one's life.

Myrtle. As a flower of the gods, myrtle is a magical plant that symbolizes spiritual initiation, peace, joy, and the feminine principle. As an evergreen, it symbolizes long life and immortality; it is also the breath of life that ensures the ongoing cycle of birth, death and rebirth. In war, it denotes victory without bloodshed. In classical mythology, myrtle is associated with Dionysus, the vegetation god who symbolizes the living force of nature.

Other meanings: 1) Virginity. 2) Love.

Nail. Piercing, binding. In a positive sense, nails represent the strength to bind and hold together. In a negative sense, they represent a painful binding.

Nails—especially three in number—also represent wounding, after Christ's wounds from being nailed to the cross. (See **Wound**.)

Other meaning: Getting stuck on something, not making progress.

Nakedness. See **Nudity**.

Names. The names of persons in a dream usually refer to other people by the same name, or to the qualities, attributes or talents associated with famous or mythological persons by the same name. For example, someone named Mary may be a symbol of the Blessed Virgin Mary, or the Madonna, the feminine principle or anima (see **Madonna, The**). Other associations with names include memories, activities, decisions, fears, hopes, etc. A name may also be a play on words for something going on in one's life, or it may be intended to direct the dreamer's attention to a certain situation.

To have no name is to be indistinct or formless, or to have no real qualities or attributes.

Other meaning: One's secret description of oneself.

Natural disasters. See **Disasters, natural.**

Nature. It is our conscious awareness that separates us from the rest of nature which represents our unconscious. In the earliest religions nature was felt to be alive with a multitude of spirits. The nature spirits were individually worshipped in order to maintain a harmony with them. Civilization has inhibited our contact with those elemental spirits and energies.

Our dreams may take us on a shamanistic journey through the realm of the nature spirits where we confront the various elements of our individual and collective unconscious. To go into nature is to go into the wilderness of the unconscious, where one encounters primordial instincts.

Nausea. See **Indigestion**.

Navel. A center of life, life on earth, and the cosmos. A nexus where all things come together, where heaven and earth are united. As a center, a navel is the source of the outflowing of life energy, and is a refuge and haven.

See **Spiral**.

Near-sightedness. See **Glasses**.

Neck. The neck is fragile and a weak point in the body; thus, dreams involving the neck often have to do with weaknesses, vulnerabilities and risk-taking.

To protect the neck is to avoid risks, while sticking it out is to take risks. To be strangled or choked may parallel similar situations in life.

Necktie. Dreams about tying neckties, or of neckties that are askew, too loose, or too tight, often occur as symbols

Necktie

of anxieties, especially about getting married. Neckties also relate to fears or anxieties concerning job and career, or formal social situations. A necktie that is too tight might symbolize a feeling of being constricted, choked or suffocated by people or circumstances.

See **Clothing**.

Needle. The power or ability to mend one's problems or one's life, albeit with some piercing and, probably, some pain.

Other meaning: The ability to pierce through the surface of things and get to the heart of the matter.

Nest. The home base; safety. Nests symbolize safety and security, especially that afforded by the mother.

Other meanings: 1) The womb. 2) Parenthood. 3) Home-making activities.

Net. Nets have both positive and negative associations. As a positive symbol, they protect us and provide safety, catching us when we fall from great heights. On the negative side, nets entangle and entrap. In mythology, the Mother Goddess is sometimes portrayed as the goddess of nets; thus nets may symbolize her destructive aspects.

New year. A new beginning; starting fresh. A rebirth of spirit.

Newspaper. Public disclosure or exposure. Information, truths and secrets revealed to the world.

Night. The unknown, which is full of unformed fears. The night is ruled by the Mother Goddess, and can symbolize the terrifying unknown depths of the unconscious. It also can represent the darkness of the womb, which is protective and nourishing.

Night also symbolizes the alchemical darkness that is the destruction of the old, the death that precedes rebirth.

Nightmare. The psyche's drastic way of trying to get your attention.

Noose. Being caught or trapped in a strangling situation.

North. Primordial chaos; darkness; and night. Ignorance and emotional darkness.

North also is associated with winter, old age and death (as in the ending of a phase of life) and with the Devil's

powers (materialism and base pursuits).
See **Night**.

Nose. Curiosity; meddling. Also, instinct and intuition, especially if an animal nose. The ability to accurately size up a situation.

Notebook. A collection of memories and records of life. Perusing a notebook may symbolize a review of one's deeds or one's life, a reflection of past events, a toll taking. Consider the emotions associated with notebooks, such as nostalgia, fondness, happiness, sadness, bitterness, etc. Do the notebooks contain any information useful to present situations or events?

Storing a collection of notebooks, especially in a box, drawer, closet or out-of-the-way place, may represent avoidance or a repression of things in one's past.

Nuclear contamination. A symbol of unresolved anxieties over changes in life that threaten to overwhelm.
See **Disasters, Natural**.

Nudity. Vulnerability; openness; sincerity; naiveté; embarrassment. Dreams of appearing nude in public are common in many cultures. Such dreams are associated with feeling unprepared, or being afraid of exposing emotions.

Nudity as a symbol of vulnerability occurs in dreams related to stage two of recovery, especially from separation or divorce. In stage two, the dreamer feels depressed, angry and in despair, especially if he or she is the one left behind.

Nudity also may symbolize a change of identity in the making, prior to the acquisition of new clothes.
See **Clothing**.

Numbers. Archetypal symbols representing the self, the dynamics of the psyche, and stages of growth and devel-

Numbers

opment. Number symbolisms are important to myths, fairy tales, alchemy, and other esoteric teachings. According to Jung, these aged, root symbolisms are expressed unconsciously in dreams.

Dream numbers must be considered in a variety of ways. Esoteric meanings may have significance for the dreamer. Numbers may also represent time spans, phases and ages. For example, the number 3 might have significance concerning events that occurred three years earlier, or when the dreamer was three years old. In his work with patients, Jung often added and divided numbers—such as sums of money, sequences of numbers, addresses and dates—to ascertain if their sums or parts might have a significance to the dreamer.

Numbers also can be represented by quantities of people, animals and objects, by geometric shapes (the square, triangle, cross, etc.), by phases (seasons, months, days of the week, hours of the day) and by repetitions of actions (such as trying twice to accomplish something).

Odd numbers have masculine properties and associations, while even numbers are feminine. The following are number symbolisms most significant to dreams:

0. The unmanifested, the nothingness which precedes all things, the cosmic egg which is the container of all life, the Mother Goddess who brings forth all life. Zero has associations with the circle, the symbol of wholeness, perfection and eternity. See **Circle; Egg.**

From a colloquial perspective, zero in a dream might equate with emptiness, worthlessness, a waste of time or all for naught: "nothing but a big zero."

1. The beginning and end of all things, the source, the mystic center, divinity, the spiritual unity which unites all beings. One is auspicious, pointing to creation, unity, light, spirit and mind.

Although it is an odd number, 1 is not masculine; it is hermaphroditic, because 1 added to an even number makes an odd number, and 1 added to an odd number makes an even number. All numbers, and thus all things, emanate from 1.

The ship and the chariot are symbols related to 1. See **Ship.**

2. Duality and balance. In alchemy, 2 is the number of opposites, which are dissolved and recombined to create the philosopher's stone. In dreams, 2 often represents the emergence of something out of darkness and into consciousness—the dawning of spiritual light. This symbolism appears in myth and fairy tale in the form of twins or two siblings.

Two is associated with horns, which in turn are associated with the moon and the Mother Goddess. Thus 2 in a dream might also represent birth and nurturing intuitive faculties or emotions.

In Christian symbolism, 2 represents the dual nature of Christ (God and human). In Kabbalistic symbolism, it represents wisdom and self-consciousness.

3. The generative force, creative power and forward movement. Three expresses a totality in terms of a beginning, middle and end, which occurs in myth, folklore and fairy tales as the triad: three wishes, three sisters, three brothers, three chances, blessings done in threes, and spells and charms done in threes. In the Three Fates of mythology, 3 has associations with past, present and future and knowledge of all things. Three is an important number in mysticism, as expressed in the Christian Trinity, the threefold nature of man (body, mind and spirit) and the name of the mythical author of the Hermetica, Hermes Trismegistus ("Thrice-greatest Hermes").

Jung, however, observed that the totality of 3 is relative, for 3 is one short of the completion of 4. Thus three symbolizes a stepping stone toward 4. He also said that 3 can represent either the higher consciousness of the self or the unexpressed shadow, for 3 forms a triad and the complement of a triad is an opposite triad.

4. Wholeness and completeness, which in dreams usually refers to the self. 4 is conscious totality; it also symbolizes the earth (solidity), the physical, the completion of a spiritual evolution, foundations, hard work, toil and tangible achievement.

Four has a strong association with the square, another symbol of completeness. The presence of 4 in a dream can indicate the process of becoming whole or stabilized. See **Cross; Square.**

5. The number of natural humankind, the microcosm and materialism: the physical body and its five senses; the body with four limbs plus a head; the four cardinal points with a mystic center, the four elements plus a fifth element of ether, the universal vitalizing substance. In the Tarot, 5 is the number of the Hierophant. Five also represents equilibrium, because it divides 10, the perfect number, in two.

Five is expressed in the pentagram, a five-pointed star which in occultism represents the dominion of mind over the lower nature. To the Greeks, the pentagram symbolized light, health and vitality.

The number 5 is often expressed by five-leaved plants, such as the rose, lily or vine.

6. Equilibrium, balance, harmony, health and time. The six-sided figure, the hexad, and the hexagram, are formed by two triangles in a union of opposites; thus 6 is the number of creation, marriage, generation and evolution.

The Pythagoreans considered 6 the form of forms, the perfection of all the parts, and associated it with immortality. In Christian symbolism, 6 also is a number of perfection, for God created the world in six days. In the Kabbalah, 6 represents beauty and creation.

7. A universal sacred number. Seven is the macrocosm and divinity. It is the number of mystical man, the sum of 3 (spirit) and 4 (material), thus making the perfect order. In alchemy, seven metals make up the work, the creation of the philosopher's stone.

Seven also is associated with magical, psychic and healing powers. In initiatory rites, it represents the highest stage of illumination.

There are seven notes in the musical scale, and seven colors in the spectrum (a rainbow, the mythical bridge between earth and heaven).

When the number 7 occurs in a dream, it often indicates the search for wisdom, the growth of spirit, the need to rely upon intuition or the need to meditate on what has been learned.

8. A higher order of the number 4. Eight represents re-generation and achievement of a spiritual goal. It is associated with the lemniscate (an ellipse), the symbol of eternity, infinity, the alpha and omega, infinite wisdom and higher consciousness. Eight also is associated with the spiral, which symbolizes evolution, growth and flexibility, and with the serpent, a symbol of illumination, and, in dreams, sometimes the self. See **Snake.**

The octagon, the eight-sided figure, represents a transition between the square and the circle, symbols of completion and unity.

9. A higher order of the number 3. Nine is a powerful number, incorruptible, representing attainment and fulfillment. It is spiritual and mental achievement. The Hebrews considered it to be the number of truth, because when multiplied it reproduces itself. In Kabbalism, it represents the foundation. It is also a number of humankind, symbolizing the nine months of gestation before physical birth. In the Eleusinian Mysteries, there were nine spheres through which the consciousness had to pass before it could be born anew.

Nine is represented by an inverted triangle within an upright triangle, expressing the union of opposites.

10. The number of perfection, heaven and earth and the law; the paradigm of creation, for it contains all numbers. The four basic building blocks, 1, 2, 3 and 4, add up to 10. There are ten emanations to the Tree of Life, ten names of God and ten commandments.

Ten also is a number of completion and a return to origins ($10 = 1 + 0 = 1$). Odysseus returned home from his wanderings in the tenth year, and Troy, besieged for nine years, fell in the tenth.

11. An unstable and imperfect number, 11 represents sin and transgression and the striving to become 12.

12. Often a time symbol, as expressed in the twelve

months of the year, the hours of the day and night, and the signs of the zodiac. Twelve turns the wheel of the heavens and represents the cosmic order of things; it is a higher aspect of the number 4.

One may also find spiritual significance in 12 by relating it to the apostles of Christ, the tribes of Israel or the fruits of the Tree of Life.

13. An unlucky and unstable number because it exceeds 12 by 1. In Christian symbolism, 13 is associated with the betrayal of Christ: Christ plus his twelve disciples made thirteen, until one disciple betrayed him.

Thirteen also has lunar associations, for there are thirteen full moons in a calendar year. See **Moon.** Some magical and neopagan traditions consider 13 a lucky number because of its lunar associations and because 13 is the traditional number of witches in a coven.

Thirteen also can be interpreted from an alchemical perspective, for $13 = 1 + 3 = 4$. It is not the wholeness of 4, but the striving toward it.

40. A period of spiritual incubation, trial and initiation. There are numerous Biblical references to 40: the period of the Deluge, the reign of David, the days Moses spent on Mt. Sinai, the years the Jews wandered in the desert, the days Jesus spent fasting in the wilderness, and the elapsed time of the Resurrection. In alchemy, the initial phase of the work, the *nigredo*, the blackening, takes about forty days to complete. Persons undergoing a spiritual crisis (sometimes called "spiritual emergence" or "spiritual emergency") often spend forty days in an awakening stage.

Nun. Spiritual purity, relating especially to the anima, or to a woman in one's life. Nuns also symbolize withdrawal from the material world, and healing, especially of the spirit.

In addition, there may be many personal associations

Nun

with nuns, based upon one's experiences in, and feelings about religion and religious education. Persons who attended Catholic school, for example, may have definite positive or negative associations with nuns.

Nurse. A healing taking place or a desire to be healed, especially spiritually. Nurses may symbolize the dreamer's own anima, or a woman in the dreamer's life who has a capacity to heal a problem.

Other meaning: A desire to be taken care of.

Nut. Spiritual wisdom, truth. Also, a symbol of fertility and the generative force.

In Christian symbolism, nuts represent humanity: the kernel, or soul, is encased by the shell, or flesh and bone.

Other meanings: 1) The heart of the matter. 2) New life or rebirth.

Oak. A sacred tree in many mythologies, revered for its strength, durability, majestic size and spread, and its ability to draw lightning (spiritual illumination). The oak is the foundation of the earth and the material.

Oaks also symbolize wisdom and truth; the Druids worshipped the oak because of the gods believed to reside in the trees, who were consulted for their advice.

Other meanings: 1) Fertility and the generative force. 2) The world axis that connects earth to heaven and the underworld.

Oar. Power, with which one plies the waters of the unconscious. Oars also represent skill and knowledge, and are comparable to the rod or wand. They are phallic symbols, representing the masculine principle of intellect.

Oasis. A respite from the harsh world. Emotional sustenance (water) amidst the aridity of intellect and the material.

Reaching an oasis in a dream also may indicate that a rest or a break from routine is needed. Take care of oneself, pay attention to emotion.

Oats. Sexual energy or activity.

Obesity. Low self-esteem; insulation or protection that keeps one from being too close or intimate with others, especially due to fear of rejection.

Observer. Detachment or distance from what is unfolding in one's life. Disconnection from emotions. Passivity.

Observers other than oneself—who could be animals as well as human beings—may represent parts of the self, including the shadow. One can try to connect with these parts by role-playing in the imagination.

Ocean. The unconscious; the primordial waters; the Goddess Mother. Oceans represent the unplumbed, mysterious and seemingly impenetrable depths of one's psyche.

Traveling across an ocean symbolizes navigating through life. Consider the condition of the ocean: smooth, beautiful, placid, choppy, stormy, tempest, etc. Consider also the means of transit: a raft (little support system in place); a small vessel; a large boat; a leaky vessel, etc.

To be pulled down into the ocean is to be pulled into the unconscious. Monsters in the ocean represent unformed or irrational fears and anxieties. To float on the ocean is to be supported by emotions and the unconscious.

The ocean also represents the waters of life, and thus is a symbol of the womb, and of birth.

See **Water.**

Octopus. Possessive, clinging entanglements, especially relating to a mother figure. The octopus also may symbolize a desire to be possessive in a relationship.

As a "monster" of the deep, it also symbolizes irrational fears that threaten to drag one down.

See **Animals.**

Office. One's station in the world; one's career, job or profession. A collective place where one is judged by others. Offices represent the advancement—or loss—of professionalism, ambition, self-esteem, self-image and financial security. They also represent planning and organization. A corporate office is a symbol of authority.

Officials. Authority figures who represent controlling factors in life, or collective influences upon one's choices and actions. An official also may symbolize a specific person in one's life, such as a parent, teacher, supervisor or some other individual with power.

Ogre. The Terrible Father, a destructive, oppressive archetypal force that threatens to devour individuality. Ogres often appear in dreams in relation to discipline problems. They may concern father-child relationships or may pertain to self-discipline issues for the dreamer.

Oil. Lubricant that symbolizes the smoothing out of difficulties and the easing of troubles.

Oil is also slippery; something covered in oil in a dream may represent a situation that is difficult to grasp.

Oil has played a role in sacred ritual since ancient times and thus has spiritual meanings. To anoint with oil is to bestow new life or confer wisdom. Oil also is used in consecrations and dedications. It sometimes is a symbol of the soul.

Old Man. Mortality, or the passage of time. The appearance of an archetypal Old Man in a dream may serve as a prompt to action or resolve indecision. The message is that time passes and mortality draws near.

An Old Man with hourglass and scythe is an archetypal representation of death, and may refer to a phase of life that is coming to an end.

On a mundane level, an old man in a dream may represent a real person in life. He may represent attitudes toward, or fears about, aging held by the dreamer, or characteristics (negative or positive) associated with growing old, such as physical deterioration, illness, wisdom, insight, etc.

See **Old Woman.**

Old Woman. The mature wisdom of the feminine principle or the Mother Goddess. The Old Woman is an archetypal figure. As the Crone, she is the wise but destructive aspect of the Mother Goddess, the witch, the devourer— that force which brings about the death of the old, such as a phase in life.

See **Old Man.**

Olive, olive branch. Peace; also, immortality. In the Bible, a dove returns to Noah's ark with an olive branch to signify God's peace with humanity. Olives in a dream may symbolize the resolution of conflict in life.

The olive also is a symbol of wisdom, and in classical mythology and Renaissance art it was associated with the goddess Minerva.

Onion. Layers upon layers that hide or protect a central truth or secret. Onions may represent a probing or a need to probe.

The roundish shape of the onion lends it a symbolic meaning of wholeness and unity.

In folklore, the onion is sometimes substituted for garlic as an amulet against the powers of evil.

Other meaning: Crying and tears.

See **Vegetables.**

Onyx. See **Jewels.**

Opal. See **Jewels.**

Operating theater. Sterility, antiseptic conditions, emergency treatment.
See **Hospital.**

Operation. The need to make a change, or to get rid of something harmful which is threatening inner well-being or is impeding growth. Operations are performed when illness or injury threatens one's physical life or health; they are radical measures.

Operations may be compared to ritual dismemberment, in which an initiate is symbolically dismembered and reconstructed to symbolize the destruction of the old self and the rebirth of a new self.

Other meaning: Individuals who have undergone operations, or who have lost family or friends during operations, associate them with different feelings, states and conditions, which in turn may have those symbolizations in dreams. These can include fear, helplessness, trust in others, teamwork, salvation, healing, relief, pain, grief, or loss.

Orange. Fruitfulness, fertility; juiciness, as in vitality.

In mythology, the orange is a symbol of immortality. In Christian art, it sometimes substitutes for an apple as a symbol of the Tree of Knowledge, also of the Fall.
See **Colors.**

Orchid. Love, luxury, beauty; being in full bloom. Since antiquity, orchids have been regarded as aphrodisiacs and have been ingredients in love potions. In a dream, an orchid may relate to a need for "love magic" to revitalize a relationship, or may symbolize a desire for a love relationship.

Operation

Orgy. Something in life that is out of control, especially pertaining to the physical and material. Orgies represent dissolution and chaos. They also represent regeneration (the sowing of seed), and thus, like the *nigredo* state of alchemy, symbolize the disintegration that precedes renewal, or at least the potential for renewal.

Orphan. An archetypal symbol that generally represents fears of being unloved, misunderstood, homeless, left out or abandoned. These fears may pertain to spiritual matters as well as to the mundane.

The orphan is a wounded and needy child; thus in a dream an orphan may be associated with old and perhaps unresolved childhood memories or fears.

See **Child/children.**

Ostrich. Ignoring (at one's own peril) what is going on in one's life, especially unpleasantries.

Ostrich feathers symbolize truth and justice in Egyptian mythology.

The ostrich also represents the dragon, a symbol of psychic transformation.

See **Animals; Dragon.**

Ouroboros. See **Snake.**

Oven. The womb. The oven is a symbol of the Mother Goddess, where life is created and brought forth; it is associated with the mysteries of life, death and rebirth. In alchemy, the oven is the athanor in which spiritual transmutation takes place. In dreams, ovens may represent new projects in the making, or new phases of life about to come into being.

Overweight. See **Obesity.**

Owl. A symbol of either wisdom or death. The owl is a messenger from heaven; within the context of a dream, this might represent the presentation of information that needs to be brought into conscious awareness.

In mythology, owls are death omens, and their presence presages a death in a family or household. As a harbinger of death, the owl in a dream heralds the *nigredo,* the blackening stage of alchemy, which represents the death of the old that is necessary for the new to come to life. Such a death may be of an old phase of life or an old influence.

See **Birds.**

Ox. Toil; hard physical labor. Working very hard toward a goal, but making slow progress. Patience and brute strength.

The ox is a good-natured animal that shares with the bull a symbolism of fertility. In classical and Biblical times, it was worthy of divine sacrifice. Occasionally, the ox is a symbol of sloth, one of the seven deadly sins characterized by mental inactivity, melancholia and creative inactivity.

See **Animals.**

Oyster. Secrecy; hidden treasure. Oysters also may represent having a hard, outer shell in dealing with others. An oysters without its shell means having no protection.

The creation of pearls through irritation of the oyster's insides may warn of irritation in one's own innards, such as the stomach or intestines.

In myth, oysters represent the womb and the life-giving forces of the Mother Goddess or feminine principle; they give birth to something of great beauty and value—the pearl. They are denizens of the deep, and thus have associations with the unconscious, particularly the literal "hidden treasure" that lies buried below waking consciousness.

Oysters are considered aphrodisiacs, and thus may represent sexual allure or sexual desires.

See **Jewels.**

Packing. Putting one's belongings, i.e. inner self, in order. Packing may relate to having too much inner clutter, or too much activity in waking life—things need to be better organized or disposed of. Packing to put something away may relate to repression. Packing in preparation, such as for travel, anticipates change in life. Unpacking may relate to bringing something from the unconscious into light.

Paddle. See **Oar.**

Paint, painting. Paint or the act of painting can symbolize either a desire to enhance and beautify something, or to cover something up. Painting a house relates to the psyche (see **House**). For the painting of objects, see individual entries.

The color of the paint has symbolic meaning. Gold paint, for example, relates to spiritual or intellectual matters. Black paint signifies the end of something in life. See **Colors.**

Palm. See **Hands.**

Palm tree. Victory, valor, triumph, blessings, exultation. The palm originally was a symbol of military victory, but in Christianity came to represent Christ's triumph over death. It may refer to mundane matters, such as triumph over adversity.

The palm also is a phallic symbol, and represents fertility.

See **Tree.**

Paralysis. A symbol of anxieties over stresses due to grief or major changes in life, especially separation or divorce. Dreams of being paralyzed characterize the first stage of recovery, shock and denial, when one is still struggling to come to terms with the change, and feels overwhelmed.

Parents. See **Father; Mother.**

Passport. See **Identification.**

Path. A course one sets out upon to journey through life or to attain a particular goal. Paths typically are small and narrow, often winding, and one travels them alone. The conditions of a path provide clues to the message in a dream. An easy, open path in a tranquil environment reflects a different psychic state from one that is steep and rocky or obscured by overgrowth. Paths through unknown territory that seems frightening may symbolize fears and uncertainties about a direction one has taken or is contemplating taking. Paths that seem to lead nowhere may indicate the dreamer has taken a wrong turn, or is wandering through life and needs a new direction. Paths through familiar environments, either present or past, are likely to have personal associations, such as a period in one's life that relates to the issue presented in the dream.

See **Traveling companions.**

Pearl. See **Jewels.**

Penis. The penis, as phallus, is a universal symbol for generation and fertility. It represents the life force, and resurrection and renewal. It also represents creative drive, potency, and manifestation in the physical plane.

The penis may also indicate problems with sexuality that would depend on the gender of the dreamer.

See **Sex and Sexuality, Urination.**

Peridot. See **Jewels.**

Physician. See **Doctor.**

Pink. See **Colors.**

Planetary disaster. The existence of a threat to one's own world or life. The possibility of major changes; things coming apart.

Plowing. The fertilizing, creative force. Plowing is a metaphor for sex, especially the impregnating of a woman by a man.

Other meaning: Preparation, making ready, especially for mental faculties of thoughts and inspiration.

Plumb line. Spiritual balance and uprightness; knowing that one is right about something.

Other meaning: The world axis that connects heaven, earth and the underworld, and provides a means of accessing those realms.

Plumbing. The workings of the unconscious; the hidden structure of the psyche (see **House**). Leaks, rotting plumbing, or convoluted plumbing indicate that attention needs

Police

to be paid to something in the unconscious. The process of making repairs to plumbing indicates healing work taking place on an unconscious level.

Police. Figures representing the collective authority and body of rules. Police do not make the rules, but enforce them. Mistakes, crimes and grievances are reported to them for rectification. Their appearance in a dream signifies a reminder or warning that one is overstepping limits, is not following proper procedures or behavior, or is going out of control. They also may bring to attention feelings that one "should" do something because it's expected or proper. It may be wise to examine one's motives.

Poison, poisoning. Danger, especially to one's physical health. Dreams of being poisoned sometimes occur to people who are suffering serious or life-threatening illness, especially cancer (see **Contamination**).

Poisoning something or someone in a dream also may symbolize a desire to rid oneself of something troubling.

Other meaning: Harmful emotions, such as hatred, envy and greed, that literally poison one's psyche.

Potato. Simplicity, plainness; a staple of life, especially community life; a provider of concentrated energy.

Potatoes have lowly natures, and, like all members of the vegetable kingdom, represent the "vegetable soul." Because they are shaped liked testes, potatoes also have an aphrodisiacal nature; yet, to be likened to a potato is to be insulted, humiliated or scorned as a lump.

See **Vegetables.**

Preparation, lack of. Anxiety. Lack of preparation is a common dream, and often involves facing an unexpected exam, or taking a test feeling unprepared. Such dreams may represent a fear of being judged by others in authority, or by one's parental self. In rare cases, especially involving terminal illness, the ultimate concern may be a spiritual preparation for death.

President. A supreme authority figure, one who establishes rules and has power over one's welfare and status.

Prison. Being confined, pinned down, limited in options and activity. Having one's back pressed against the wall. Dreams of being imprisoned sometimes are a psychic balancing that follows a period of great or spontaneous activity.

Dreams of being imprisoned may occur during the first stage of recovery from major upheavals in life that bring a sense of profound loss or disorientation. During the shock and denial of stage one, the dreamer may feel powerless to regain control of life; circumstances have literally created a prison. When the reality of the situation has been accepted, one can move on toward complete recovery.

Other meanings: 1) Protection, refuge from the unknown, a retreat from the pressures of the world and the need to make decisions. Prison life is routine, regular, predictable and defined. Rules are set by a collective authority. 2) Fear or expectation of punishment. 3) Guilt.

Prune. Anxiety over aging; showing the effects of aging. Prunes also might symbolize relief of spiritual blockage.

Pumpkin. Empty-headedness; foolishness. When double, a symbol of the material world and the underworld (consciousness and unconscious). Even as a single gourd, the pumpkin has associations with the underworld, as it plays a role in fall harvest rites and the dying of the natural world.

As a gourd, a pumpkin also may be likened to an alchemical cauldron, especially of the ''vegetable soul.''

Other meaning: Black comedy.

See **Vegetables.**

Purple. See **Colors.**

Purse. See **Identification.**

Q

Quarrel. Arguments in dreams often mirror inner conflicts. Or, they may represent real disagreements in situations in life.

Consider the individual quarreling in the dream. A quarrel between the dreamer and a woman may indicate a conflict involving the anima, while an argument with a man may represent conflict involving the animus. Men and women, even if strangers in a dream, also may represent father and mother figures, siblings, co-workers or supervisors, authority figures, spouses or lovers, etc.

Issues involved in a dream quarrel, if they are not clear, can be symbolic. An argument over a house relates in some way to the psyche, while disagreement over food relates to spiritual nourishment.

Queen. A symbol of the Mother Goddess in her full powers of fecundity and nurturing. The queen is the bounteous earth, the plenty of nature, the ripeness of fruit and grain. She is the ultimate mother, as well as the ultimate authority, who presides over the mysteries of life, death and rebirth. Through her, one can attain a higher consciousness.

The queen also rules the night. She is the moon who illuminates the mysterious landscape of the unconscious.

In her benevolent aspect, the queen is love, nurturing, guidance, fullness and generosity. In her malevolent aspect, she is jealousy, vindictiveness, destruction, dryness and barrenness.

See **Mother.**

Quicksand. A destructive aspect of the unconscious. Being pulled down by quicksand symbolizes losing one's emotional footing and being consumed or overwhelmed by emotions, fears and anxieties. Such dreams are common during times of stress and upheaval.

Other meaning: A shifting, unpredictable and potentially dangerous emotional landscape.

R

Rabbit. See **Hare.**

Rags. Material poverty that hides an inner, spiritual wealth. The triumph of the spiritual over the material.

See **Clothing.**

Rain. The unconscious. In dreams, any kind of contact with water can be seen as contact with the unconscious. When the unconscious comes to us in the form of rain, it is demanding our attention, perhaps seeking to engage us in something we have failed to recognize or have avoided. When the unconscious is represented by a body of water, we can often control our immersion in it, or avoid it altogether. But we cannot control the elements, and when it rains we can get wet.

See **Roof; Umbrella; Water.**

Rainbow. A common symbol of a promise.

The rainbow also is a universal symbol of the bridge between earth and heaven, humankind and God or the gods. It is the path traveled by the souls of the dead to the afterlife. In mythologies, good souls traverse the rainbow with no problem, while unworthy souls are rejected or are consumed by fire.

The rainbow also has mythical associations with a cos-

Rain

mic serpent—a symbol of wisdom and fertility—that encircles the earth.

Other meanings: 1) A sign of God's covenant with humanity. 2) Reconciliation with God. 3) Transfiguration.

See **Bridge; Snake.**

Rat. A symbol of disease, illness, misfortune, death and decay; a bad omen. In European folklore, the rat also is associated with witches and such malevolent supernatural beings as demons and goblins.

As an allegorical figure, the rat is deceitful and tricky, and will turn on one when one is off-guard.

See **Animals.**

Raven. Like all birds, the raven is a messenger between God and humankind. Ravens are also associated with death and the underworld, and are often considered omens of death because they gather at battlefields and houses where someone is about to die, and symbols of impurity because they feed on corpses. Thus, they are messengers of the dark side of God. However, ravens in mythology and fairy tales are neither good nor evil, but express the blunt truth of the unconscious. Talking ravens are agents of prophecy. In a dream, a raven may be bringing messages from the Higher Self or from the unconscious.

In alchemy, the raven is the darkness that precedes the light. It represents the nigredo, the mortification that represents the dying to the material world that is necessary in order for spiritual purification and illumination to take place.

Other meanings: 1) In Christianity, the raven symbolizes sin and the Devil, and is the opposite of the dove. 2) Warfare and bloodshed. 3) In magic, a familiar, a shapeshifter.

See **Birds; Crow.**

Red. See **Colors.**

Retirement. The end of a phase of life.

Rhubarb. Astringency; medicinal qualities; an antidote for spiritual constipation.

The juice of the rhubarb is like sap, and is associated with semen and the generative principle. Rhubarb can go wild, and thus may represent something gone out of control, or which needs to be tended and cut back.

Other meaning: Absurd humor.

See **Vegetables.**

Rice. A staple of spiritual nourishment; food of the gods. Rice also represents magical replenishment, fecundity (the reason it is thrown at weddings), rebirth and immortality. It is associated with the sun and illumination. Alchemists used it to represent bitter sulphur, a dissolving agent in the Great Work.

See **Vegetables.**

Right hand, right-handedness. Rational thought. Using the right hand in a dream symbolizes reliance upon or the functioning of rational thought. If you are left-handed, it may indicate a need for more rational thought and less emotion.

River. The flux of the manifest world and the passage of life are to be found in the symbolic river. The serpentine river reminds us of the twists of fate.

If we are standing on the bank of a river then life is passing us by. In trying to cross a river, we must have a spiritual initiation before reaching the goal on the other side. Whether the currents in the dream river are peaceful or raging might indicate how we feel we are going along in life. To be swimming in a fast river without life support might represent vulnerability and feelings of being overwhelmed. To be tossed about by rough waters represents upheavals of emotion, or a feeling that fate is dealing us a harsh turn. Drifting along on lazy currents in a boat might represent feelings of coasting in life, getting by with a minimal effort, or taking a break.

See **Ship; Water.**

Roadblock. An obstacle preventing you from staying on your present course; a need to change direction.

Robbery. The loss of valuables—i.e., one's identity, self-esteem, emotions. Robbery dreams can occur during the first stage of recovery (shock and denial) following a major upheaval, such as loss, separation, divorce or serious illness, during which one feels an irretrievable or insurmountable loss.

See **Valuables.**

Roof. A covering that separates the conscious from the unconscious. Leaking roofs are a common dream image, and usually represent an invasion of the conscious by the waters of the unconscious. In this way, the unconscious seeks to force our attention to something.

Other meanings: 1) Misery; 2) Discomfort.

Room. Like the house, the room often symbolizes the dreamer's own person, but narrows the focus to specific areas needing attention. Rooms also are womb-like containers and represent protection, separation from the collective.

Interpretations depend on the type of room, the atmosphere in it, the people and objects in it, what takes place in the room and the emotional tone of the dream. If dream rooms are familiar, i.e., in a present or former home or school, consider events which occurred there in the past which might have a bearing on present situations. The presence, or lack, of objects in a room, and their condition may reflect the feelings of the dreamer. Objects which are bright, shiny and in good condition indicate a positive tone, while shabby and dull objects indicate negativity.

The most common room images in dreams are hidden, back, secret, basement or underground rooms, locked rooms and closed rooms. All of these images usually point to the shadow, and call attention to a need to acknowledge and integrate repressed material into the consciousness. Hidden, secret and inner rooms also symbolize womblike places where one feels safe and protected from the outside world. In addition, hidden rooms symbolize unexplored areas of one's consciousness, talents or abilities. Locked and closed rooms often hold something frightening. See **Door; Key; Lockout.**

Other room associations are:

Classrooms, libraries and study rooms: learning, growth process taking place.

Family rooms, living rooms, dens and activity rooms: relationships, dealing with problems and everyday affairs.

Kitchens, dining rooms: relationships in terms of decorum of behavior, role expectations; preparation, digestion of ideas, transmutation.

Nurseries, childhood rooms: birth and nurturing of ideas and creativity; or, calling attention to events at those periods in life.

Bathrooms: release or blockage of emotions and creative energies; cleansing, release of problems or things no longer needed. See **Defecation; Urination.**

Bedrooms: privacy, intimacy, sexual matters. See **Bed/Bedroom.**

Upstairs rooms: higher consciousness.

Utility and work rooms, garages: basic needs, foundations, fundamentals in life.

Rooms newly constructed or under construction, or newly discovered: new areas of creativity, talent, ability opening up.

Crowded or cluttered rooms: confusion, disorganization, loss of control, overcommittment.

Confining rooms: limitations, boundaries, sense of being suffocated. Also, protection. See **Prison; Suffocation.**

Empty rooms: lack of fulfillment, sense of loss, low self-esteem.

Mazes of rooms: feeling lost, disoriented, unanchored, uncertain of one's self; or, journey of discovery.

Holy and sacred rooms: entry symbolizes re-entry into a womb, a reversal of the birth process which in mysticism signifies being spiritually reborn.

See **House.**

Roots. See **Tree.**

Rose. A complex symbol with numerous meanings. The rose in dreams often represents the true, archetypal Self, the highest expression of consciousness. Roses in bloom indicate the dreamer is opening to higher awareness, while withering roses indicate that a path to growth is being left untaken.

The rose is a feminine symbol, and thus representative of fertility, passion, creation, life, beauty and the eternal cycle of birth, death and rebirth. It is the symbol of Venus, goddess of love.

In alchemy, the rose is a symbol of wisdom; red and white roses together are an alchemical symbol of the union of opposites, part of the process of individuation.

In Western mysticism, the rose symbolizes God, Christ, the mystic center, the heart center and universal love; along with the lily, it is the equivalent of the lotus of Eastern mysticism. Jung compared the rose to a mandala, the symbol of wholeness.

The rose's thorns are a Christian symbol of sin. Renaissance artists often used garlands of roses to symbolize the rosary of the Blessed Virgin Mary; they adorned angels, saints and mystics in wreaths of roses to symbolize heavenly bliss.

Colors of roses have significance: a white rose represents purity and innocence, a red rose martyrdom and charity, a blue rose the unattainable.

See **Flowers; Lily.**

Ruby. See **Jewels.**

Rust. A symbol of an unresolved situation, or unresolved emotions, fear or anxieties that are corroding one's life. Rust also symbolizes something no longer useful in one's life.

S

Salt. Purity, incorruptibility, especially of the spirit; moral and spiritual powers. The preservative powers of salt, and its necessity to life, also give it the symbolism of life, immortality and permanence. Since ancient times, it has been a universal charm against evil.

In alchemy, salt unites water and fire and is a rectifying agent. It is also a symbol of the body uniting with spirit and soul.

Salt dissolving in the ocean symbolizes the merging of the individual into the absolute. Salt with food, especially bread, is a symbol of friendship and hospitality.

Other meanings: 1) The bitterness in life. 2) Wit.

Sap. The vital life force, especially that which flows through the "vegetable soul." Sap is likened to semen or mother's milk; it is the generative force, the nurturing food. Sap brings strength and vitality.

See **Vegetables.**

Sapphire. See **Jewels.**

School. Going through a learning experience; learning one of life's lessons. All of life is a school. Attending school in a dream might reflect feelings that one lacks certain types of experience needed to round out the curriculum of life.

School

School dreams especially are likely to occur during major changes and transitions in life.

Teaching at school often represents having assimilated a lesson, or "graduated" to a position of authority concerning matters in life.

Scientist. The intellect; rational, logical thought processes. Scientists are thinkers and experimenters.

See **Laboratory.**

Sea. See **Ocean.**

Seed. Latency, potentiality and hope. The seed is also the sacred center out of which grow the tree of life and the

World Tree. The seed is the link between past and future generations.

Seminar. An educational experience—as an attendee in a seminar one has something to learn; as an instructor, one has something to teach, impart or disseminate to others.

Serpent. See **Snake.**

Service station. A way station along the journey of life, where one can stop, rest, refuel, revitalize oneself, ask directions and get assistance. A service station may represent a refuge, or a plateau for reorientation.

Sewer. The destructive aspects of the unconscious, filled with cast-off waste. In alchemical terms, a sewer is the *nigredo,* the darkness of the soul, the self-reflection that comes with depression and dissolution.

Sex and Sexuality. Frequently, the symbol of two energies joining together. Dreams of sexual encounters with persons of the same sex are sometimes mistaken as repressed homosexuality, but instead they usually symbolize a need to be more in touch with one's own anima or animus.

Sometimes sexual dreams are metaphors for repression of emotion, or liberation of emotion, especially erotic feelings. They also reflect anxieties about commitment (such as prior to marriage) or worries that a relationship has gone stale or is coming to an end. Sexual liaisons with other persons, especially strangers or persons whom we know but have no intimate relationship with, may portray one's own anima or animus.

Dreams of sex with members of one's family are not completely without reference to actual physical desire;

Sex and Sexuality

nonetheless they must be examined from an alchemical perspective.

See **Infidelity.**

Sexual rejection. Dreams of being sexually rejected usually mirror one's real fears of being rejected in a relationship, or of being inadequate.

Such dreams are common in situations where one has entered into a separation or divorce, especially if the other party initiated the split. They also occur when infidelity is suspected or discovered. The dreamer feels abandoned, rejected and vulnerable, and these emotions are reflected in sexual rejection dreams. Sometimes the dream involves the partner, and sometimes it involves old flames from the past.

Sexual rejection dreams are most likely to occur during the second stage of recovery, which involves anger, depression and despair.

Shell. A feminine symbol associated with womb and water. A cornucopia. A shell is something that we can pull back into to recuperate or when we are threatened.

Snake

Ship. An important dream symbol with archetypal associations, the ship is a means of transport across the waters of the unconscious.

Snake. One of the most common dream symbols, and one with many and complex meanings depending upon the context of the dream. Generally, the snake is a symbol of great power indicating change, renewal and transformation. Jung considered the snake to represent a potent archetype of psychic energy, power, dynamism, instinctual drive and the entire process of psychic and spiritual transformation. In dreams, the snake may indicate a transformative process already underway, but often calls attention to the need to move to a new level of consciousness. The dreamer may fear it, as he or she may fear change itself, but the snake must be seen as a positive sign and not a negative one. Even a snake bite in a dream can be positively interpreted as being ''bitten'' by a new awareness.

In mythology, snakes are powerful magical and mystical

creatures. They are universal symbols of renewal and re-birth because of their unique ability to shed their old skin for new. The ouroboros, the snake which forms a circle by biting its own tail, symbolizes the eternal cycle of life, death and rebirth. In its carnal aspect, the snake represents a phallus and its associations of the life force, sexuality and sensuality. As a phallic symbol, the snake often is associated with pregnancy in imagery and mythology. In dreams, such pregnancy also may refer to a state of psychic trans-formation: pregnant with ideas, possibilities, changes, events about to happen.

As a creature which crawls along the earth and lives in holes in the ground, the snake has connections to the un-derworld, the unconscious and humankind's instinctual drives. Mythical snakes guard the sleep of both the living and the dead; thus, they are creatures at the gateway to new consciousness. The snake also is a universal companion to goddesses, and thus can symbolize the feminine, the anima, the womb, the dark, intuition, emotion and all the aspects of the Goddess Mother. See **Mother.**

The coils of the snake represent the cycles of manifes-tation: life and death, good and evil, wisdom and blind passion, light and dark, healing and poison, protection and destruction. In kundalini yoga, a psychic force called the "serpent power" is said to reside coiled near the base of the spine, and in the transformation to enlightenment the energy rises up the spine to the crown.

In alchemy, the snake is the *serpens Mercurii,* the quick-silver that represents the constant driving forward of psy-chic life forces: living, dying and being reborn. The snake is the prima materia, the unformed and dark chaos, from which order and life spring. Alchemical art often shows the snake wearing a gold crown, gem, diadem, or light to depict its expanded spiritual consciousness, which, like the serpent power of kundalini yoga, arises from the same energy as sexuality.

The snake is a symbol of healing, which also is part of the transformation process. Aesclepius, the Greek god of healing, appears in the form of a snake, and domesticated snakes were kept at the sacred healing temples of the classical world. Dream experiences were an integral part of the ancient healing therapies at these temples. The healing power of serpents is cited in Numbers 21:8, in which Moses is instructed to set a fiery serpent upon a pole, so that all who look upon it shall live.

Snakes also are associated with water, the symbol of the unconscious, and trees, the symbol of wisdom and knowledge. A snake climbing up a tree represents the process of becoming conscious, or going through psychic transformation. See **Tree; Water.** Two serpents twine up the caduceus staff of Hermes (Mercury), the classical god who escorts the souls of the dead and delivers messages to the gods. The caduceus is a symbol of enlightenment and of healing.

In Christian symbolism, the snake represents evil or the Devil, the tempter who entices humankind to eat the fruit of the Tree of Knowledge and thus fall from grace. However, the Gnostics considered the snake as the Saviour himself, who initiates humankind into consciousness and raises it up out of a primitive, nature-identified unconsciousness.

Dragons often carry the same symbolisms as snakes. See **Dragon.**

Snake bite. Initiation, penetration by a content. A snake bite in a dream is the equivalent of an injection administered by a doctor: one is forcibly administered a substance that will bring about some kind of healing or new spiritual awareness. To be stalked or pursued by a snake intent on biting indicates that the unconscious is attempting to bring

Snow

something into waking awareness.

See **Wound.**

Snow. Feelings, talents or abilities that are frozen, buried or inaccessible. Snow also can represent the absence of emotion. Similarly, melting snow means a cold heart beginning to warm.

Spear. A phallic symbol; the warrior and hunter. The spear is power and strength; it also represents virtue. In myth, the spear is the *axis mundi,* the world axis that connects the physical world to the underworld and the heavens.

In Christian symbolism, the spear is associated with the Holy Grail and victory over evil, because Christ was pierced by a spear as he hung upon the cross.

Spider. The spider represents two aspects of the Goddess Mother: the weaver of fate and the destroyer. The spider spins the web of time and fate, and captures all things in it. The web also can represent illusion.

The spider can represent the destructive aspects of the Goddess Mother because its web is used to catch and kill. Thus the spider uses its creative power to spin fate, which binds the living and eventually claims their lives. This is the cycle of birth, life and death. The spider in a dream can represent a phase in the cycle of change, depending on whether it is spinning, catching or killing.

See **Insects.**

Spiral. Spirals represent both the masculine and feminine waxing and waning cyclical powers of the cosmos: fertilization, birth, growth, decline, death. Spirals take many shapes, and can indicate a winding up or a winding down. A spiral also is a center of life, and a vortex of energy. In a dream spirals may represent a need for change, a growth process that is taking place, or the withering away of something no longer needed.

Spirals have numerous associations. Mazes, labyrinths and lightning, navels, s-link chains, fire and the caduceus are forms of spirals. All life that grows in coils, s-shapes and spirals represent the symbolism of the spiral, such as seashells, tree cones, serpents, trailing and vining plants, snails, ferns, and octopi. Animals with horns can be interpreted in terms of the spiral, as well as any animal which curls (coils) itself up.

See **Circle; Fire; Horns; Lightning; Maze; Shell; Snake.**

Square. Stability, solidity and materiality. There are the four classical elements (earth, air, fire and water), and the cardinal points of the compass. The square is one face of a solid block. Thus, squares in dreams often represent the solid, material world, and a sense of security.

Stairs. Access to higher and lower realms of consciousness. Ascending stairs (such as to attics or towers) is a symbol of transcendence. Descending stairs (especially into basements or caves) means to go down into the uncon-

Stairs

scious. Winding stairs represent mysteries; spiral stairs are
a symbol of growth, or of the cycle of rebirth.

On a more mundane level, stairs in a dream may represent ascent or descent in one's career or social standing.

See **Ladder; Spiral.**

Storm. As a destructive force of nature, and thus linked to
the earth, storms are a shadow symbol of the emotions and
instincts. They may point to a repression of emotions which
builds to a point where they become released in the fury
of a thunderstorm, tornado, hurricane and so on. Storms are

Storm

accompanied by downpours of water (the unconscious, the reservoir of emotions, instincts and intuitions). One seeks shelter from a storm by going within (reconnecting to one's emotional/instinctual nature), such as to a house, cave, building or the underground.

Storms also may mirror horrendous or violent events that have happened in life; they symbolize feelings of being out of control or overwhelmed as a result.

Subway. A collective symbol of the unconscious, penetrated by planned routes.

Suffocation. Being pinned down, confined, restricted, prevented from taking action. Having one's options limited.

Suffocating in a small space occurs in dreams during pregnancy, especially during the third trimester, and anticipates the physical birthing.

Sun. Life, energy, the light of consciousness and active intellect, the all-seeing eye. The sun god is the hero and the emperor. Sunset corresponds to the death of the hero. As the sun ascends out of darkness to the zenith, so does ego consciousness awaken and overcome the dark forces of the unconscious.

The dual aspect of solar (masculine) and lunar (feminine) energy must be kept in balance, so that one is not parched by too much of the sun.

Swaddling clothes. See **Baby.**

Swan. Partaking of both air and water, the swan is often a symbol of the soul. Its dying song is heard by the poet, to whom the swan signifies solitude and peace. In myth, the transformation of people and divinities into swans represents a purification of spirit. As with Leda's swan, amorousness may also be signified.

Sweater. One's total being, body and Self.
See **Clothing.**

Swimming. Navigating through the waters of the unconscious. Swimming in an ocean or a vast lake indicates more of an opening up of uncharted territories in the unconscious than swimming in a pond or a pool. The depth of the water, the current or waves, and the ability of the swimmer are all factors reflecting one's feelings concerning the unconscious. Currents, riptides or monsters threatening to pull one under represent fears residing within the unconscious.

Swimming also is a symbol of birthing. It may represent a spiritual birthing of a new awareness or higher plane of consciousness—a new Self. Swimming dreams also occur to both men and women during a pregnancy.

Swimming pool. A symbol of a restricted unconscious. Swimming pools are artificial constructions, which gives them associations with collectivity. They have boundaries and known depths, and offer relatively safe encounters with water. Symbolically, such safe encounters are with only a restricted part of the unconscious, unlike the unbounded depths of the ocean or the great depths of a lake. A swimming pool at a home takes on a more personal significance than a swimming pool in a public facility such as a gym or school, the latter of which operates under collective rules.

See **Water.** Compare to **Lake; Ocean; River.**

Sword. A masculine symbol representing authority, power, sovereignty, truth and justice. It is also a weapon, but does not connote aggression so much as the fight for, or defense of, "right." The sword is the instrument of action, dynamism and the intellect. It is the symbol of the king, a father or authority figure; the hero, who quests for truth; and the warrior, who seeks justice. It also is a ritual tool of the magician, the intermediary between the heavenly realm of spirit and the earthly realm of instinct.

The sword cuts and separates. It divides right from wrong, good from bad, healthy from unhealthy. As an alchemical symbol, it represents *separatio,* in which the whole is divided into its basic parts prior to recombining or reassembling into a better whole.

Tears. The healing waters of the unconscious. In alchemy, tears are associated with *solutio*, "dissolve and coagulate." In psychotherapy, this occurs when the ego is dissolved (but not obliterated) in a descent into the unconscious, and coagulated into a new form.

Teeth. One of the most common dream motifs. Teeth have a variety of meanings depending upon the context of the dream.

Teeth can be symbols of attack, hostility, war and defiance, as in baring one's teeth. While biting is an aggressive act, it also can symbolize sensuality and the act of love. The teeth, representing the male, penetrate the flesh, or the female. See **Biting.**

As part of the mouth, teeth are also symbols of speech, and in dreams may reflect the impact of what one says to others. Loose teeth, for example, may represent loose or careless talk, especially speaking without thinking or making wild statements.

As one of the most enduring and indestructible parts of the body, teeth symbolize death and rebirth. Baby teeth being replaced by mature teeth represent the process of psychic transformation.

Losing teeth represents a loss of power or potency, mat-

Telephone

uration, the process of growing older, or physical or emotional injury.

See **Dentist**.

Telephone. Communication with the inner self, the unconscious. Telephones also represent one's communication with others. Dreaming about someone hanging up on you symbolizes fears of abandonment, rejection or unavailability.

Terminal illness. See **Illness**.

Thieves. See **Robbery; Valuables.**

Threshold. See **Door; Gate.**

Thunder. The voice of the gods. Thunder denotes creativity and fertilizing power (the rain brought by thunderstorms), as well as divine anger and fury. Like lightning, the other great tool of sky gods, it may mean generation, regeneration, or destruction. In myth, thunderbolts are both the weapon and the personification of gods. They also symbolize flashes of divine inspiration and enlightenment.
See **Hammer; Lightning.**

Tidal wave. See **Waves.**

Tides. See **Water; Waves.**

Time. Pressure against deadlines. A period allotted one for projects, goals, life in general. Dreams of time running out are anxiety dreams that usually occur when one is under stress or pressure. The dreams may be showing that priorities need to be re-examined, or some projects or activities scaled back or dropped.

Time dreams are likely also to occur during life passages, when we suddenly realize we haven't accomplished everything we set out to do. In cases of grave illness, time running out symbolizes a fear of death, and sometimes impending death.
See **Eleventh hour.**

Tomb. See **Grave.**

Topaz. See **Jewels.**

Tornado. See **Storm.**

Totem pole. A repository of sacred stories—of one's life, of the cosmos; repository of sacred wisdom.

Train

Other meanings: 1) The protective forces of nature. 2) Something that must be deciphered. 3) A phallic symbol.

Tower. Masculine symbol of the intellect. A repository of wisdom, but isolated from the earth (feminine symbol of emotions and the physical). Exclusive domain, retreat of the select.

Other meanings: 1) A symbol of the father. 2) A phallic symbol, the masculine generative and creative power. 3) A place of imprisonment and punishment.

Train. A collective symbol, a means of traveling through life by a planned route and schedule.

See **Bus.**

Trapped. A feeling of being trapped by people, a job, circumstances or situations in waking life.

Being trapped in a small space is a typical dream motif during pregnancy, especially in the third trimester.

Traveling companions. In dreams, one is sometimes accompanied by a mysterious or magical traveling companion. This being, who may be human or may have fantastical or supernatural attributes, sometimes is a silent companion, at other times provides guidance and direction. The traveling companion is an archetypal representation common to myth and folktale. Essentially, it symbolizes both the goal of the journey and one's own higher wisdom that will enable one to complete the journey. It is a part of the Self.

Tree. An archetypal symbol of the Self and its process of individuation, as represented by growth and branching out. In mythology, the tree is an important symbol of growth, life and knowledge. Its roots reach deep into the soil and its branches reach toward the heavens. Thus, the World Tree is the *axis mundi* connecting the three cosmic spheres of spirit, earth and underworld. The fruit of the tree is wisdom.

Roots of a tree symbolize buried or unrecognized potentialities.

Other meanings: 1) A symbol of Mother Nature or of the Goddess Mother; the divine feminine. 2) Family matters, as in one's family tree.

Trunk. Where repressed and unresolved emotions and memories are shut away. Opening a trunk in a dream may be akin to opening Pandora's box: whatever is released will have to be dealt with.

Tree

Tunnel. Access to and egress from the unconscious. Tunnels are underground and underwater, both symbols of the unconscious. Emerging from a tunnel is a symbol of birthing of a new Self out of the unconscious. Going into a tunnel symbolizes self-reflection and introspection.

Tunnels may be twisted or dangerous, or filled with monsters, which are symbols of unresolved fears. Twisted tunnels may have associations with mazes and labyrinths (see **Maze**).

Tunnel dreams commonly occur during pregnancy, especially the last stages, and symbolize the physical birthing process.

Turquoise. See **Jewels.**

Twilight. A time of uncertainty, when things are not clear and when shadows appear over the landscape of the psyche. Darkness approaches. Twilight may indicate that one is uncertain, undecided, confused or fearful about events or a state of affairs.

Twilight also is the final stage before entry into the darkness of change and transformation. In alchemy, the nigredo, or blackness, involves a dissolution that must occur in order for a reconstruction into something greater to occur. The Christian mystic, St. John of the Cross, conceived of the "dark night of the soul"—a stage of turmoil and despair during which significant transformation occurs to yield a higher, enlightened spiritual state.

See **Dawn.**

Twins. The appearance of twins, people or animals in twos, heralds the emergence of something into the consciousness. Twins and pairs are a common motif in mythology. In the story of the Flood and Noah's ark, for example, the pairs of animals are symbolic of the start of a new world order.

The appearance of two-of-a-kind in a dream also may indicate the presence of duality or conflict.

U

Umbrella. Protection, especially from the waters of the unconscious in the form of rain. If the unconscious cannot engage us through immersion, such as in a body of water, then it may attempt to reach us from above through rain. Umbrellas prevent, or at least limit, contact.

Unicycle. Riding a unicycle symbolizes being on one's own, especially in terms of marital or love relationships.

Urination. A bodily function which in dreams symbolizes psychic states and experiences. Urination generally represents the expression of emotion and feelings. Often it harkens back to a time in early life when feelings were more fluid and easily expressed. Urination by a child symbolizes the naiveté and spontaneity of childhood. Urination in copious quantities, or in great frequency, may parallel a great outflow of emotion taking place in waking life. Urine that spills out of control may mean overwhelming emotions. Hot urine may represent emotions difficult to cope with. The inability to urinate may indicate blocked feelings.

Other meanings: 1) Creative output. Urine is associated with water, which is representative of the unconscious and creativity. See **Water.** Within an alchemical context, both urine and water are names for the *prima materia*, the basic material of the cosmos, which in the terms of depth psy-

Umbrella

chology is the state of conscious chaos at the beginning of the process of individuation. 2) Psychic waste. For example, a person undergoing analysis might dream of passing enormous quantities of urine, representing the release of repressed material from the shadow. 3) Transmutation. In alchemy, the urine of an uncorrupted boy is an ideal solvent in the alchemical process. 4) Sexuality. A Freudian interpretation that views urination dreams accompanied by the physical urge to urinate as really caused by sexual stimuli. The urination dream is a regression to the infantile form of urethral eroticism.

See **Defecation.**

V

Valuables. One's identity; emotions. Dreams of loss of valuables, such as money or jewelry, are common symbols of anxieties over major changes in life, such as marriage, separation, divorce, grief, serious illness or job loss. These dreams especially occur during the first stage of recovery, when one is suffering from shock and denial.

Finding, carrying and losing valuables are common symbols in the dreams of pregnant women.

Vegetables. The vegetable kingdom is much maligned, and is often used as a metaphor for inactivity, dullness, lack of vitality, low intelligence, absence of emotion, lack of will, melancholy and bad humor. In fact, the symbolisms of vegetables are much more profound and go deep into the souls of humankind and nature.

The root of the word "vegetable" means the very opposite of dullness and inactivity: to animate, invigorate, enliven, grow, refresh and vivify. The concept of a vegetable soul that nourishes all living things goes back to classical Greece; it passed then into the Hermetic and alchemical philosophies of the Renaissance. Humankind is viewed as having a tripartite soul, including the vegetable, animal and rational.

The vegetable soul grounds the rational soul, and is the mediator between the conscious and the unconscious. It is dark and downward-pulling, connecting us directly and intimately to our ancestral roots and to the roots of the earth and nature. The vegetable soul is part of the anima mundi, the world soul, that which animates all things.

Physically, the vegetable soul is connected to the human body's autonomous nervous system, the unconscious, unthinking force that rules metabolism, digestion and primitive functions. Jung observed that plants are nourished by the elements; therefore the vegetable kingdom represents the very deepest level of the unconscious, where one encounters the roots of one's real self, and where the fundamental life-energy of all things originates. Wilhelm Reich believed that ''vegetative energies'' could become bound up in people, and that their release brought about a state of wholeness.

Because it is elemental, material, of the earth and in the earth, the vegetable has numerous associations with the mysteries of death and rebirth. Vegetation deities are all associated with these mysteries: that from the vitality of death, rebirth and new growth are possible. Various societies have mystery rites around certain totemic foods, such as corn, wheat, rice, yams, coconuts, breadfruit and taro root. Such totemic foods—indeed all vegetables—are vessels for the gods, representing the complexities of their manifestations in the material world.

Vegetables in general are totemic in a social sense, reflecting cultural, religious and political attitudes. For example, potatoes were shunned by Puritans because they are not mentioned in the Bible. Thus, vegetables place us in a social context.

It is these associations that make the vegetable the most widespread metaphor for spiritual growth. On a simple level, the vegetable is plain, a staple. It is dark and melancholic. On a higher level, it is the foundation of the animating force of the cosmos.

Within the vegetable kingdom is a hierarchy of symbolisms. The lowly cabbage signifies dullness and solidity, while trees are the alchemists' gold. Nuts are hidden wisdom, the generative principle. Fruits and flowers are transcendental symbols. Some vegetables, such as beans, are ascribed magical properties in myth and fairy tale—they become talismans that take human consciousness into another realm.

In dreams, vegetables are seldom dramatic, but their appearance may have profound meaning. In the broadest sense vegetables are a connection to one's family, community and ancestral roots. Vegetables pull us down, bring us back to earth, force us down into the depths of our unconscious.

Eating vegetables (see **Food**) signifies the taking in of spiritual nourishment of the most fundamental kind; the subsequent process of digestion is the absorption and assimilation of this nourishment into the psyche. Cooking vegetables is an alchemical process. Growing vegetables indicates fertility and renewal. Rotting vegetables—a symbol of death—are a precursor to renewal and growth. Seeing rows and rows of neatly planted vegetables could mean immobility or fear of immobility or a loss of will—or a sense of orderliness and solid organization. Wild vegetables are disorganization, chaos, the vegetable soul out of control. Frozen vegetables show a state of suspended spiritual animation. Processed vegetables have had some or all of their spiritual nutrients removed.

See **individual vegetable listings.** See also **Gardener.**

Vehicles. A vehicle is what carries us on our journey through life, or into the unconscious or spirit realm. It may symbolize one's physical body, or one's ego. Note the type of vehicle and any unusual features that demand attention. An automobile driven by one's self or others has different meanings than being a passenger on a public conveyance, such as a train, which is limited in where it can go and how fast. Also note if there are companions.

See **Automobile; Journey; Ship; Travelling companions.**

Victimization. Dreams of being victimized commonly are a symptom of severe depression, such as occurs following a separation or divorce. Such dreams indicate self-blame for everything that has gone wrong.

Victimization dreams also may symbolize a feeling of being oppressed by others or by circumstances in life. Again, the dreamer is projecting self-blame onto the situation.

Violence. Murder, bloodshed, mutilation of bodies, massacres and other horrendous physical violence symbolize the alchemical state of *mortificatio*, in which ingredients are cut apart and ground to their common elements before being recombined into something better. Thus, violence may indicate the beginning stages of transformation, in which the old must be rent apart to make way for creation of the new.

Dreams of violence often symbolize feelings of being out of control or overwhelmed as a result of major upheavals. They may also represent rage and anger toward others.

Violet. See **Colors.**

Volcano. Like the mountain, the volcano is an archetypal symbol of the Self. Its potential for eruption, for spewing forth great quantities of material, signals impending or potential drastic inner change.

Vomiting. Revulsion; a desire to get rid of something unpleasant or poisonous in one's life.

Wallet. See **Identification.**

Walnut. Because of its shape, the walnut is a symbol of the brain and, by association, intellectual activity. It also represents the general symbolism of nuts as hidden wisdom, the heart of a matter, and fertility.

War. Inner conflict, especially of a serious nature, not being acknowledged or resolved.

The particular weapons used in a dream war can shed additional light on the nature of the conflict. Swords and knives are symbols of severance and separation, and may indicate an inability to separate one's self from a situation. Guns, grenades and bombs are symbols of anger; the latter two may also indicate a threatening buildup of inner pressure. Nuclear weapons (as well as large-scale warfare) are symbolic of great frustration and anger which may be directed at ideas, beliefs and concepts.

Washing. Cleansing one's self of "dirt," such as unhappy situations or circumstances, or emotional baggage. Getting clean in a dream often represents newness and renewal—we scrub up our egos, self-images and sense of worth. Not being able to get clean might represent frustration or inability to make changes.

Water

Uncleanliness in certain body parts also can be a harbinger of serious physical illness.

See **Baptism; Body, body parts; Dirt, dirtiness; Disinfectant.**

Washing machine. A washing machine may appear in a dream involving one's identity (see **Clothing**), and relate to changing or improving the identity.

A washing machine also is a common symbol in dreams during pregnancy, and represents the watery inner space of a pregnant womb.

Other meanings: 1) A purification process going on in the unconscious. 2) Turbulence, agitation.

Water. The unconscious; emotions. To get wet in dreams is to enter the unconscious. Many persons undergoing crises or life passages have dreams in which they are doused by rain or forcibly immersed in bodies of water, such as by falling or dunking. These might indicate feelings of being overwhelmed by emotion. Being caught in a tidal wave might symbolize a feeling of being overwhelmed by emotion to the point of destruction.

Water signifies the source of being in most cosmologies, and so it is symbolic of birth and the Mother Goddess. Submerging into water is to disolve the old and give birth to the new.

Water has its magical aspects as in baptism and initiation. The abyssal waters represent ultimate mystery and may evoke fear, but they might also signify profound wisdom. Water can also connote forgetfulness.

Waves. Being buffeted or engulfed by waves commonly represents feelings of being emotionally overwhelmed, especially during times of crisis or major life change. Tidal waves reflect extreme upheaval in life. Being lapped by gentle waves or tides represents peace and tranquility in the womblike waters of the unconscious.

Dreams involving waves are common during pregnancy, and represent the womb.

Wedding. See **Initiation; Marriage.**

Well. The deep layers of the unconscious; contact with the underworld. Nature spirits (the forces of nature) dwell near and protect wells.

Wells also are a source of spiritual refreshment and powers of healing.

Other meanings: 1) The womb of the Mother Goddess. 2) A woman's womb.

See **Water.**

Wellness. Dreams of good health and wellness are not uncommon among persons who are terminally ill. Such dreams may symbolize the desire for recovery. They also symbolize impending death, and recovery in the afterlife.

Dreams in which deceased persons appear well and perhaps younger and more vital—especially if they died of illness or in a debilitated state—are difficult to interpret. They may represent the desire on the part of the living to see the deceased restored to life, or they may be a symbol of one's acceptance of the deceased's transition from life. However, it cannot be ruled out that such dreams may also represent a picture of the afterlife.

Wheat. A symbol of the mysteries of death and resurrection; the Mother Goddess; fecundity; the bounty of the earth; and prosperity. Wheat is associated with the womb of the earth, which brings forth life and takes in death to resurrect life anew. Wheat was used by the ancient Egyptians to represent Osiris rising from the dead, and by the Greeks as a symbol of Demeter in the Eleusinian mysteries.

In Christianity, wheat represents the Christ risen from the dead; and symbolizes the Virgin Mary, who is the grain from which the flour of the host is made. Wheat also suggests the human nature of Christ.

See **Vegetables.**

Wheel. Dynamism; change; the relentless turning of time; the course of life; the seasons; the cycle of birth, death and rebirth; the sun (illumination) rotating through the heavens. Like the circle, the wheel also symbolizes completion and wholeness (see **Circle**); becoming and passing away.

In alchemy, a wheel represents *circulatio*, the rotation of the universe, the ascension of humankind into God and the descent of God into humankind.

The wheel also represents the pattern set in motion by the psyche, in terms of the manifestation of inner potential in real events.

On a mundane level, the wheel represents fortune: the ups and downs of life.

A spoked wheel should be considered in terms of number symbolisms (see **Numbers**).

Whip, whipping. Domination, superiority, authority; also punishment, degradation and abuse.

The whip is both a symbol of male virility and the generative force, and female fecundity and the dark aspect of the Mother Goddess, or Terrible Mother. In ancient times, people and fruit and nut trees were whipped to ensure fertility, and to drive away evil spirits.

In a dream, whips or whipping may represent the germination of creativity or something new. It also may mean a form of punishment or self-punishment, and relate to one's relationships, job or other circumstances.

White. See **Colors.**

Window. Consciousness; one's perception or perspective on the world. Looking in a window can symbolize insight; looking out a window can mean one's outlook on the world.

Windows also are symbols of openings to other levels of consciousness.

In dreams related to impending death, windows can symbolize transformation to another state of being.

Wine. Vitality; truth; the blood of the gods. Like blood, wine has a transforming power. Ritually, it has been used in offerings to chthonic deities, giving it a symbolic connection to the realm of the unconscious. It also is associated with the vegetation gods Dionysus and Bacchus, and thus represents intoxication, divine ecstasy, the vital powers of nature, and the "vegetable soul" (see **Vegetables**).

Wine is associated with the masculine principle, the sun (illumination) and fire (purification).

Wine is also a symbol for blood, especially in the context of sacrifice. In Christianity, it symbolizes the blood of Christ.

See **Blood.**

Wise Old Man/Woman. These figures represent the Higher Self or guardian spirit that may be called up in times of crisis. They are often represented by grandparents, teachers and persons in authority. They are the wisdom that has been accumulated in life, and the superior knowledge of the Higher Self in guiding us through life's trials. Wise Old Men and Wise Old Women in dreams often are trying to call our attention to important information or considerations.

The Wise Old Man and Wise Old Woman also can symbolize the goal of the integrated self that is prepared for the spiritual journey at the end of life.

Witch. The destructive side of the feminine principle; the Terrible Mother. A witch often symbolizes destructive, malevolent acts or nature of a mother, wife or lover; or, of one's shadow.

Wolf. Devouring forces; diabolic forces; the principle of evil; fierceness; craftiness; gluttony. The wolf frequently appears in mythology and fairy tale as a negative force, but it has its positive, spiritual associations as well.

The wolf is a chthonic animal, the companion of gods of the underworld (the unconscious) and psychopomp of the souls of the dead. Like the dog, the wolf has lunar associations and thus is connected to the Mother Goddess, especially her dark aspects.

In its positive aspects, the wolf is a symbol of light because it can see in the darkness. It also is a symbol of valor and victory.

In alchemy, the wolf is the dual nature of Mercurius, which is in all things.

In Christian symbolism, the wolf represents the evil powers that tempt and threaten the faithful.

Other meaning: Devouring fear.

See **Animals; Dog.**

Wood. Solidity; hardness; the raw material of building and new construction. In alchemy, wood is the first matter, the *prima materia*, from which all things are shaped, and from which the philosopher's stone is derived. It is a mother symbol with associations of protection and carrying; it is a repository of the vital force that animates the universe.

The burning of wood has magical properties in sacrificial rites, signifying wisdom and death; its ashes symbolize rebirth. Thus, wood is related to the symbol of fire, and to the alchemical process of *calcinatio*, or purification through a burning away.

See **Fire; Tree; individual listings for trees.**

Worm. Death; decay; dissolution; rotting. Also, the earth, or the material.

Jung viewed the worm as a libidinal figure that kills rather than gives life. In alchemy, the worm is key to *putrefactio*, the blackening and decay that precedes resurrection and light. Similarly, worms aerate rotting compost which becomes the fertilizer of new life.

The worm also is a symbol for the world serpent (see **Snake**) and for the Devil, or the principle of evil.

Because of its association with rot, decay and stench, the worm in dreams also may symbolize pollution—of one's life, environment, or literally the air.

Other meanings: 1) Untrustworthiness; 2) Low moral character.

Wound. A symbol of initiation. Also, unresolved emotions, anxieties or fears.

Dreams of mortal wounds commonly occur during the

Wound

stresses of midlife crisis, and represent fear of letting go of the old self to make way for a new self.

See **Death**.

Wounded children. See **Child/children**.

Y

Yam. A phallic symbol because of its shape. Like potatoes, yams are a staple of life and community life. They also are an important totemic vegetable, tied to the mysteries of death and rebirth.

See **Vegetables.**

Yard. A personal boundary associated with family, home and security; a place where games are played—a child's world; a place of innocence, where the real world is the yard, while the mysterious and possibly dangerous unknown lies beyond.

Yellow. See **Colors.**

Yew. An evergreen that is a symbol of long life and immortality. In folklore, the yew is a magical charm against bewitchment. In its destructive aspect, the yew is a symbol of death and mourning, because its needles and seeds are poisonous.

Yoke. Union; being connected or bound to something in a balance.

Yokes also carry negative connotations of slavery, bondage, obedience, toil, and being treated like an animal.

Z

Zircon. See **Jewels.**

Zone. A bounded space that implies territoriality, limited access or activity, or sovereignty. Zones are collective symbols, the rules for which are set by collective authority.

Zoo. Confined or imprisoned animal nature, urges or instincts.
Other meaning: Chaos.

Bibliography and Recommended Reading

Bishop, Peter. *The Greening of Psychology: The Vegetable World in Myth, Dream and Healing.* Dallas: Spring Publications, 1990.

Blackmore, Susan. *Beyond the Body: An Investigation of Out-of-Body Experiences.* London: Heinemann, 1990.

Broadribb, Donald. *The Dream Story.* Toronto: Inner City Books, 1990.

Chetwynd, Tom. *How to Interpret Your Own Dreams.* New York: Bell Publishing, 1972.

Cirlot, J. E. *A Dictionary of Symbols.* New York: Philosophical Library, 1971.

Clift, Jean Dalby, and Wallace B. *The Hero Journey in Dreams.* New York: Crossroad, 1988.

———. *Symbols of Transformation in Dreams.* New York: Crossroad, 1989.

Cooper, J. C. *An Illustrated Encyclopedia of Traditional Symbols.* London: Thames & Hudson, 1978.

Crisp, Tony. *Do You Dream?* New York: E.P. Dutton, 1971.

Delaney, Gayle. *Living Your Dreams.* Rev. ed. San Francisco: Harper & Row, 1988.

Devereaux, George (ed.). *Psychoanalysis and the Occult.* New York: International Universities Press, 1953.

Dunne, John W. *An Experiment with Time.* New York: Macmillan, 1927.

Eliade, Mircea. *Patterns in Comparative Religion.* New York: New American Library, 1958.

———. *From Primitives to Zen: A Thematic Source Book of the History of Religions.* San Francisco: Harper & Row, 1977.

———. *The Myth of the Eternal Return, or, Cosmos and History.* Princeton, N.J.: Princeton University Press, 1954.

———. *Rites and Symbols of Initiation.* New York: Harper & Row, 1958.

———. *Shamanism.* Princeton, N.J.: Princeton University Press, 1964.

———. *Myths, Dreams, and Mysteries.* New York: Harper & Row, 1960.

————. *Symbolism, the Sacred & the Arts*. Diane Apostolos-Cappadona (ed.). New York: Crossroad, 1988.

Edinger, Edward F. *Anatomy of the Psyche*. LaSalle, Ill.: Open Court, 1985.

Epstein, Gerald. *Waking Dream Therapy: Dream Process As Imagination*. New York: Human Sciences Press, 1981.

Faraday, Ann. *Dream Power*. New York: Berkley Books, 1972.

————. *The Dream Game*. New York: Harper & Row, 1974.

Ferris, Timothy. *Coming of Age in the Milky Way*. New York: William Morrow, 1988.

Fontana, David. *Dreamlife: Understanding and Using Your Dreams*. Longmead, U.K.: Element Books, 1990.

Fosshage, James L., and Clemens A. Loew. *Dream Interpretation: A Comparative Study, Revised Edition*. New York: PMA Publishing Corp., 1987.

Fox, Oliver. *Astral Projection*. New York: University Books, 1962.

Freeman, Lucy, and Kerstin Kupferman. *The Power of Fantasy*. New York: Continuum, 1988.

Freud, Sigmund. *The Interpretation of Dreams*. New York: The Modern Library, 1950. First published 1900.

Gackenbush, Jayne and Stephen LaBerge (eds.). *Conscious Mind, Sleeping Brain: Perspective on Lucid Dreaming*. New York: Plenum Press, 1988.

Gackenbush, Jayne, (ed.). *Dreams: A Sourcebook*. New York: Garland Press, 1989.

Gackenbush, Jayne, and Jane Bosveld. *Control Your Dreams*. New York: Harper & Row, 1989.

Garfield, Patricia. *Creative Dreaming*. New York: Ballantine, 1974.

————. *The Healing Power of Dreams*. New York: Simon & Schuster, 1991.

Gendlin, Eugene T. *Let Your Body Interpret Your Dreams*. Wilmette, Ill.: Chiron Publications, 1986.

Green, C. E. *Lucid Dreams*. London: Hamish Hamilton, 1968.

Grossinger, Richard (ed.). *The Alchemical Tradition in the Late Twentieth Century*. Berkeley: North Atlantic Books, 1983.

Guiley, Rosemary Ellen. *Harper's Encyclopedia of Mystical and Paranormal Experience*. San Francisco: Harper San Francisco, 1991.

Hall, Calvin S., and Vernon A. Nordby. *A Primer on Jungian Psychology*. New York: New American Library, 1973.

Hall, James A. *Jungian Dream Interpretation: A Handbook of Theory and Practice*. Toronto: Inner City Books, 1983.

————. *Patterns of Dreaming: Jungian Techniques in Theory and Practice*. Boston & London: Shambhala, 1977, 1991.

Hall, Manly P. *Dream Symbolism.* Los Angeles: Philosophical Research Society, 1965.

Hartmann, Ernest. *The Nightmare.* New York: Basic Books, 1984.

Hillman, James. *The Dream and the Underworld.* New York: Harper & Row, 1979.

Holzer, Hans. *The Psychic Side of Dreams.* Garden City, N.Y.: Doubleday, 1976.

Hunt, Harry T. *The Multiplicity of Dreams: Memory, Imagination and Consciousness.* New Haven: Yale University Press, 1989.

Jacob, W. Lindsay. *Interpreting Your Dreams.* Coraopolis, Pa.: J. Pohl Associates, 1988.

Johnson, Robert A. *Inner Work.* San Francisco: Harper & Row, 1986.

Jones, Ernest M. *On the Nightmare.* New York: Liveright Publishing Corp., 1951.

Jung, C. G. *The Archetypes and the Collective Unconscious.* 2nd ed. Bollingen Series XX. Princeton: Princeton University Press, 1968.

————. (ed.). *Man and His Symbols.* New York: Anchor Press/Doubleday, 1988. First published in the United States 1964.

————. *Mandala Symbolism.* Princeton: Bollingen/Princeton University Press, 1972. First published 1959.

————. *Memories, Dreams, Reflections.* Ed. Jaffé, Aniela. Translator Winston, Richard & Clara. New York: Vintage Books, 1963.

————. *Psychology and Alchemy.* Rev. ed. Princeton: Princeton University Press, 1968.

————. *Aion.* 2nd ed. Princeton: Princeton University Press, 1968.

————. *Dreams.* From *The Collected Works of C. G. Jung,* Vols. 4, 8, 12, and 16. Princeton: Princeton University Press, 1974.

————. *Mysterium Coniunctionis.* 2nd ed. Princeton: Princeton University Press, 1970.

Jung, Emma, and Marie-Louise von Franz. *The Grail Legend.* Boston: Sigo Press, 1986. First published in English 1970.

Kaplan-Williams, Strephon. *The Jungian-Senoi Dreamwork Manual.* Berkeley: Journey Press, 1980.

Kelsey, Morton. *Dreams: A Way to Listen to God.* New York: Paulist Press, 1978.

Kossowski De Rola, Stanislas. *The Golden Game: Alchemical Engravings of the Seventeenth Century.* New York: George Braziller, 1988.

Krippner, Stanley, and Joseph Dillard. *Dreamworking: How to Use Your Dreams for Creative Problem-Solving.* Buffalo, N.Y.: Bearly Limited, 1988.

Krippner, Stanley (ed.). *Dreamtime and Dreamwork.* Los Angeles: Jeremy P. Tarcher, 1990.

LaBerge, Stephen. *Lucid Dreaming.* New York: Ballantine Books, 1985.

LaBerge, Stephen, and Howard Rheingold. *Exploring the World of Lucid Dreaming.* New York: Ballantine Books, 1990.

Langs, Robert. *Decoding Your Dreams.* New York: Henry Holt & Co., 1988.

Layard, John. *The Lady and the Hare: A Study in the Healing Power of Dreams.* Boston & Shaftesbury: Shambhala, 1988.

Lenz, Frederick. *Lifetimes: True Accounts of Reincarnation.* New York: Bobbs Merrill, 1979.

Lincoln, Jackson S. *The Dream in Primitive Culture.* Baltimore: Williams and Wilkins, 1935.

Mattoon, Mary Ann. *Understanding Your Dreams.* Dallas: Spring Publications, 1990.

Maybruck, Patricia. *Pregnancy & Dreams.* Los Angeles: Jeremy P. Tarcher, 1989.

McDonald, Phoebe. *Dreams: Night Language of the Soul.* New York: Continuum, 1987.

McLean, Adam (ed.). *The Rosary of the Philosophers.* Magnum Opus Hermetic Source Works #6. London: The Hermetic Research Trust, 1980.

Meier, C. A. *Healing Dream and Ritual.* Einsiedeln, Switzerland: Daimon Verlag, 1989.

Parker, Russ. *Healing Dreams: Their Power and Purpose in Your Spiritual Life.* New York: Crossroad, 1989.

Piotrowski, Zygmunt A., with Albert M. Biele. *Dreams: A Key to Self-Knowledge.* Hillsdale, N.J.: Lawrence Erlbaum Associates, 1986.

Powell, Neil. *Alchemy, the Ancient Science.* London: The Danbury Press, 1976.

Rhine, Louisa E. *The Invisible Picture: A Study of Psychic Experiences.* Jefferson, N.C.: McFarland, 1981.

Rogo, D. Scott. *The Search for Yesterday: A Critical Examination of the Evidence for Reincarnation.* Englewood Cliffs, N.J.: Prentice-Hall, 1985.

Ryback, David, with Letitia Sweitzer. *Dreams That Come True.* New York: Dolphin/Doubleday, 1988.

Sanford, John A. *Dreams and Healing: A Succinct and Lively Interpretation of Dreams.* New York: Paulist Press, 1978.

―――. *Dreams: God's Forgotten Language.* San Francisco: Harper & Row, 1968, 1989.

Savary, L. M., P. H. Berne and S. K. Williams. *Dreams and Spiritual Growth: A Christian Approach to Dreamwork.* Ramsey, N.J.: Paulist Press, 1984.

Schulman, Sandra. *Nightmare.* New York: Macmillan, 1979.

Schwartz-Salant, Nathan, and Murray Stein (eds.). *Dreams in Analysis.* Wilmette, Ill.: Chiron Publications, 1990.

Scott, Walter (ed. & trans.). *Hermetica.* Boston: Shambhala, 1985.

Sechrist, Elsie. *Dreams: Your Magic Mirror.* New York: Cowles Education Corp., 1968.

Siegel, Alan B. *Dreams That Can Change Your Life.* Los Angeles: Jeremy P. Tarcher, 1990.

Stevenson, Ian. *Telepathic Impressions: A Review and a Report of 35 New Cases.* Charlottesville, Va.: University of Virginia, 1974.

———. *Children Who Remember Previous Lives: A Question of Reincarnation.* Charlottesville, Va.: University of Virginia Press, 1987.

Tart, Charles T. (ed.). *Altered States of Consciousness: A Book of Readings.* New York: Wiley, 1969.

Taylor, Jeremy. *Dream Work.* New York: Paulist Press, 1983.

Tedlock, Barbara (ed.). *Dreaming: Anthropological and Psychological Interpretations.* Cambridge, England: Cambridge University Press, 1987.

Thomas, Keith. *Religion & the Decline of Magic.* New York: Charles Scribner's Sons, 1971.

Thurston, Mark. *Dreams: Tonight's Answers for Tomorrow's Questions.* San Francisco: Harper & Row, 1988.

Tylor, Edward Burnett. *Religion in Primitive Culture,* Vol. 2. New York: Harper Torchbooks, 1958.

Ullman, Montague, and Claire Limmer (eds.). *The Variety of Dream Experience.* New York: Continuum, 1987.

Ullman, Montague, and Stanley Krippner, with Alan Vaughan. *Dream Telepathy: Experiments in Nocturnal ESP.* Baltimore: Penguin, 1973.

Ullman, Montague, and Nan Zimmerman, *Working With Dreams.* Los Angeles: Jeremy P. Tarcher, 1979.

Vance, Bruce A. *Dreamscape: Voyage in an Alternate Reality.* Wheaton, Ill.: Quest Books, 1989.

Von Franz, Marie-Louise. *Alchemy.* Toronto: Inner City Books, 1980.

———. *On Dreams and Death.* Boston & London: Shambhala, 1986.

———. *Dreams.* Boston & London: Shambhala, 1991.

von Grunebaum, G. E., and Roger Callois (eds.). *The Dream and Human Societies.* Berkeley and Los Angeles: University of California Press, 1966.

Waite, Arthur Edward (trans.). *The Hermetic Museum: Restored and Enlarged.* York Beach, Maine: Samuel Weiser, Inc., 1973.

Whitmont, Edward C., and Sylvia Brinton Perera. *Dreams, A Portal to the Source.* London: Routledge, 1990.

Windsor, Joan. *The Inner Eye: Your Dreams Can Make You Psychic.* Englewood Cliffs: Prentice-Hall, 1985.

———. *Dreams & Healing.* New York: Dodd, Mead & Co., 1987.

Wolman, Benjamin B. (ed.). *Handbook of Parapsychology.* New York: Van Nostrand Reinhold, 1977.

Woods, Ralph L., and Herbert B. Greenhouse (eds.). *The New World of Dreams.* New York: Macmillan, 1974.

Yamamoto, Gary K. *Creative Dream Analysis: A Guide to Self-Development.* Tucson: Harbinger House, 1988.

Zeller, Max. *The Dream: The Vision of the Night.* Boston: Sigo Press, 1975.

Zohar, Danah. *Through the Time Barrier: A Study in Precognition and Modern Physics.* London: Heinemann, 1982.